Four Corners

Jack C. Richards · David Bohlke

4

Student's Book

CAMBRIDGE
UNIVERSITY PRESS

CAMBRIDGE UNIVERSITY PRESS
Cambridge, New York, Melbourne, Madrid, Cape Town,
Singapore, São Paulo, Delhi, Mexico City

Cambridge University Press
32 Avenue of the Americas, New York, NY 10013-2473, USA

www.cambridge.org
Information on this title: www.cambridge.org/9780521127615

First published 2012
3rd printing 2013

Printed in Lima, Peru, by Empresa Editora El Comercio S.A.

A catalog record for this publication is available from the British Library.

ISBN 978-0-521-12761-5   Full Contact 4 with Self-study CD-ROM
ISBN 978-0-521-12765-3   Teacher's Edition 4 with Assessment Audio CD / CD-ROM
ISBN 978-0-521-12763-9   Class Audio CDs 4
ISBN 978-0-521-12756-1   Classware 4
ISBN 978-0-521-12762-2   DVD 4

For a full list of components, visit www.cambridge.org/fourcorners

Art direction, book design, photo research, and layout services: Adventure House, NYC
Audio production: CityVox, NYC
Video production: Steadman Productions

Authors' acknowledgments

Many people contributed to the development of *Four Corners*. The authors and publisher would like to particularly thank the following **reviewers**:

Nele Noe, **Academy for Educational Development, Qatar Independent Secondary School for Girls**, Doha, Qatar; Yuan-hsun Chuang, **Soo Chow University**, Taipei, Taiwan; Celso Frade and Sonia Maria Baccari de Godoy, **Associaçao Alumni**, São Paulo, Brazil; Pablo Stucchi, **Antonio Raimondi School** and **Instituto San Ignacio de Loyola**, Lima, Peru; Kari Miller, **Binational Center**, Quito, Ecuador; Alex K. Oliveira, **Boston University**, Boston, MA, USA; Elisabeth Blom, **Casa Thomas Jefferson**, Brasilia, Brazil; Henry Grant, **CCBEU – Campinas**, Campinas, Brazil; Maria do Rosário, **CCBEU – Franca**, Franca, Brazil; Ane Cibele Palma, **CCBEU Inter Americano**, Curitiba, Brazil; Elen Flavia Penques da Costa, **Centro de Cultura Idiomas – Taubate**, Taubate, Brazil; Inara Lúcia Castillo Couto, **CEL LEP – São Paulo**, São Paulo, Brazil; Geysa de Azevedo Moreira, **Centro Cultural Brasil Estados Unidos (CCBEU Belém)**, Belém, Brazil; Sonia Patricia Cardoso, **Centro de Idiomas Universidad Manuela Beltrán**, Barrio Cedritos, Colombia; Geraldine Itiago Losada, **Centro Universitario Grupo Sol (Musali)**, Mexico City, Mexico; Nick Hilmers, **DePaul University**, Chicago, IL, USA; Monica L. Montemayor Menchaca, **EDIMSA**, Metepec, Mexico; Angela Whitby, **Edu-Idiomas Language School**, Cholula, Puebla, Mexico; Mary Segovia, **El Monte Rosemead Adult School**, Rosemead, CA, USA; Dr. Deborah Aldred, **ELS Language Centers, Middle East Region**, Abu Dhabi, United Arab Emirates; Leslie Lott, **Embassy CES**, Ft. Lauderdale, FL, USA; M. Martha Lengeling, **Escuela de Idiomas**, Guanajuato, Mexico; Pablo Frias, **Escuela de Idiomas UNAPEC**, Santo Domingo, Dominican Republic; Tracy Vanderhoek, **ESL Language Center**, Toronto, Canada; Kris Vicca and Michael McCollister, **Feng Chia University**, Taichung, Taiwan; Flávia Patricia do Nascimento Martins, **First Idiomas**, Sorocaba, Brazil; Andrea Taylor, **Florida State University in Panama**, Panamá, Panama; Carlos Lizárraga González, **Grupo Educativo Angloamericano**, Mexico City, Mexico; Dr. Martin Endley, **Hanyang University**, Seoul, Korea; Mauro Luiz Pinheiro, **IBEU Ceará**, Ceará, Brazil; Ana Lúcia da Costa Maia de Almeida, **IBEU Copacabana**, Copacabana, Brazil; Ana Lucia Almeida, Elisa Borges, **IBEU Rio**, Rio de Janeiro, Brazil; Maristela Silva, **ICBEU Manaus**, Manaus, Brazil; Magaly Mendes Lemos, **ICBEU São José dos Campos**, São José dos Campos, Brazil; Augusto Pelligrini Filho, **ICBEU São Luis**, São Luis, Brazil; Leonardo Mercado, **ICPNA**, Lima, Peru; Lucia Rangel Lugo, **Instituto Tecnológico de San Luis Potosí**, San Luis Potosí, Mexico; Maria Guadalupe Hernández Lozada, **Instituto Tecnológico de Tlalnepantla**, Tlalnepantla de Baz, Mexico; Greg Jankunis, **International Education Service**, Tokyo, Japan; Karen Stewart, **International House Veracruz**, Veracruz, Mexico; George Truscott, **Kinki University**, Osaka, Japan; Bo-Kyung Lee, **Hankuk University of Foreign Studies**, Seoul, Korea; Andy Burki, **Korea University, International Foreign Language School**, Seoul, Korea; Jinseo Noh, **Kwangwoon University**, Seoul, Korea; Nadezhda Nazarenko, **Lone Star College**, Houston, TX, USA; Carolyn Ho, **Lone Star College-Cy-Fair**, Cypress, TX, USA; Alice Ya-fen Chou, **National Taiwan University of Science and Technology**, Taipei, Taiwan; Gregory Hadley, **Niigata University of International and Information Studies, Department of Information Culture**, Niigata-shi, Japan; Raymond Dreyer, **Northern Essex Community College**, Lawrence, MA, USA; Mary Keter Terzian Megale, **One Way Línguas-Suzano**, São Paulo, Brazil; Jason Moser, **Osaka Shoin Joshi University**, Kashiba-shi, Japan; Bonnie Cheeseman, **Pasadena Community College** and **UCLA American Language Center**, Los Angeles, CA, USA; Simon Banha, **Phil Young's English School**, Curitiba, Brazil; Oh Jun Il, **Pukyong National University**, Busan, Korea; Carmen Gehrke, **Quatrum English Schools**, Porto Alegre, Brazil; Atsuko K. Yamazaki, **Shibaura Institute of Technology**, Saitama, Japan; Wen hsiang Su, **Shi Chien University, Kaohsiung Campus**, Kaohsiung, Taiwan; Richmond Stroupe, **Soka University, World Language Center**, Hachioji, Tokyo, Japan; Lynne Kim, **Sun Moon University (Institute for Language Education)**, Cheon An City, Chung Nam, Korea; Hiroko Nishikage, **Taisho University**, Tokyo, Japan; Diana Peña Munoz and Zaira Kuri, **The Anglo**, Mexico City, Mexico; Alistair Campbell, **Tokyo University of Technology**, Tokyo, Japan; Song-won Kim, **TTI (Teacher's Training Institute)**, Seoul, Korea; Nancy Alarcón, **UNAM FES Zaragoza Language Center**, Mexico City, Mexico; Laura Emilia Fierro López, **Universidad Autónoma de Baja California**, Mexicali, Mexico; María del Rocío Domíngeuz Gaona, **Universidad Autónoma de Baja California**, Tijuana, Mexico; Saul Santos Garcia, **Universidad Autónoma de Nayarit**, Nayarit, Mexico; Christian Meléndez, **Universidad Católica de El Salvador**, San Salvador, El Salvador; Irasema Mora Pablo, **Universidad de Guanajuato**, Guanajuato, Mexico; Alberto Peto, **Universidad de Oxaca**, Tehuantepec, Mexico; Carolina Rodriguez Beltan, **Universidad Manuela Beltrán, Centro Colombo Americano**, and **Universidad Jorge Tadeo Lozano**, Bogotá, Colombia; Nidia Milena Molina Rodriguez, **Universidad Manuela Beltrán** and **Universidad Militar Nueva Granada**, Bogotá, Colombia; Yolima Perez Arias, **Universidad Nacional de Colombia**, Bogota, Colombia; Héctor Vázquez García, **Universidad Nacional Autónoma de Mexico**, Mexico City, Mexico; Pilar Barrera, **Universidad Técnica de Ambato**, Ambato, Ecuador; Deborah Hulston, **University of Regina**, Regina, Canada; Rebecca J. Shelton, **Valparaiso University, Interlink Language Center**, Valparaiso, IN, USA; Tae Lee, **Yonsei University**, Seodaemun-gu, Seoul, Korea; Claudia Thereza Nascimento Mendes, **York Language Institute**, Rio de Janeiro, Brazil; Jamila Jenny Hakam, **ELT Consultant**, Muscat, Oman; Stephanie Smith, **ELT Consultant**, Austin, TX, USA.

The authors would also like to thank the Four Corners editorial, production, and new media teams, as well as the Cambridge University Press staff and advisors around the world for their contributions and tireless commitment to quality.

No classes: May 27 June 3 July 1

Kosta (404) 901-0506 KDalageorgas @gmail.com

Scope and sequence

Functional language	Listening and Pronunciation	Reading and Writing	Speaking

Interactions:
Agreeing with an opinion
Disagreeing politely
	Listening:
	Today's news
	News reports based
	  on viewer-submitted
	  photos
	Pronunciation:
	Reduced vowel sounds
		Reading:
		"Citizen Journalism"
		A magazine article
		Writing:
		Become a citizen
		  journalist
			• Information exchange about news stories
			• *Keep talking:* Interview about news-reading habits
			• Opinions on reading the news
			• Information exchange about headline news
			• *Keep talking:* Question practice
			• A news blog

Interactions:
Expressing interest
Offering options
	Listening:
	Options for English
	  classes
	Favorite methods of
	  communication
	Pronunciation:
	Unreleased final
	  consonant sounds
		Reading:
		"Too Much Information"
		A magazine article
		Writing:
		A conversation in writing
			• Discussion of improving English to communicate
			  successfully
			• *Keep talking:* "Find someone who" activity about recent
			  experiences
			• Role play about language class options
			• Personal anecdotes about communicating
			• *Keep talking:* Role play of body language
			• Class survey about most popular ways of communicating

Interactions:
Giving a recommendation
Accepting a
  recommendation
	Listening:
	Healthy eating habits
	The San Francisco
	  Gourmet Chocolate
	  Tour
	Pronunciation:
	Linked consonant and
	  vowel sounds
		Reading:
		"Chocolate – From Forest
		  to Factory"
		A company brochure
		Writing:
		A recipe
			• List of popular street foods
			• *Keep talking:* Description of festival foods
			• Role play about finding time to cook
			• Description of an original snack
			• *Keep talking:* Interview about fun food facts
			• A plan for a food tour

Interactions:
Expressing an expectation
Acknowledging an
  expectation
	Listening:
	Cross-cultural differences
	Radio talk show about
	  acts of kindness
	Pronunciation:
	Reduction of *have*
		Reading:
		"Make Someone Happy"
		A magazine article
		Writing:
		An act of kindness
			• Interviews about reactions to different situations
			• *Keep talking:* Information exchange about reaction to
			  dilemmas
			• Information exchange about customs in different
			  countries
			• Information exchange about past hypothetical situations
			• *Keep talking:* Discussion of right and wrong decisions
			• Discussion about kind acts

Interactions:
Reporting a problem
Responding to a problem
	Listening:
	Hotel problems
	City festivals
	Pronunciation:
	Linking of same
	  consonant sounds
		Reading:
		"Welcome to Medellín,
		  Colombia – The City of
		  Everlasting Spring"
		A website
		Writing:
		Creating a home page
			• Comparison of different cities
			• *Keep talking:* Travel adventures game
			• Role play about a hotel situation
			• Advice for foreign visitors
			• *Keep talking:* Interview about solutions to travel problems
			• A plan for a town festival

Interactions: Interrupting politely Agreeing to an interruption	**Listening:** Type A and Type B personalities Guided imagery **Pronunciation:** Stress in thought groups	**Reading:** "Therapies That Work!" An article **Writing:** About relaxation	• Discussion about job and personality matches • *Keep talking:* Discussion of birth order and personality • Discussion about personality • Information exchange about making wishes • *Keep talking:* Board game about wishes • Brainstorm creative ways to relax

LEVEL 4	Learning outcomes	Grammar	Vocabulary

Functional language	Listening and Pronunciation	Reading and Writing	Speaking
Interactions: Eliciting an idea Suggesting a solution	**Listening:** Unusual solutions to unusual problems i-Cybie, a robot dog **Pronunciation:** Emphatic stress	**Reading:** "Technology Helps Japan's Elderly" An article **Writing:** An invention	• Discussion of inventions • *Keep talking:* Promoting creative products • Vote on inventive solutions • Discussion of improvements to early innovations • *Keep talking:* Discussion of product improvements • Description of an original invention
Interactions: Expressing worry Reassuring someone	**Listening:** Worrisome situations Memorable days **Pronunciation:** Reduction of *had*	**Reading:** "The Story of My Life" A book excerpt **Writing:** About a memorable day	• Information exchange about past experiences • *Keep talking:* Picture story • Role play about difficult situations • Description of personal experiences that might have been different • *Keep talking:* Discussion of possible outcomes in different situations • Description of a memorable day
Interactions: Expressing probability Expressing improbability	**Listening:** Mind-reading "The Magpies and the Bell," a Korean folktale **Pronunciation:** Intonation in embedded questions	**Reading:** "How the Kangaroo Got Its Pouch" A myth **Writing:** An origin myth	• Discussion of possible explanations for unusual everyday events • *Keep talking:* Speculations about pictured events • Information exchange about probability • Discussion of possible explanations for historical mysteries • *Keep talking:* Descriptions and speculations about unsolved mysteries • Story-telling from different cultures
Interactions: Changing the topic Returning to a topic	**Listening:** Three conversations about sports Interview for the Proust Questionnaire **Pronunciation:** Linked vowel sounds with /w/ and /y/	**Reading:** "The Proust Questionnaire" An interview **Writing:** Questionnaire results	• "Whisper the sentence" game to report what people say • *Keep talking:* "Find the differences" activity about eyewitness reports • Discussion about sports • "Find someone who" activity about famous people • *Keep talking:* Survey about general topics • Questionnaire about thoughts and values
Interactions: Taking time to think Closing an interview	**Listening:** Plans to get things done A job interview **Pronunciation:** Reduction of *will*	**Reading:** "Jobs of the future" An article **Writing:** A letter of interest	• Discussion about ways to prepare for an interview • *Keep talking:* Match the places and the activities • Role play about a job interview • Discussion of future goals • *Keep talking:* Survey about life in the future • Information exchange about career interests
Interactions: Supporting an opinion Not supporting an opinion	**Listening:** Bottled water and the environment How people help solve community issues **Pronunciation:** Rise-falling and low falling tones	**Reading:** "The Elephant Men" A magazine article **Writing:** A letter to a community leader	• Discussion of environmental trends • *Keep talking:* Board game about the environment • Comparison of opinions about issues • Discussion about ways to improve the quality of life of people in the community • *Keep talking:* A plan for a community improvement project • Information exchange about raising awareness

Classroom language

A 🔊 Complete the conversations with the correct sentences. Then listen and check your answers.

✓ Do you think this is correct? ✓ Is it all right if I . . .
✓ Do you want to join our group? ✓ Which number are we on?
✓ I'm sorry for being late. ✓ Would you mind explaining that to me?

1.
A: *Do you want to join our group?*
B: That'd be great. Thanks.

2.
A: Would you mind explaining that to me.
B: Sure. I think I understand it.

3.
A: Is it right if I leave five minutes early tomorrow? I have a doctor's appointment.
B: Of course.

4.
A: I'm Sorry for being late. My last class ended late.
B: That's OK. Take your seat.

5.
A: Which number are we on?
B: We just finished question two, so we're on number three now.

6.
A: Do you think this is correct?
B: I don't think so. I think you need to use the past tense here.

B **Pair work** Practice the conversations.

The news

Warm-up

A Look at the pictures. How are the people getting their news?

B How do people you know get the news? How do *you* get the news?

1 Vocabulary News sections

A 🔊 Listen to the names of news sections. In which news sections can you find the pictures? Compare your answers with a partner.

a. Business	c. Health	e. Local	g. Technology / Science	i. Weather
b. Entertainment	✓d. Lifestyle	f. Sports	h. Travel	j. World

1. d

2. b

3. g

4. h

5. c

6. i

"I think you can find the first picture in the Lifestyle section."

B Pair work In which news section can you find these news stories? Discuss your ideas.

the best new applications for phones	a meeting among world leaders
last night's soccer scores	a new coffeehouse in your town

2 Language in context In the news

A 🔊 Read the headlines and the beginning of each story. Match the headlines to the news sections in Exercise 1A where you can find these stories.

PHOTOS SHOW ANCIENT MARTIAN LAKE _g_ ☐

New photos suggest that Mars had a large lake billions of years ago.

Town Recovering from Storm ____ ☐

The town of Jasper is slowly recovering from last week's storm.

OPEN FOR BUSINESS ____ ☐

Hawaii hopes to attract more business travelers.

Jason Parker Debuts New CD at Lucid's ____ ☐

Jason was playing his new songs to an excited audience until 2:00 a.m.

B What about you? Are you interested in these stories? Rank them from 1 to 4 in the order you would read them.

3 Grammar 🔊 Verb tenses – statements

Simple present: Hawaii **hopes** to attract more business travelers. *daily habits or usual activities, general statements of fact (P, P, F)*

Present continuous: *(D progressive)* Jasper **is recovering** from last week's storm. → *A activity that is in progress right now*

Simple past: Mars **had** a large lake billions of years ago. *Situations that began and ended in the past (yesterday, last night, two days etc.)*

Past continuous: Jason **was playing** songs all night.

⊛ Present perfect: Café Bella **has opened** in Pelham. *Meaning something happed before now at an unspecified time*

Future with will: The Winter Olympics **will begin** next Monday.

① *Present Perfect Progressive. expresses the duration (length of time) of an activity That began in the past and is in progress right now exemple: Po has been sitting in class since nine o'clock*

⊛⊛ *Past Perfect*

⊛ The present Perfect expresses an activity that occurred before now at an unspecified time in the past Example: I am not hungry now. I have already eaten.

⊛⊛ expresses an activity that Occurred before another time in the past. exemple. I had already eaten.

Complete the news stories with the correct forms of the verbs. Then compare with a partner.

1. The *Austin Sun Times* ____**has closed**____ (close) its doors – for now. The newspaper ____printed____ (print) its last newspaper last Sunday, but it ____Will open____ (open) again next month as an Internet-only paper. Staff members ____are learning____ (learn) about digital publishing now, so they ____are going to be____ (be) ready next month. Sadly, the *Austin Gazette* ____is____ (be) now the city's only "paper" newspaper.

2. Pink ____is____ (be) a playful color, and it ____makes____ (make) people smile. But last night William Maddox ____didn't smile____ (not / smile) when he ____stopped____ (stop) a fight in his store. "Two people ____had argued____ (argue) for about five minutes over the last pink T-shirt in my store. I ____asked____ (ask) them to leave and then ____closed____ (close) the store for the day," said Maddox.

3. Fifteen-year-old Kate Moore ____Will be____ (be) the country's newest texting champion. Last Tuesday, she ____had competed____ (compete) against 20 other contestants and ____won____ (win) $50,000 for her fast and accurate texting. But even Kate ____got____ (get) one question wrong. No one ____Knows____ (know) the meaning of the abbreviation "PAW." It ____means____ (mean), "I can't talk now. My parents ____are watching____ (watch)."

4 Speaking News stories

A Pair work Think of a story from the news, or make one up. Complete the chart.

What happened?	Our plane arrived late Yesterday
What else was happening at the time?	I was sleeping when it happen.
What has happened since?	I have been traver in treen.
What's happening now?	My family and I move to another City.

B Group work Share your stories. What will happen in the future?

5 Keep talking!

Go to page **123** for more practice.

I can *tell news stories.* ☑

B *I totally agree.*

1 Interactions　Agreeing and disagreeing

A Do you agree with this statement? Why or why not?

"The best place to get news is online."

B 🔊 Listen to the conversation. Why can't Carl check the news headlines?
Then practice the conversation.

> **Carl:** Hey, Jim. Catching up on the news?
>
> **Jim:** Oh, hi, Carl. Yeah, I like to know what's going on in the world.
>
> **Carl:** I feel exactly the same way. Do you read the paper every day?
>
> **Jim:** Every day. It's the best way to get the news.
>
> **Carl:** Really? I don't know about that. I get all my news online. I check the news several times a day, so I always know what's happening.
>
> **Jim:** Online news is OK, but I prefer reading an actual newspaper. So, what are the latest headlines online – right now?
>
> **Carl:** Let's see. . . . Oh, no! I can't get online. I guess there's no wireless signal here. Say, would you mind sharing your paper?
>
> **Jim:** No problem!

C 🔊 Read the expressions below. Complete each box with a similar expression from the conversation. Then listen and check your answers.

Agreeing with an opinion	Disagreeing politely
_____	_____
I couldn't agree with you more. I totally agree.	I'm not sure about that. I'm not sure that's really true.

D Pair work Check (✓) the statements you agree with. Then give your opinions and agree or disagree with your partner.

☐ It's important to read the news every day.

☐ The Internet is a better way to get news than newspapers.

☐ Newsmagazines are more interesting than newspapers.

☐ There's not enough positive news these days.

A: *I think it's important to read the news every day.*
B: *I totally agree. It's important to know what's going on.*

2 **Pronunciation** Reduced vowel sounds

A 🔊 Listen and repeat. Notice the reduced vowel sound /ə/ in unstressed syllables.

agree   totally   even   happening

B 🔊 Listen. Underline the reduced vowel sounds. Then practice with a partner.

signal   about   magazine   travel   section   television

3 **Listening** Agree or disagree

A 🔊 Listen to Ted and Carrie discuss today's news. What news are they talking about? Number the pictures from 1 to 4.

B 🔊 Listen again. Does Carrie agree or disagree with Ted? Circle the answers.

1. agree / disagree   2. agree / disagree   3. agree / disagree   4. agree / disagree

4 **Speaking** What do you think?

A Check (✓) the statements you agree with, and mark an ✗ next to the statements you disagree with. Then write a supporting sentence for your opinion.

Statement	Supporting sentence
☐ News bloggers don't provide real news.	
☐ International news stories don't affect me.	
☐ It's important to follow local news.	
☐ Getting news 24 hours a day is helpful.	
☐ Newspapers hurt the environment.	

B Class activity Walk around the class. Share your opinions with your classmates. Agree or disagree politely.

A: *In my opinion, news bloggers don't provide real news. They write opinions, not facts.*

B: *I'm not sure that's true. A lot of bloggers are really newspaper writers.*

I can *agree and disagree with opinions.* ☑

C Survival stories

1 Vocabulary Actions in the news

A 🔊 Match the news headlines and the pictures. Then listen and check your answers.

a. Shark **Attacks** Local Surfer	e. Boat **Overturns** – All Swim to Safety
b. Bear **Chases** Hiker Up Tree	f. Firefighter **Rescues** Family Cat
c. Pilot **Crashes** Plane – No One Hurt	g. Hiker **Survives** Week in the Mountains
d. Lightning **Misses** Golfer by One Foot	h. Fire **Threatens** Historic Town

1. e   2. g   3. d   4. f

5. h   6. c   7. a   8. b

B Pair work Use each verb in Part A in a new headline.

"Swimmer Survives Three Days in Ocean"

2 Conversation Shark attack!

A 🔊 Listen to the conversation. How did Wade stop the shark?

Reporter: Wade, what happened?
Wade: A shark attacked me! Can you believe it?
Reporter: How are you feeling? Are you OK?
Wade: Oh, I feel great! I survived a shark attack. That's pretty cool.
Reporter: What were you doing when it happened?
Wade: I was riding a killer wave.
Reporter: Did you actually see the shark?
Wade: Not at first. But then I fell off my board. The shark tried to bite me, so I hit it with my surfboard.
Reporter: Have you seen your surfboard?
Wade: Yeah. It has a big shark bite in it.
Reporter: Amazing! So, what will you do next?

B 🔊 Listen to the rest of the interview. What will Wade do next? When?

3 Grammar 🔊 | Verb tenses – questions

Wh- questions	Yes / no questions
Simple present: When **do** you **plan** on surfing? ①	**Do** you **plan** on surfing today?
Present continuous: How **are** you **feeling**?	**Are** you **feeling** OK?
Simple past: What **did** you **see**?	**Did** you **see** the shark?
Past continuous: What **were** you **doing**?	**Were** you **surfing**?
Present perfect: How long **have** you **surfed**? ②	**Have** you **surfed** for a long time?
Future with will: What **will** you **do** next?	**Will** you **go** back in the water soon?

(handwritten annotations:)
Present Progressive
was, were + ing
① Do I, you, we, they
   Does He, she, it.
② Actividad que pasa en un inespecifico tiempo en el pasado
   have, has + been

A Look at the *yes/no* questions the reporter asked Wade. Complete the questions with the correct forms of the verbs. Then compare with a partner.

1. __Do__ you __go__ (go) surfing every day?
2. __Did__ anyone __see__ (see) the shark before it attacked you?
3. __Didn't__ other people __surf__ (surf) around you?
4. __Will__ you __buy__ (buy) a new surfboard soon?
5. __Didn't__ you __speak__ (speak) with your family yet?
6. __Do__ you __have__ (have) any advice for other surfers?

B Read the answers. Write *Wh-* questions about the underlined words. Then practice with a partner.

1. *Where did she crash the plane?* — She crashed the plane <u>in a forest</u>.
2. How long timer He has been in the desert? — He's been in the desert <u>for a week</u>.
3. How the firefighter felt? — The firefighter felt <u>very proud</u>.
4. When the fire will threaten the town center? — The fire will threaten the town center <u>tonight</u>.
5. When the boats overturned? — They <u>were fishing</u> when the boat overturned.
6. What He is thinking writing about? — He's thinking about writing a <u>survival book</u>.

4 Speaking   Tell me about it.

Pair work Role-play a reporter and a survivor of one of the news stories in Exercise 1. Then change roles.

Student A: Choose a headline from Exercise 1, and read it to your partner. Answer your partner's questions.

Student B: Ask your partner five questions about what happened.

A: *Who were you sailing with?*
B: *I was sailing with some friends.*

Questions
1. *Who were you sailing with?*
2. *How exactly did the boat overturn?*
3. *How often do you go sailing?*
4. *Have you ever . . . ?*
5.

5 Keep talking!

Go to page **124** for more practice.

Go to page **124** for more practice.

I can ask questions and talk about a news story. ✓

D | Creating news

1 Reading ◀))

A Look at the logos of the news websites in the article. Which websites have you looked at? What other news websites do you know?

B Read the article. Check (✓) the main idea of the article.

☐ Traditional news organizations are upset with citizen journalists.

☐ Technology allows anyone to be a reporter, anytime and anywhere.

Citizen **Journalism**

Arpita has just updated her news blog. The winners of a local election in Mumbai have just been announced, and she has listed their names on her blog. On the website of a local newspaper, Liat has recently posted a "digital story," a series of photos and descriptions of a whale rescue. And hundreds of people in the Dominican Republic are tweeting on their cell phones to describe a hurricane that is threatening the country.

What do these stories have in common? Technology is giving people the chance to be news reporters. More than ever before, technology is allowing everyone to share opinions, ideas, stories, photos, and videos from anywhere in the world. If there is **breaking news**, you can be sure that someone is reporting it.

Wikinews, iNewsit, CNN's iReport, and MSNBC's FirstPerson are just a few of the websites where "citizen journalists" can write their news reports. More and more people are blogging texts, photos, and videos. They're sharing their personal thoughts and news

reports with the world on these websites. And the increased **prevalence** of cell phones and cameras has made it even easier for people to share news.

Many media organizations such as CNN now have entire sections of these news stories on their websites. News editors used to decide what was news. Now *you* decide.

There has been some **criticism** of citizen journalism, however. For example, there are often mistakes in these stories, including incorrect facts, spelling, and grammar. These stories may not be as **neutral** as regular news organizations' stories usually are. Moreover, when people **instantly** upload stories and images, they cannot know how other people will use them later. But it seems that news by the people and for the people is here to stay.

C Find the words in **bold** in the article. Circle the correct meaning.

1. **breaking news**   a. news happening now   b. news about problems
2. **prevalence**   a. lower cost of   b. frequent use
3. **criticism**   a. high costs   b. opinions on what's wrong
4. **neutral**   a. written well   b. fair
5. **instantly**   a. immediately   b. done without thinking

D What's your opinion about citizen journalism? Do you think it's a good thing? Do you agree with the criticisms in the article? Do you have other ideas?

2 **Listening** Photos of the day

A 🔊 Listen to a TV newscaster discuss photos that four viewers have sent in. Number the photos from 1 to 4.

B 🔊 Listen again. Answer the questions.

1. When did Rafael take the photograph? _____

2. How much of a discount was the store offering? _____

3. How long does it usually take Yumiko to get home? _____

4. What did Arlo do when he saw the animal? _____

C Which news stories in Part A interest you? Why? Where can you find out more about them?

3 **Writing and speaking** Become a citizen journalist

A Complete one of these headlines.

HUGE STORM TO ARRIVE _____

_____ **Threatens High School**

LOCAL TEEN RESCUES _____ IN FOREST

Lightning Misses _____

Technology Changes _____

Students Ask _____ for _____

B Write a short news blog. Use your headline from Part A and the model to help you.

> *Huge Storm to Arrive Friday*
> *A huge storm is coming on Friday. Everyone is preparing for it. Most people have already bought food and water. . . .*

C **Group work** Share your news blogs. Ask questions to find out more information about each story.

I can *discuss a news story.* ☑

Wrap-up

1 Quick pair review

Lesson A **Find out!** What are two sections of the news both you and your partner like to read? You and your partner have one minute.

A: *I read the World section of the newspaper. Do you?*
B: *No, I don't. I read the Travel section. Do you?*
A: *Yes, I do.*

Lesson B **Do you remember?** Write A for expressions that show agreeing with an opinion and D for expressions that show disagreeing with an opinion. You have one minute.

_A_ 1. I feel exactly the same way.   _____ 4. I don't know about that.

_____ 2. I couldn't agree with you more.   _____ 5. I totally agree.

_____ 3. I'm not sure about that.   _____ 6. I'm not sure that's really true.

Lesson C **Brainstorm!** Write the question "Where do you shop?" in as many different tenses as you can. You have two minutes.

Lesson D **Guess!** Describe something newsworthy for each item, but don't say where it happened. Can your partner guess the place? Take turns. You and your partner have three minutes.

> something you did yesterday
> something you do every day
> something you will do tomorrow

A: *Yesterday I ate at a great café. I had tacos and rice and beans.*
B: *Were you at Café Mexicana?*
A: *Yes, I was.*

2 In the real world

What is a breaking news story in your area? Go online or read a newspaper, and find an article in English about it. Then write about it.

- What section did you find the article in?
- What happened?

> *Oil Spill Threatens Animals*
> *The national news reported an oil spill in the Gulf of Mexico. The oil will harm fish and birds.*

Communicating

Warm-up

A Look at the pictures. What do you think the people are saying?

B Imagine you are going to travel to an English-speaking country. What do you think are the most useful English phrases or questions to know? Why?

A Language learning

1 Vocabulary Language-learning tips

A 🔊 Complete the chart with the correct tips. Then listen and check your answers.

Tips for Successful Language Learning
Watch online video clips.
Keep a vocabulary notebook.
✓ Make flash cards.
Talk with native speakers.
Watch movies with subtitles.
Talk to yourself out loud.

To remember vocabulary
Make flash cards.

To increase speaking fluency

To improve listening comprehension

B **Pair work** What's your number one language-learning goal? Which tips in Part A do you use to reach your goal? Tell your partner.

"My number one goal is to improve my listening comprehension. I often watch online video clips in English."

2 Language in context Improving communication skills

A 🔊 Read this online chat between a teacher and some of his students. What are they discussing?

Mr. Phillips: I hope you've been enjoying your vacation. And I hope you haven't forgotten your English! So, what have you been doing recently to improve your English?

Luisa: Hello, Mr. Phillips. Hi, everybody! I've been reading magazines and comic books in English.

Mr. Phillips: Excellent!

Jin: I've been making vocabulary flash cards. They really work! And I've been keeping a vocabulary notebook.

Marcus: I've been chatting online in English.

Mr. Phillips: Fantastic! Have you been doing anything to improve your speaking?

Pedro: I have. Omar and I have been starting conversations with native speakers. We were nervous about it at first, but we've been making new friends that way.

Luisa: I've been having the best conversations of all. I've been talking to myself out loud in front of a mirror.

Marcus: Very funny! ☺

Mr. Phillips: But very helpful, too. Good job, everyone! I'll see you in class on Monday.

B What about you? Which tips would you like to try? Which would you probably not want to try? Why?

3 Grammar 🔊 **Present perfect continuous**

Use the present perfect continuous to emphasize the duration of an action that is in progress. How long, recently, *and* lately *are often used with the present perfect continuous.*

What **have** you **been doing** recently?

  I**'ve been reading** magazines.

How long **has** he **been writing** in his notebook?

  He**'s been writing** in it for about a month.

Have they **been talking** to native speakers lately?

  Yes, they **have**. No, they **haven't**.

Remember: some verbs are not usually used in the continuous form.

believe	like
belong	love
forget	need
hate	own
hope	remember
know	want

A Complete the conversations with the present perfect continuous forms of the verbs. Then practice with a partner.

1. **A:** ___have___ you ___been doing___ (do) anything recently to improve your vocabulary?

   B: Yes, I ___have___ . I ___have been keeping___ (keep) a vocabulary notebook.

2. **A:** How long ___have___ you ___been studing___ (study) English?

   B: I ___have been studing___ (study) English since last year.

3. **A:** What ___have___ you ___been doing___ (do) in class lately?

   B: We ___have been making___ (make) vocabulary flash cards.

B Pair work Ask the questions in Part A. Answer with your own information.

4 Speaking Communicating successfully

A Group work What have these people been doing lately to improve their English? What language goals do you think they have been trying to reach?

B Class activity What else can you do to improve your speaking? learn more vocabulary? improve listening comprehension? Discuss your ideas and make a class list of tips.

5 Keep talking!

Go to page 125 for more practice.

I can give and discuss language-learning tips.

B One possibility is . . .

1 Interactions — Interests and options

A How good is your English? Rate these areas 1 (good), 2 (fair), or 3 (not very good).

☐ reading ☐ writing ☐ speaking ☐ listening
☐ vocabulary ☐ grammar ☐ pronunciation ☐ idioms

B ◄))) Listen to the conversation. What idiom did Ralph learn? Then practice the conversation.

Ralph: Excuse me. Do you have a minute?

Mr. Hill: Of course, Ralph. What's up?

Ralph: Well, I'm trying to find a way to learn English idioms. Can you help me?

Mr. Hill: Well, how about taking one of our conversation courses? I know Ms. Davis teaches a lot of idioms.

Ralph: OK.

Mr. Hill: But why are you so interested in idioms?

Ralph: Oh, a friend and I were making plans, and he said, "Let's play it by ear." I asked him to repeat it, but I still didn't understand.

Mr. Hill: I see. Well, "play it by ear" means you don't make plans ahead of time. You decide what seems best at the time.

Ralph: Oh, I know that now. I looked it up online. But that's why I need to learn idioms.

C ◄))) Read the expressions below. Complete each box with a similar expression from the conversation. Then listen and check your answers.

Expressing interest

_____
I'm interested in . . .
I'm looking for . . .

Offering options

_____
One possibility is . . .
You might want to consider . . .

D **Pair work** Express interest in improving your skills in one of the areas in Part A. Your partner offers course options. Take turns.

Podcasting in English	Advanced Grammar	Academic Test Prep
Vocabulary for Science	Intermediate Listening	Pronunciation Workshop

2 Pronunciation Unreleased final consonant sounds

A 🔊 Listen and repeat. Notice how the final sounds /b/, /g/, /d/, /p/, /k/, and /t/ are not fully pronounced before other consonant sounds.

Film Club Group Discussions   Advanced Grammar   Travel Blog Writing

Intermediate Conversation   Academic Listening   Test Prep Course

B 🔊 Listen. Cross out the final sounds that are not fully pronounced. Then practice with a partner.

Create flash cards.   Set realistic goals.   Join group discussions.

Read books in English.   Memorize verb tenses.   Write a blog for practice.

3 Listening Fun classes

A 🔊 Listen to a man ask about options for English classes. Write the class names.

	Class name	One interesting thing
1.		
2.		
3.		
4.		

B 🔊 Listen again. Write one interesting thing about each class. Then circle the class the man chooses.

4 Speaking Consider all the options!

Pair work Role-play the situation. Then change roles.

Student A: You are a new student at a language school. Student B has been taking classes at the school for a year. Ask about class options and choose one.

Student B: You have been taking classes at your language school for a year. Student A is a new student. Help Student A find the right class from the classes below.

Academic Listening	Vocabulary for Science	Reading for Business	Advanced Speaking
Tue. & Thur., 4:00–6:00 p.m.	Mon. & Fri., 7:00–8:30 a.m.	Wed., 2:00–5:00 p.m.	Tue. & Thur., 6:00–8:00 p.m.
Practice note-taking and intensive listening.	Learn science vocabulary and academic skills.	Practice reading notes, memos, and reports.	Improve your speaking skills.

A: *I'm interested in a way to improve my reading.*
B: *One class possibility is Reading for Business. They practice reading memos.*
A: *Really? I don't know about that. . . .*

> *I can express interests.* ☑
> *I can offer options.* ☑

C Have her text me.

1 Vocabulary Communicate . . . or not?

A 🔊 Label the phrases C (ways to communicate) or A (ways to avoid communicating). Then listen and check your answers.

1. answer the phone __C__
2. call (someone) back ____
3. don't check voice mail ____
4. ignore a text ____
5. leave (someone) a voice message ____
6. let the call go to voice mail ____
7. respond to an email ____
8. screen your calls ____
9. turn off the phone ____
10. update your status online ____

B Pair work How do you usually communicate? What things do you sometimes do to avoid communicating?

"I update my status online every day. That way my friends know what I'm doing."

2 Conversation Where's Beth?

A 🔊 Listen to the conversation. How has Pete been trying to contact Beth?

Akemi: Hello?

Pete: Hi, Akemi. It's Pete.

Akemi: Oh, hi, Pete. How are things?

Pete: Good, thanks. Listen, have you seen Beth? I've left her a lot of voice messages, but she hasn't returned my calls.

Akemi: That's strange. Maybe she's busy and just isn't checking her voice mail.

Pete: She's probably screening her calls. It's too bad, because I really need to ask her to help me with something.

Akemi: Have you tried emailing her?

Pete: Several times, but so far she's ignored my emails – and my texts. That's not like her.

Akemi: You know, I usually see her at the gym on Sundays.

Pete: Oh, really? Could you ask her to call me back or to text me?

Akemi: Sure, I can do that.

B 🔊 Listen to a conversation between Pete and Beth. Why hasn't Beth been answering her phone? What's Pete planning?

3 Grammar 🔊 Verb + object + verb

Some verbs are commonly followed by an object and the base form of another verb.	Some verbs are commonly followed by an object and an infinitive (to + verb).
Would you **let** me **help**?	I **invited** you **to come**.
Please **make** them **be** quiet.	I'll **ask** her **to help** me.
Could you **have** her **text** me?	Would you **tell** her **to call** me?
Please **help** me **call** people.	Could you **remind** them **to come** early?

Auxiliary
+
To
+
Simple form of a Verb.

A Circle the correct forms of the verbs. Then compare with a partner.

1. You're talking to a friend on the phone and you get another call. What do you do?
   a. I tell the caller **call** / to call me back later.
   b. I have my friend **call** / to call me back.

2. Your grandmother can't input numbers into her cell phone. What do you do?
   a. I have someone input / **to input** the numbers for her.
   b. I say, "Let me **help** / to help you."

3. Your phone rings in the middle of the night. What do you do?
   a. I let the call **go** / to go to voice mail.
   b. I answer but ask the person call / **to call** back in the morning.

4. An uninvited stranger shows up at your party. What do you do?
   a. I invite the person **come** / to come in.
   b. I make the person **leave** / to leave.

5. A friend is always phoning you in class. What do you do?
   a. I remind my friend call / **to call** later.
   b. I ask my friend **stop** / to stop calling.

6. Your sister has been secretly using your phone to send texts. What do you do?
   a. I make her **pay** / to pay for using my phone.
   b. I let her continue / **to continue** to use my phone.

B Pair work Ask and answer the questions in Part A. Make the answers true for you.

have to tell her
I ought to be
have to study
have got to study
ought to study

4 Speaking Chat about it.

Group work Answer the questions. Give more information.

- Do you ever get texts, emails, or calls from companies trying to sell things? What do you do to make them stop calling?

- Has your computer or phone ever stopped working? Did you have someone fix it for you? Who?

- Would you let a stranger borrow your phone? Do you ever ask to borrow someone's phone? When?

- Have you ever sent an email to the wrong person? Who did you send it to? Did this person respond to your email? What did he or she say?

"I sometimes get calls from companies. I ask them to stop calling."

5 Keep talking!

Go to pages **126–127** for more practice.

I can talk about ways of communicating. ☑

Modern communication

1 Reading ◄))

A Read the first paragraph of the article. What is "communication overload"?

TOO MUCH INFORMATION

Computers and cell phones let people communicate with each other by voice or text anytime, anywhere. The result: too much information! So let me offer these tips. They could help you manage communication overload.

TIP 1 – *Stick to a schedule.* Do you have a calendar? Use it to schedule study times, meetings, and appointments. But also, use it to schedule times to respond to email, read status updates, and check voice mail. How about also using it to schedule quiet time? That is, **set aside** time for no email, no texts, no phone calls, nothing! Then **stick to it**!

TIP 2 – *Text or phone call?* Texts are great for short messages, but not for long messages with emotional **content**. Phone calls are fine when you want a more personal touch, but not when you need to save information about a conversation. In those cases, an email or a letter may be better.

TIP 3 – *Let it ring.* You don't have to answer every phone call. If you don't want to talk, screen your calls and let the caller leave a message. Or turn off your phone. The same is true for text messages. It's usually OK to make people wait for your answer.

TIP 4 – *Keep your in-box empty.* After you've answered an email, delete it or file it. If you need to save an email, create folders – for school, for work, for friends. Find a way to organize your messages that works for you, and follow it.

TIP 5 – *Pick one primary network.* Many people have a **profile** on a social network site, like Facebook. Some people have profiles on many different sites. Choose one site as your **primary** place to communicate with people. Keep your profiles on the other sites, but check those sites less frequently.

TIP 6 – *Choose your friends carefully.* If you belong to a social network site, are all your "friends" on the site real friends and family, or are some just **casual acquaintances** or even strangers? Limit the number of "friends" you welcome into your social network, and you will limit communication overload from people you don't care about.

Source: Adapted from www.ariadne.ac.uk/issue56/houghton-jan/

B Read the article. Find the words in **bold**. What do they mean? Write the words next to the correct definition.

1. main ___*primary*___
2. continue to do it ___profile___
3. people you don't know well __casual acquaintances__
4. save for later ___set aside___
5. information about yourself ___content___
6. subject matter ___stick to it.___

C Check (✓) the statements the author would probably agree with.

☐ It's always better to call.
☑ Create several email folders.
☐ It's OK to be on more than one social network site.
☐ You should always communicate with people.

D Do you think you suffer from communication overload? Why or why not?

2 Listening Communication preferences

A 🔊 Listen to four friends describe their favorite method of communicating. Write the method each person prefers.

	Method	Why he or she prefers it
Lynn		☐ It's fast, cheap, and easy. ☐ She dislikes checking her voice mail.
Alex		☐ He forgets to answer texts. ☐ He can talk to the person right away.
Anita		☐ She can communicate with a lot of people at the same time. ☐ She can see what her friends are doing.
Dean		☐ It's more personal. ☐ He can respond to email by phone.

B 🔊 Listen again. Check (✓) why they prefer their method of communication.

3 Writing A conversation in writing

A Write an answer to the question "What's the best way to communicate with people?" Use the model to help you.

B **Group work** Pass your answer to the classmate on your right. Read and respond to your classmate's answer. Continue to pass, read, and respond to all of the answers in your group.

C Read the answers and responses. Which way to communicate is the best?

> **Ming:** The best way to communicate with people is to talk in person.
> **Ella:** I don't think so. Sometimes people are too far away.
> **Justine:** Then one possibility is calling the person to talk.
> **Eduardo:** *I'm not sure about that. . . .*

4 Speaking How I communicate

A **Group work** Answer the questions. Give more information.

- What is your primary way of communicating?
- Who do you use it to communicate with?
- What do you like about it? Is there anything you dislike about it?
- Has your way of communicating with people changed in the past year? How?
- Do you think you'll still use this method in one year? five years? Why or why not?

"I usually use my phone. I talk to everyone this way. . . ."

B **Class activity** Take a class survey. What's the most popular way of communicating among your classmates?

> *I can discuss my communication preferences.* ☑

Wrap-up

1 Quick pair review

Lesson A **Test your partner!** Say three sentences in the present continuous. Can your partner say them correctly in the present perfect continuous? Take turns. You and your partner have two minutes.

A: *I'm reading a good book.*
B: *I've been reading a good book lately.*

Lesson B **Do you remember?** Complete the sentences with the correct phrases to express interest and offer options. Write the letter of the correct phrase. You have two minutes.

1. **A:** I'm interested _____
   B: You might want to consider _____
2. **A:** I'm looking _____
   B: One possibility is _____
3. **A:** I'm trying to find a way _____
   B: How _____

   a. getting an English-speaking tutor.
   b. to understand English recipes.
   c. in learning English for travel.
   d. about taking a cooking class in English?
   e. for a way to improve my pronunciation.
   f. getting an English travel magazine.

Lesson C **Brainstorm!** Make a list of ways to communicate and ways to avoid communicating. You have two minutes.

Lesson D **Find out!** Who are two people both you and your partner send text messages to – or would like to send messages to? You and your partner have one minute.

A: *I send text messages to my mom. Do you?*
B: *No, I don't. She doesn't have a cell phone. I send text messages to my sister. Do you?*
A: *Yes, I do.*

2 In the real world

How did your grandparents use to communicate with their friends and family? Talk to one of your grandparents or an older friend. How did they communicate before there were computers and cell phones? Write about it.

> *How My Grandparents Used to Communicate*
>   *My grandmother talked to her friends on a phone in her house. She also wrote them letters.*

Food

LESSON **A**	LESSON **B**	LESSON **C**	LESSON **D**
• Food preparation • Present passive	• Giving a recommendation • Accepting a recommendation	• Tastes and textures • Time clauses	• Reading: "Chocolate – From Forest to Factory" • Writing: A recipe

Warm-up

A Describe the pictures. What foods do you see?

B What have the foods been made into?

A | *Street food*

1 Vocabulary Food preparation

A 🔊 Match the words and the pictures. Then listen and check your answers.

a. bake	c. fry	e. melt	g. roast
b. boil	d. grill	f. microwave	h. steam

1. e 2. b 3. d 4. g

5. h 6. c 7. a 8. f

B Pair work What food can you prepare with each method in Part A? What food can't you prepare with each method? Tell your partner.

"You can melt cheese, but you can't melt fish."

2 Language in context On every street corner

A 🔊 Read the descriptions of popular street foods. What ingredients are mentioned?

Empanadas are a typical street snack in the Dominican Republic. They're dough that is filled with meat, vegetables, cheese, or a combination of all three. Then they're fried.

Bagels are a kind of bread that is sold by street vendors all over New York City. Bagels are boiled and then baked. They're often eaten with butter or cream cheese.

Satay is very popular in Indonesia. There are many types of satay, but usually meat is put on wooden sticks and then grilled. Satay is often served with peanut sauce.

B What about you? Do you have similar foods where you live? Which would you like to try right now?

3 Grammar 🔊 Present passive

The active voice places the focus of a sentence on the doer of an action. The passive voice places the focus on the receiver of the action. Use the passive voice when the doer is not known or is not important.

Active. The mouse (ate) the cheese.
Passive. The cheese (was eaten) by the mouse

Active

You **serve** satay with peanut sauce.
The cook **fries** the empanadas.
The vendor **boils** and then **bakes** the bagels.

Passive

Satay **is served** with peanut sauce.
The empanadas **are fried**.
Bagels **are boiled** and then **baked**.

A Complete the sentences with the present passive voice. Then compare with a partner.

1. Tamales are a traditional Mexican food. They __are selled__ (sell) on street corners all over the country. They __are maked__ (make) by filling dough with meat or vegetables. Then the dough __are wraped__ (wrap) in corn husks and it __is steamed__ (steam).

2. Crepes __are ate__ (eat) as a street snack all over France. Flour, eggs, and milk __are mixed__ (mix) together to make a batter. The batter __is poured__ (pour) onto a hot, flat pan, and then it __is cooked__ (cook). Crepes _____ (fill) with a variety of ingredients, such as cheese, chocolate, or vegetables.

3. In Japan, *taiyaki* is a popular snack that _____ (shape) like a fish. The sides of a mold _____ (cover) with batter. Then a filling such as sweet red bean paste _____ (add) to the mold. The mold _____ (close), and the taiyaki cakes _____ (cook) until they are golden brown.

B Pair work What similarities can you find among the street foods in Exercises 2 and 3? Tell your partner.

"Both empanadas and crepes are filled."

4 Speaking Popular street foods

Group work List three popular street foods. Then discuss these questions for each one.

- How is it made?
- What is it served with?
- Where is it sold?
- How much does it cost?
- When is it usually eaten?
- What do you like about it?

"Lamb shish kebabs are popular in Turkey. Pieces of lamb are put on a stick and grilled."

5 Keep talking!

Go to page **128** for more practice.

I can describe ways food is prepared. ☑

1 Interactions — Recommendations

A Do your friends or family ever give you recommendations for good places to eat? Do you ever recommend places to them? What qualities do you look for in a restaurant?

B ◄ѹ) Listen to the conversation. What is each person probably going to order? Then practice the conversation.

Ralph: I'm really glad we could meet for dinner.

Mai: So am I. I've been studying so much lately. All I've been eating is junk food.

Ralph: I know what you mean. Well, this is one of my favorite restaurants.

Mai: Everything looks so good. I have no idea what to get.

Ralph: Why don't you try the fish? This place is famous for it. It's grilled and served with fried rice or a baked potato, and a salad.

Mai: That's a good idea. Are you going to get the same?

Ralph: I'm not sure. I might try the roasted lamb with grilled vegetables.

Mai: Oh, that sounds delicious. Will you let me try some?

C ◄ѹ) Read the expressions below. Complete each box with a similar expression from the conversation. Then listen and check your answers.

Giving a recommendation	*Accepting a recommendation*
_____	_____
If I were you, I'd . . .	Sounds good to me.
My recommendation would be to . . .	OK, I think I'll do that.

D **Pair work** Have a conversation like the one in Part B. Use these foods.

2 Pronunciation Linked consonant and vowel sounds

A 🔊 Listen and repeat. Notice how consonant sounds are often linked to the vowel sounds that follow them.

if I were you   a good idea   for a long time   rice or potatoes

B 🔊 Listen to the conversation. Then practice with a partner. Pay attention to the linked sounds.

> **A:** If I were you, I'd order the steak and shrimp.
>
> **B:** That's a good idea. Where's our waiter?

3 Listening Eating habits

A 🔊 Listen to Tom talk to a nutritionist about his eating habits. Write the number of servings of each food Tom eats.

Food group	Number of servings	Recommendation
Grains (rice, bread, pasta, cereal, etc.)		more / less
Fruits (apples, berries, bananas, etc.)		more / less
Vegetables (lettuce, corn, carrots, etc.)		more / less
Dairy (milk, yogurt, cheese, etc.)		more / less
Protein (meat, fish, eggs, nuts, etc.)		more / less
Fats and oils (butter, olive oil, etc.)		more / less

B 🔊 Listen again. Does the nutritionist recommend that Tom eat more or less of each food group? Circle your answers.

4 Speaking Good recommendation!

A Read the situation. Check (✓) your recommendations and add other ideas.

My friend has no time to cook. My recommendation would be to . . .

- ☐ buy frozen dinners
- ☐ order takeout
- ☐ move back home with parents
- ☐ find a roommate who can cook
- ☐ visit friends at dinnertime
- ☐ other: _____
- ☐ other: _____
- ☐ other: _____

B Pair work Role-play the situation. Then change roles.

Student A: You have no time to cook. Listen to Student B's recommendations. Accept one recommendation.

Student B: Student A has no time to cook. Give some recommendations.

A: *I have no time to cook. I don't know what to do.*
B: *If I were you, I'd buy frozen dinners.*
A: *But I don't have a microwave.*
B: *Well, why don't you . . . ?*

I can give and accept recommendations.

1 **Vocabulary** Tastes and textures

A 🔊 Label the pictures with the correct words. Then listen and check your answers.

Tastes				
bland	salty	sour	spicy	sweet

Textures				
chewy	creamy	crunchy	juicy	sticky

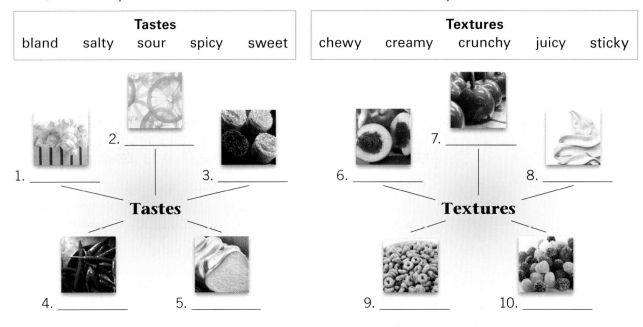

Tastes

1. _____ 2. _____ 3. _____

4. _____ 5. _____

Textures

6. _____ 7. _____ 8. _____

9. _____ 10. _____

B Pair work What are some foods that are both salty and crunchy? sweet and juicy? spicy and sticky? sour and chewy? bland and creamy? Tell your partner.

"Peanuts are both salty and crunchy."

2 **Conversation** A guest chef

A 🔊 Listen to the conversation. What ingredients are in cheese popcorn?

Host: Our guest today is chef Todd Brown. Welcome.

Todd: Thank you. Today we're going to make a salty, spicy, and super crunchy snack – cheese popcorn.

Host: Sounds good. What do we do first?

Todd: Well, we need to make a cheese sauce. But before we do that, we need to make the popcorn. I have some here that I've already microwaved.

Host: OK, so after you make the popcorn, you start the cheese sauce. And how do you do that?

Todd: Heat some cheese and butter in a pan until they melt. Once the cheese and butter are melted, add some salt and red pepper.

Host: Do you need to let the sauce cool?

Todd: No. As soon as it's done, pour it over the popcorn. Then bake it for about 20 minutes.

B 🔊 Listen to the rest of the conversation. What ingredients are in trail mix? How is it described?

3 Grammar 🔊 **Time clauses**

Use time clauses to show the order of events.

Before you start the cheese sauce, you make some popcorn.
After you make the popcorn, you start the cheese sauce.
Heat some cheese and butter in a pan **until they melt**.
Once they're melted, add some salt and red pepper.
As soon as it's done, pour it over the popcorn.

A Read the recipe. Circle the correct words in the sentences below the recipe.
Then compare with a partner.

Peruvian ceviche

Ingredients	Directions
1 kilogram of fresh fish 8 cloves of garlic 1 chili pepper juice from 10 limes salt 1 red onion	Cut the fish into small pieces. Put them in a bowl. Chop the garlic and chili pepper. Add them to the fish. Pour the lime juice in the bowl. This "cooks" the fish. Add salt. Then mix everything together. Slice the onion. Place it on top of the mixture. Let everything sit in the refrigerator for two hours. Mix and serve immediately with crunchy corn chips.

1. **Before / As soon as** you put the fish in a bowl, cut it into small pieces.
2. **Once / Until** the fish is in the bowl, chop the garlic and pepper.
3. **Before / After** you chop the garlic and pepper, add it to the fish.
4. Add salt **after / before** you pour the juice over the mixture.
5. Don't mix the onion with the fish **until / once** you remove it from the refrigerator.
6. **As soon as / Until** you mix the onion with the fish, serve it and enjoy!

B Pair work Close your books. Tell your partner the recipe for ceviche.

4 Speaking A new snack

A Pair work Use the food in the picture, or other food you know, and create an original snack. Give your snack a name, and describe how to make it.

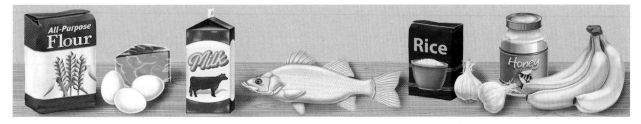

"Here's how to make Spicy Egg Surprise. Boil two eggs until they are done. Once . . ."

B Class activity Tell the class how to make your snack. Then vote on the best snack.

5 Keep talking!

Go to page 129 for more practice.

I can describe steps in a recipe.

D Chocolate!

1 Reading 🔊

A Do you like chocolate? What ingredients can you name in a chocolate bar?

B Read the article. Where do you think it comes from? Check (✓) the answer.

☐ a news blog ☐ a textbook ☐ a company brochure ☐ a newspaper

Chocolate – From Forest to Factory

Born in the rain forests
From Brazil to Indonesia to Ghana, you can find a very special tree – the cacao tree. Inside each fruit of this tree are 20 to 40 cocoa beans. These beans give chocolate its special taste.

Drying the beans
First the beans are removed from the fruit. After the beans are removed, they are dried. During this time, the familiar cocoa flavor develops. Then the beans are sent to the chocolate factory.

Liquid chocolate
At the factory, the beans are roasted. A machine then separates the shell from the bean. The insides of the beans are then ready for a process that makes them liquid (called chocolate liquor). As soon as the beans become liquid, they are ready for the rest of the ingredients.

Mixing it up
The primary ingredients in chocolate are chocolate liquor, cocoa butter, sugar, and milk. Milk is mixed with sugar, and this mixture is dried until it becomes thick. The chocolate liquor is combined with the milk and sugar mixture. This new mixture is then dried.

Perfecting the product
Once the new mixture has dried, cocoa butter is added. This gives the chocolate its special taste and creamy texture. A paste is created and poured into huge containers until it is cooled.

Wrapping it up
Chocolate bars are made by pouring the paste into molds. Finally, the paste is cooled until it becomes a candy bar. Now it's ready to wrap. And then unwrap . . . and eat!

Join our free tour to find out more!

Source: Adapted from www.hersheys.com/discover/chocolate.asp#

C Number the steps in the chocolate-making process from 1 to 6.

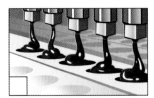

D **Pair work** Describe your favorite chocolate. What color is it? How does it taste? Does it have other ingredients in it?

2 Writing A recipe

A Make a list of your favorite dishes. Which dish is the most difficult to make? Which is the easiest?

B Write a simple recipe for one of your favorite dishes. Include the ingredients and the directions.

C Pair work Share your recipe with a partner. Are the steps clear?

> **Chocolate-covered strawberries**
>
> 20 strawberries
> 4–5 chocolate bars
> chopped nuts
>
>
>
> Wash and dry the strawberries.
> Boil some water, and then turn off the heat.
> Place the chocolate in a bowl over the water.
> Stir until it's melted. Remove the bowl from the heat.
> Dip each strawberry in the chocolate. Then dip into the nuts.
> Put in the refrigerator for 30 minutes.

3 Listening A tour for chocolate lovers

A 🔊 Listen to Yumiko get information about the San Francisco Gourmet Chocolate Tour. Check (✓) the things that the tour includes.

- ☐ a chocolate factory that makes chocolate bars
- ☐ the winner of *SF Weekly*'s "Best Chocolate" Award
- ☐ chocolate that's made using fresh ingredients from local farms
- ☐ a newsstand that sells 225 different kinds of chocolate
- ☐ a sculpture that's made of both white and dark chocolate
- ☐ hot chocolate that's prepared by one of the best chocolate makers in the city
- ☐ a Swiss chocolate maker who is famous for chocolate truffles
- ☐ a Mexican chef who makes a sauce from chocolate and chilies

chocolate truffles

B 🔊 Listen to the rest of the conversation. Complete the information.

Cost	Meeting place	Times	Group size

4 Speaking A food tour

A Pair work Plan a food tour of a restaurant, a farmers' market, or another place where you live. Answer these questions, and add your own ideas.

- What food will your tour include?
- What places will you visit?
- What will your tour do there?
- Who will lead the tour?
- What will be the cost, meeting place, time, and group size?

A: *Everyone likes ice cream. My recommendation would be to create an ice-cream tour.*

B: *That's a good idea. Or we could do something more unusual. How about a chili-pepper tour?*

B Class activity Share your tour plan. Which tours are the most interesting? Why?

> *I can plan and describe a food tour.* ☑

Wrap-up

1 Quick pair review

Lesson A Brainstorm! Make a list of food-preparation verbs. How many do you know? You have one minute.

Lesson B Find out! What are two things both you and your partner would eat at a food fair? Give and accept recommendations to find out. You and your partner have two minutes.

A: *I want something fried.*
B: *Me, too. My recommendation would be to try a fried candy bar.*
A: *That's a good idea.*

Lesson C Guess! Give simple directions for a cooking recipe. Use time clauses. Can your partner guess the food? You and your partner have two minutes.

A: *Before you pop it, heat oil in the pan.*
B: *Is it popcorn?*
A: *Yes.*

Lesson D Give your opinion! What do you think of these foods? Check (✓) *Easy to make* or *Hard to make*. Write a description of the taste and texture. Then discuss. You and your partner have three minutes.

	Easy to make	Hard to make	Taste	Texture
pizza				
lemon cake				
rice				
onion rings				

A: *I think pizza is easy to make!*
B: *I think it's hard to make, but it tastes good. It's spicy and chewy.*

2 In the real world

What's your favorite food? Go online or look in a magazine, and find a recipe for it in English. Then write about it.

- What is it?
- What are the ingredients?
- How do you make it?

Chicken and rice
Ingredients: chicken, rice, peanuts, oil, vegetables
Heat the oil. Fry the chicken and vegetables in the oil. Cook the rice. Put the peanuts on top and serve.

Behavior

LESSON **A**	LESSON **B**	LESSON **C**	LESSON **D**
• Polite and impolite behavior • Second conditional	• Expressing an expectation • Acknowledging an expectation	• Word partners • Past modals for hypothetical situations	• Reading: "Make Someone Happy" • Writing: An act of kindness

Warm-up

A Look at the picture. Which people are not behaving well?

B Is there behavior at the movies that makes you angry? Would that behavior be OK in a different place?

A The right thing to do

1 Vocabulary Polite and impolite behavior

A 🔊 Label the phrases P (polite behavior) or I (impolite behavior). Then listen and check your answers.

1. cut in line

2. admit a mistake

3. drop litter

4. talk loudly in public

5. give someone a compliment

6. offer someone your seat

7. keep someone waiting

8. give someone a gift

B Pair work Have you done any of the things in Part A? What happened?

2 Language in context Typical behavior

A 🔊 Read the survey. Which answer did more than half of the people agree with?

1. **What would you do if a stranger dropped litter in front of you?**

   20% said, "I would talk to the person."

   28% said, "I would pick it up."

   40% said, "I wouldn't do anything."

   12% said, "Other."

   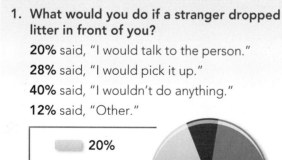

2. **If a stranger were talking loudly behind you in a theater, what would you do?**

   60% said, "I would ask the person to be quiet."

   20% said, "I would change seats."

   4% said, "I wouldn't do anything."

   16% said, "Other."

   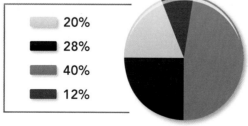

   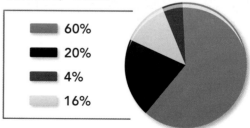

B What about you? Do the responses surprise you? What do you think some of the "other" responses were for each question?

3 Grammar 🔊 Second conditional

Second conditional sentences describe "unreal" or imaginary situations. Use a past tense verb in the if clause (the condition). Use would *in the main clause. Use* were *for the past tense of* be *in the condition.*

If a stranger **were talking** loudly behind you in a movie theater, what **would** you **do**?

    I**'d change** seats. I **wouldn't ask** the person to be quiet.

If a stranger **dropped** litter in front of you, **would** you **pick** it up?

    Yes, I **would**. I**'d** probably **throw** it away.

How **would** you **feel** if someone **gave** you a gift for no reason?

    If someone **gave** me a gift for no reason, I**'d feel** happy.

A Complete the conversations with the second conditional. Then practice with a partner.

1. **A:** If someone _*were playing*_ (play) loud music on the subway, what
   ____*would*____ you _____*do*_____ (do)?

   B: I _____ (ask) the person to turn it down.

2. **A:** What _____ you _____ (do) if a friend _____ (give) you a compliment?

   B: I _____ (thank) him.

3. **A:** If someone _____ (cut) in line in front of you, what _____ you _____ (say)?

   B: I _____ (not / say) anything. I _____ (wait) for my turn.

4. **A:** What _____ you _____ (do) if an elderly man _____ (stand) on your bus?

   B: I _____ (offer) him my seat.

B Pair work Ask and answer the questions in Part A. Answer with your own information.

4 Speaking What would you do?

A Complete this question:

"What would you do if _____?"

B Class activity Talk to different classmates and ask your question. Take notes on their answers.

    A: *What would you do if a friend gave you an unusual gift?*
    B: *I'd probably laugh.*
    C: *I wouldn't do that. I'd smile and say thank you.*

C Group work Share what you found out. What were the most polite answers?

5 Keep talking!

Go to page 130 for more practice.

I can discuss how I would react to a situation.

B I didn't realize that.

1 Interactions — Expectations

A Have you ever made a mistake because you didn't know a custom?

B 🔊 Listen to the conversation. What mistake did Ruben make?
Then practice the conversation.

Diana: So, Ruben, how do you like it here?
Ruben: Oh, I love it. The people, the food – but can I ask you something?
Diana: Sure, anything.
Ruben: Well, last night I was invited to a classmate's house for dinner. It was the first time. And I think I made a mistake.
Diana: What happened?
Ruben: Dinner was at 7:30. As usual in my country, I arrived a little after 8:00. My friend seemed kind of surprised.
Diana: Here it's the custom to arrive on time or no more than 10 minutes late.
Ruben: Really? I didn't realize that.
Diana: Well, you'll know for next time.

C 🔊 Read the expressions below. Complete each box with a similar expression from the conversation. Then listen and check your answers.

Expressing an expectation	Acknowledging an expectation
_____	_____
You're supposed to . . .	Oh, I didn't know that.
You're expected to . . .	Oh, really? I wasn't aware of that.

D **Pair work** Talk about expectations. Use this information and take turns.

the United States	Japan	Argentina
Leave a tip of 15 to 20 percent in most restaurants.	Take off your shoes before you enter someone's home.	Begin to eat only after the host or hostess invites you to.
China	**Morocco**	**Russia**
Greet the oldest person in a group first.	Bargain for lower prices on souvenirs in markets.	Bring a small gift if you are invited to someone's home.

A: *In the United States, it's the custom to leave a tip of 15 to 20 percent in most restaurants.*
B: *Oh, really? I wasn't aware of that.*

2 **Listening** Cross-cultural differences

A 🔊 Listen to four people talk about customs in their country. Write the country name.

1. _____
   You're expected to _____
   _____
   _____

2. _____
   You're supposed to _____
   _____
   _____

3. _____
   It's the custom to _____
   _____
   _____

4. _____
   You're not supposed to _____
   _____
   _____

B 🔊 Listen again. What is the custom in each country? Write the sentences.

3 **Speaking** Good things to know

A Think about a country you know. Choose three topics below. What are the expectations for polite behavior there? How would you tell a visitor to behave?

receiving gifts	eating in a restaurant	pointing and gesturing
cutting in line	giving gifts	talking loudly in public
doing business	greeting people	visiting someone's home
dropping litter	money and shopping	walking or driving

B **Pair work** Share your ideas.

A: *In China, you're not supposed to open gifts immediately.*
B: *Really? I didn't know that.*

I can *express and acknowledge expectations.* ✓

C Doing things differently

1 Vocabulary Word partners

A 🔊 Circle the verbs or verb phrases in column A that partner with the nouns in column B. Then listen and check your answers.

A	B
1. (offer)/ do /(accept)	an apology
2. tell / (ask for) / (offer)	an explanation
3. (agree with) / (disagree with) / turn down	an opinion
4. (make) / give / (turn down)	a request °ask for something to done
5. deny / (give) / accept	a compliment cumplido
6. admit / (ask for) / (return)	a favor do something for somebody,
7. (reach) / say / (suggest)	a compromise
8. say / (accept) / (turn down) rechazar	an invitation
9. (make) / offer / do	an excuse

B **Pair work** Ask and answer the question "When was the last time you . . . ?" with four different word partners from Part A.

> **A:** *When was the last time you asked for a favor?*
> **B:** *Last night. I asked my brother to help me with my homework.*

2 Conversation I feel terrible.

A 🔊 Listen to the conversation. Steve asked Paul for a favor. What was it?

Paul: I made a terrible mistake.
Lydia: Why? What happened?
Paul: Well, you know Steve, the new guy in our class?
Lydia: Yeah, I think so.
Paul: Well, yesterday he asked me for a favor. He wanted to borrow my laptop. I said I didn't think it was a good idea, and now he's upset with me.
Lydia: Really?
Paul: Yeah. Should I have lent it to him? What would you have done?
Lydia: I'm not really sure.
Paul: Well, would *you* have let him use *your* laptop?
Lydia: I don't know. I guess it would have depended. What did he need it for?

B 🔊 Listen to the phone conversation. Why does Steve call Paul? What does Paul offer Steve?

3 Grammar 🔊 Past modals for hypothetical situations

Use past modals to talk about hypothetical situations in the past. Use should have *to talk about the right thing to do,* could have *to talk about possibilities, and* would have *to imagine your behavior.*

I **should have lent** him my laptop.	**Should** I **have lent** it to him?
I **shouldn't have said** no.	Yes, you **should have**.
He **could have offered** you an explanation.	No, you **shouldn't have**.
It **would have depended**.	What **would** you **have done**?

Complete the conversations with past modals. Then practice with a partner.

1. **A:** My sister loves her new haircut. I told her I hated it. Now she's mad at me.

   B: That wasn't nice! I _**wouldn't have said**_ (wouldn't / say) that. You
   Could have given (could / give) her a compliment instead.

   [handwritten: have + P.P.]

2. **A:** _Should_ I _have invited_ (should / invite) the whole class to my party? I didn't, and now some people are angry.

   B: Yes, you _Should have_ . But your apartment is really too small.

3. **A:** My cousin asked me for a favor. He wanted to borrow my new car. What
   Would you _have done_ (would / do)?

   B: I _Would have said_ (would / say) no.

4. **A:** A few days ago, I broke the microwave at my office by accident.

   B: You _Should have offered_ (should / offer) to buy a new microwave.

4 Pronunciation Reduction of *have*

A 🔊 Listen and repeat. Notice how *have* is reduced in past modals.

You could have given her a compliment.   You shouldn't have said that. *[handwritten: Shouldn't've]*

I would have asked her for an explanation.   I wouldn't have done that. *[handwritten: Would've]*

B Practice the conversations in Exercise 3. Use the reduced form of *have*.

5 Speaking What would you have done?

A Have you done any of these things? What happened? Choose one and prepare to talk about it.

- You returned a favor.
- You disagreed with an opinion.
- You made an excuse.
- You suggested a compromise.

B Group work Share your experiences. Would you have done things differently? Discuss your opinions.

> **A:** *Last week, my friend lent me his car. When his car broke down this week, I returned the favor and gave him my car.*
> **B:** *I would have done the same thing.*

6 Keep talking!

Go to page **131** for more practice.

I can talk about past hypothetical situations.	✓

1 Reading 🔊

A Read this quote. What do you think it means?

fabulas

"No act of kindness, however small, is ever wasted." – Aesop

Make Someone Happy

A man gives a stranger his umbrella during a rainstorm. A teenager picks up litter on her way to school. A woman lets a shopper with fewer groceries cut in line at the supermarket. A man puts money into parking meters on the street so no one gets a ticket.

What do these acts have in common? They are all **random** acts of kindness, **selfless** acts that a person does to make people happy, with nothing expected in return. The acts may be **spontaneous** or planned in advance. The person who receives a random act of kindness may know the person who performed the act, but often the acts are done **anonymously**.

Random acts of kindness are often encouraged by schools and communities. In fact, in some countries, February 17 is Random Acts of Kindness Day, an unofficial holiday. For many people, it's important on this day to "pay it forward." This means if someone does something kind for you, you don't pay "back" that person by returning a kind act to him or her. Instead, you pay it "forward" to someone new. This can be a wonderful way to make both you and someone else very happy.

EXAMPLES OF RANDOM ACTS OF KINDNESS

- Give a stranger a compliment.
- Give someone a gift for no reason.
- Stop and help someone fix a flat tire.
- Let someone cut in line at the bank.
- Offer your seat, and not just to an elderly person.

- Give another driver your parking spot.
- Leave a copy of a good book on a train or a bus.
- Help someone with his or her grocery shopping.
- Offer an apology even if it isn't required.

B Read the article. Find the words in **bold**. Circle the correct meaning.

1. **random** *no rules* *no hora* a. with no pattern — *habito patron*   b. with a regular pattern
2. **selfless**   a. putting your own needs first   b. putting others' needs first
3. **spontaneous**   a. with no planning   b. large and important
4. **anonymously**   a. knowing the person's name   b. without knowing the name

C According to the article, which of these would be random acts of kindness? Check (✓) the correct answers.

- ☑ You buy a friend dinner for no reason.
- ☐ You let yourself sleep late on the weekend.
- ☐ You get a job to save money for college.
- ☐ You return a book that you borrowed.
- ☑ You help a neighbor paint his house.
- ☑ You offer your seat to someone.

D Group work Choose an act of kindness from the reading and discuss it. What would you do if someone did it for you? How would you feel? Would you "pay it forward"? How?

2 Listening For no reason

A 🔊 Listen to four callers to a radio show talk about acts of kindness. Was each act performed or received by them? Check (✓) the correct answer.

	Performed	Received	Act of kindness
1. Jared	☐	☑	*~~Line~~ Some one let him eat in line*
2. Keisha	☑	☐	*Flax tire. She helped a Woman to fix her tire*
3. Antonio	☐	☑	*A friend give a gift. for (not) reason.*
4. Mei-li	☑	☑	*Keisha fixxed her Flax tire, give parkin spot.*

[handwritten notes above header: "receiv"]

B 🔊 Listen again. What was each act of kindness? Write it in the chart.

[handwritten, right side: A woman helped her fix. she gave another driver her parting spot]

3 Writing An act of kindness

A Group work Choose one of these topics. Discuss what happened.

> something nice someone did for you
> something nice you did for someone
> something nice you'd like to do for someone

B Write a paragraph about your topic. Use the reading and the model paragraph to help you.

C Class activity Post your paragraphs around the room. Read your classmates' paragraphs. Then get more information about a paragraph that interests you.

> *An Act of Kindness*
> *This happened to me last year. I was having a really bad day, so I went to an ice cream shop. I ordered some ice cream, and when I went to pay for it, I couldn't find my wallet. Just then, the person in front of me paid for it! Then she smiled and walked away. I couldn't believe it. She did it just to be nice.*

4 Speaking Doing nice things

Group work Look at the picture. What would be some nice things to do? Discuss your ideas.

> I can discuss ways to be kind. ☑

Wrap-up

1 Quick pair review

Lesson A **Guess!** Think about your partner. How would your partner complete each sentence? Can you guess? Take turns. You and your partner have two minutes.

I _____ if I made a mistake.

If someone cut in line in front of me, I _____ .

I _____ if I didn't finish my homework.

A: *You would say you're sorry if you made a mistake.*
B: *No, I wouldn't. I wouldn't tell anyone if I made a mistake.*

Lesson B **Do you remember?** Complete the sentences with the correct words to express and acknowledge expectations. You have two minutes.

1. **A:** It's the _____ to arrive on time.

   B: Oh, really? I wasn't _____ of that.

2. **A:** You're _____ to wait in line here.

   B: Oh, I didn't _____ that.

3. **A:** You're _____ to bring a small gift.

   B: I _____ realize that.

Lesson C **Test your partner!** Say a verb or a verb phrase that partners with one of the nouns below. Can your partner choose the correct word to make a phrase? Take turns. You and your partner have two minutes.

| an apology | a compromise | an explanation | an invitation |
| an compliment | an excuse | a favor | an opinion |

"Ask for."

1. *ask for an explanation*   3. _____

2. _____   4. _____

Lesson D **Find out!** What is one random act of kindness both you and your partner have done? You and your partner have two minutes.

A: *I've given someone my seat on the bus. Have you?*
B: *No, I haven't. I've given my mother a compliment. Have you?*

2 In the real world

What's polite and impolite in different countries? Go online and find three examples of polite and impolite behavior for an English-speaking country. Then write about it.

- What is the country?
- What is the behavior?

Behavior in Australia
In Australia, it's polite to come to meetings on time. It's impolite to miss a doctor's appointment and not call first.

Travel and tourism

LESSON **A**	LESSON **B**	LESSON **C**	LESSON **D**
• Compound adjectives • Comparatives and superlatives	• Reporting a problem • Responding to a problem	• Travel talk • Reporting commands and advice	• Reading: "Welcome to Medellín, Colombia" • Writing: Creating a home page

Warm-up

1. *a*

Ulan Bator, Mongolia

2. *f*

Wellington, New Zealand

3. *c*

Damascus, Syria

4. *e*

La Paz, Bolivia

5. *d*

Reykjavik, Iceland

6. *b*

Cairo, Egypt

A Look at the capital cities. Match them to their descriptions.

a. the coldest	c. the oldest	e. the highest
b. the driest	d. the most northern	f. the most southern

B What's your capital city like? What three adjectives do you think best describe it?

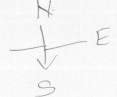

Cities

1 Vocabulary Compound adjectives

A 🔊 Complete the sentences with the correct words. Then listen and check your answers.

| culturally diverse |
| densely populated |
| fun-loving |
| high-tech |
| highly educated |
| open-minded |
| slow-paced |
| well-planned |
| world-famous |

1. Everyone knows New York City. It's a <u>world-famous</u> city with many interesting places to visit.
2. Bangalore is a very <u>high tech</u> place. It's the center of India's computer industry.
3. For a capital city, Vientiane in Laos is a <u>slow-paced</u> place. It's a great place to not be in a hurry.
4. Lagos is a very <u>densely populated</u> city. There are about 20,000 people per square kilometer.
5. Brasília is a <u>well planned</u> city. There are wide roads, a lot of green space, and great public transportation.
6. Singapore's people are <u>highly educated</u>. Many continue their studies after they finish high school.
7. The people in San Francisco are very <u>open minded</u>. They are open to new ideas, opinions, and experiences.
8. There are a lot of <u>fun-loving</u> people in San Juan, Puerto Rico. They love to go out and have a good time.
9. London is an extremely <u>culturally diverse</u> city. You can find people from all over the world there.

B Pair work Which words in Part A describe people? Which describe places? Which describe people and places? Tell your partner.

2 Language in context My city

A 🔊 Listen to three people describe their cities. Where does each person live?

I used to live in Buenos Aires, but I live in Mendoza now. It's not as crowded as Buenos Aires, so it's slower-paced here. But I think the people are pretty fun-loving and open-minded. And there's a great music scene!
– *Angela, Argentina*

I live in St. Petersburg, but I was born in Moscow. I like both cities, but I prefer St. Petersburg. In the winter, it isn't as cold as Moscow. It's a well-planned city, and I think it's even a little cheaper than Moscow.
– *Boris, Russia*

I like Osaka for its shopping, but I love it for its food. I think the food is better than in Tokyo. In fact, I think it has the best food in Japan! We have a saying here: "Eat till you drop in Osaka!" I never want to move!
– *Nozomi, Japan*

Moscow is colder than St. Peterburgs
St. Peterburgs is warner that Moscow

B Which city do you think would be good for tourists? students? businesspeople? Why?

"Osaka would be good for tourists because the food is good and tourists love to eat!"

3 Grammar Comparatives and superlatives

Comparisons	Superlatives
St. Petersburg is **cheaper than** Moscow.	. . . is **the cheapest** city in Russia.
Buenos Aires is **more crowded than** Mendoza.	. . . is **the most crowded** city.
St. Petersburg is **less expensive than** Moscow.	. . . is **the least expensive** city.
The food in Osaka is **better than** in Tokyo.	. . . is **the best** food in the world.
Traffic here is **worse than** in St. Petersburg.	. . . is **the worst** traffic I've ever seen.

(not) as . . . as

St. Petersburg is**n't as cold as** Moscow. Osaka is **as high-tech as** Tokyo.

Atlanta isn't as expensive as Miami

A Complete the sentences with the comparative form of the adjectives.

1. Today's high temperature is 29°C in Bangkok and 26°C in Chiang Mai. Bangkok is hotter that (hot) Chiang Mai.
2. The average cost of a house in Denver, Colorado, is $345,000. The average cost of a house in Salt Lake City, Utah, is $310,000. Houses in Salt Lake City are less expensive than (expensive) houses in Denver.
3. There are 7,200 people per square kilometer in São Paulo, and 5,200 people per square kilometer in Rio de Janeiro. São Paulo is more densely populary than. (densely populated) Rio.
4. Mumbai usually gets 87 centimeters of rain and very little sunshine in July. In January, there is almost no rain, and the weather is mild and sunny. The weather in July is worse than (bad) in January.

1 + Syllables (1) Adjective + than
2+ Syllables (2) more / less +
(1) hotter than, Colder than
(2) more expensive than. less expensive

B **Pair work** Say each sentence in Part A in a different way. Use *not as . . . as.*

"Chiang Mai isn't as hot as Bangkok."

C Complete the questions with the superlative form of the adjectives. Work with a partner. Ask and answer with your own information.

1. What's ***the most high-tech*** (high-tech) city in your country?
2. What's the worst (bad) restaurant in your town?
3. What's the most culturylly diverse (culturally diverse) city in your country?
4. What's the less populated (less populated) part of your country?

In Mexico city The traffic is worst than other states.

Exepciones. clever gentle friendly quiet

4 Speaking Comparing three cities

Group work Compare three cities you know. Talk about:

education	food	shopping	transportation
entertainment	people	traffic	weather

A: *Why don't we compare Curitiba, São Paulo, and Santos?*
B: *OK. São Paulo is bigger than Curitiba.*
C: *Curitiba is the most well-planned of the three.*

5 Keep talking!

Go to page 132 for more practice.

I can *make comparisons about cities.*

1 Interactions — Problems

A What do you think are the most common hotel complaints? If you had a problem with a hotel room, what would you do?

B 🔊 Listen to the conversation. What's the problem? Then practice the conversation.

Clerk: Front desk. Please hold.

· · · · · · · · · · · ·

Clerk: Thank you for waiting. How can I help you?

Lina: Um, hi. I just checked in a few minutes ago. There's a problem with my Internet connection. I can't get a wireless signal.

Clerk: I'm very sorry. I'll let someone know right away.

Lina: Thank you. I'd appreciate it.

Clerk: Is there anything else I can help you with?

Lina: Um, yeah. Can you recommend a restaurant near the hotel?

Clerk: Yes, there are several, but our hotel restaurant is one of the best in the city.

C 🔊 Read the expressions below. Complete each box with a similar expression from the conversation. Then listen and check your answers.

Reporting a problem	Responding to a problem
_____	_____
I'm having a problem with . . .	I'll get someone to take care of it.
There seems to be a problem with . . .	I'll have someone get on it right away.

D **Pair work** Have conversations like the one in Part B. Use these problems.

The air-conditioning isn't working.

The table lamp doesn't have a bulb.

The bathroom sink is clogged. Adj.
to clog→Verb

The door has a broken knob.

46

2 **Pronunciation** Linking of same consonant sounds

🔊 Listen and repeat. Notice the linking of the same consonant sounds at the end and beginning of words. The sound is pronounced only once.

There's no wireless signal.

The radio has a broken knob.

The bathroom mirror is dirty.

The table lamp doesn't have a bulb.

3 **Listening** How can I help you?

A 🔊 Listen to three people call the front desk at a hotel. Check (✓) the problem.

Problem	Response	Solved?
1. ☑ She hears a strange noise. ☐ She can't close her windows.	*I let some one*	(yes) no
2. ☑ The TV won't turn on. ☐ There's no battery in the remote.	*I get some one how take care it*	yes (no)
3. ☑ There isn't any electricity. ☐ The desk lamp needs a new bulb.	*I have some one get in right in*	(yes) no

B 🔊 Listen again. How does the man at the front desk respond to the problems? What does he say he will do? Write the sentences in the chart.

C 🔊 Listen. A hotel worker comes to solve each problem. Does he? Circle *yes* or *no*.

4 **Speaking** Problems, problems, problems

Pair work Role-play the situation. Then change roles.

Student A: Call the front desk three times to report three problems in your hotel room.

Student B: You work at the front desk. Answer the phone and respond to each problem.

A: *There's a problem with my room. There are bugs on the wall.*
B: *I'll have someone get on it right away.*

cob webs

Torn

*made →unmade
maid*

bed bugs

I can *report and respond to a problem.* ☑

C Travel experiences

1 Vocabulary Travel talk

A 🔊 Read Luke's travel blog. Complete the chart with the **bold** words in the blog. Then listen and check your answers.

LUKE'S TRAVEL BLOG

Sunday, August 25th

My trip's been full of surprises so far. First, my flight here was **delayed**. I took the next one, and I was **upgraded** to first class! *problem something wrong* Then I discovered that my visa was **expired**, but I was **issued** one at the airport on arrival. Good thing! But they lost my luggage.

When I went to my two-star hotel, I found out it was **overbooked**. But I had a reservation, and it was **guaranteed**. So they put me in a four-star hotel for the same price. *dicetener 5 start buy isn't*

I read that the museums here are always **packed** and the restaurants are **overrated** and **overpriced**. But I went to a museum early this morning, and there were only a few people there. I even got a **discounted** ticket! After that, I went to a famous restaurant for lunch. It was priced right, and it was the best meal I've ever had.

Good experiences
1. _guarant_
2. _packe_
3. _on ___
4. _discounted_

Bad experiences
5. _delayed_
6. _upgraded_
7. _expired_
8. _____
9. _____
10. _priced_

B What experiences have you had like Luke's? Which have you never had?

2 Conversation Welcome home!

A 🔊 Listen and practice. Where's Luke's luggage?

Jae-Sun: Luke! Welcome home!
Luke: Hi, Jae-Sun. Thanks for picking me up.
Jae-Sun: That's what friends are for. I read your blog. I can't believe your flight was delayed *and* your hotel was overbooked.
Luke: I know, but things turned out OK.
Jae-Sun: Hey, where's your luggage?
Luke: They never found it! The man at the airport told me to be patient.
Jae-Sun: Patient? Are you serious? You've *been* patient.
Luke: Well, he advised me to call in a few days to check on it. Anyway, look! I got you a souvenir.
Jae-Sun: Really? Thank you!

B 🔊 Listen to a phone conversation between Luke and the man at the airport. Where is Luke's luggage now? When can he expect his luggage? *Mongolia*

3 Grammar 🔊 Reporting commands and advice

mandatos y Consejos (handwritten)

These reporting verbs are followed by an object + infinitive. Notice the placement of not.

The man said:

a → use to (infinitive) (handwritten) · *infinitive* (handwritten)

"Be patient."	He **told me to be** patient.
"Don't be impatient."	He **told me not to be** impatient.
"Remember to take your room key."	He **reminded us to take** our room key.
"Don't forget your room key."	He **reminded us not to forget** our room key.
"Call in a few days."	He **advised me to call** in a few days.
"Don't carry a lot of cash."	He **warned her not to carry** a lot of cash.

Look at your friend Maria's travel advice. Rewrite her advice. Use reporting verbs. Then compare with a partner.

infinitive (handwritten)

1. "Get a good guidebook."   tell   *She told me to get a good guidebook.*
   She told me not to pack too much. (handwritten)
2. "Don't pack too much."   tell   *She advised me to buy a youth hostel card.* (handwritten)
3. "Buy a youth hostel card."   advise   *She reminded me to get a visa.* (handwritten)
4. "Get a visa."   remind   *She warned me not to go out at night alone.* (handwritten)
5. "Don't go out at night alone."   warn   *She told me to keep my passport safe* (handwritten)
6. "Keep your passport safe."   tell   *She advised me to use atm's to get cash.* (handwritten)
7. "Use ATMs to get cash."   advise   *She remieded me Not to forget to write.* (handwritten)
8. "Don't forget to write."   remind

4 Speaking Good advice

A Class activity Talk to different classmates. What advice would they give an overseas visitor to their city? Write their names and advice in the chart.

extranjeros (handwritten) · *used to / accustomed to* (handwritten)

Advice about . . .	Name	Advice
a tourist attraction to avoid	Diego	Don't go to street fairs. They're packed and overrated.
a "must-see" tourist attraction	Rocio	Do you must see stone mountain' fire works.
a restaurant to avoid	Rosa Maria	Avoid to go McDonal's restaurant fast food.
the best way to get around	Natali	You should take Martha to go aroud.
a good way to save money	Magaly	The best way to save money is use Marth for to go around to the city

B Group work Imagine you are the overseas visitor. Report the advice you heard. Does everyone agree with the advice?

"Diego advised me not to go to street fairs. They're packed and overrated."

Kosta said "Do your homework" He told us to do our homework. (handwritten)

5 Keep talking!

Go to page 133 for more practice.

I can report commands and advice.

1 Reading ◀))

A Do you like to visit new places? What things do you especially like to see and do?

B Read the headings under *Travel essentials* and *Things to see and do*. What topics are covered under *Travel essentials*? What topics are covered under *Things to see and do*?

Welcome to
MEDELLÍN, COLOMBIA
the City of Everlasting Spring

TRAVEL ESSENTIALS

Climate Medellín is located at about 5,000 feet (1,538 meters) above sea level. Its climate is not as hot as other cities located near the equator. The city's average temperature is a pleasant 72°F (22°C). Read more

Getting here Medellín has an international airport, with flights from Miami, New York, Madrid, and many other cities. There are taxis and minibuses from the airport to downtown Medellín. Read more

Getting around The quickest and cheapest way to get around Medellín is with the well-planned metro system. The modern Turibus also goes around the city, showing parks, beautiful neighborhoods, and historical sites. Read more

Where to stay There are many hotels, but hostels are also popular, especially when hotels are overbooked. Many hostels include hot showers, TV, laundry service, free Internet, private lockers, and Spanish lessons. Read more

THINGS TO SEE AND DO

Shopping Medellín is only a few hours from the coffee-growing centers of Colombia. Coffee makes a great souvenir. Medellín is sometimes called the textile capital of the country, but it is not the best place to shop for clothes. Read more

Nightlife The fun-loving people of Medellín love to dance. There are many places around the city to dance. One of the most famous is the Zona Rosa. Most clubs close at 3:00 a.m. Read more

Sightseeing There are world-famous museums in the city, but one "must-see" is the Museo de Antioquia. It has a large collection of art, including paintings and sculptures by Fernando Botero. Read more

Festivals Why not plan a trip around a festival? There's a poetry festival in July, a celebration of lights in December and January, and for two weeks in August, a flower festival – the city's most important cultural event. Read more

C Read the home page. Answer the questions.

1. How can you get from the airport to downtown? _In taxis and minibuses_
2. What's the least expensive way to get around the city? _metro System, The modern turibus._
3. What local product would make a great souvenir? _Medellín. Coffe_
4. What's one of the most famous places to go to at night? _Zona Rosa._
5. What can you find at the Museo de Antioquia? _large collection of art including painting and Sculptures_
6. When is the flower festival? _two weeks in August_

D Imagine you had only one day in Medellín. How would you spend your day?

2 Writing Creating a home page

A **Group work** What kind of information might appear on your town's home page?
Make a list of topics. Use the topics in Exercise 1 to help you.

B **Group work** Create and design a home page for your town. Have each student write a
paragraph about a topic from your list in Part A. Use Exercise 1 and the model to help you.

Shopping
Our town is a shopper's paradise! There is
something for everyone, and the prices are great.
You can buy textiles, jewelry, and the painted
wooden creatures that so many tourists love. . . .

C **Class activity** Post your home pages around the room. Which home page best
represents your town?

3 Listening City festivals

A 🔊 Listen to four people talk about city festivals. Complete the second and third
columns of the chart.

Name of the festival	Year started	Month of the festival	One thing to see or do
1. Milan Melon Festival	1958	september 1508	races, large 'atapy Brown Melon festivo
2. Pusan International Film Festival	1996	fall August - Sept- Oct	Lot thing to wach disco, diferrent films
3. Historic Center Festival of Mexico City	1985	April 9 1960 -	Event to do, Game music, teather
4. Edinburgh Festival Fringe	1947	August	Actor Perfomerd Dance — Music —

[handwritten: Thomas Edwon / Edison]

B 🔊 Listen again. Complete the chart. Write one thing to see or do at each festival.

C Which festival would you most like to attend? Why?

4 Speaking A festival to remember

A **Group work** Plan a festival for your town. Use these ideas or ideas
of your own for fun events at the festival.

a contest	a parade
a fashion show	a sporting event

A: *Our town is well known for corn.*
B: *So why don't we have a Corn Festival?*
C: *We could have a corn-eating contest.*

B **Class activity** Share your ideas.

I can discuss ideas for a festival in my town. ☑

Wrap-up

1 Quick pair review

Lesson A **Do you remember?** Match the words. You have one minute.

1. fun- _____		a. tech
2. open- _____		b. minded
3. densely _____		c. paced
4. high- _____		d. loving
5. highly _____		e. educated
6. well- _____		f. populated
7. culturally _____		g. diverse
8. slow- _____		h. famous
9. world- _____		i. planned

Lesson B **Brainstorm!** Make a list of ways to report a problem and respond to a problem. How many do you know? You have two minutes.

Lesson C **Test your partner!** Give your friend travel advice using commands. Can your partner say the sentence using reported commands or advice? Take turns. You and your partner have one minute.

A: *Make a reservation.*
B: *You told me to make a reservation.*

Lesson D **Find out!** How would you and your partner answer these questions? You and your partner have two minutes.

- What's the most expensive restaurant in your town?
- What's the best festival in your country?
- What's the most high-tech building in your town?

A: *I think the most expensive restaurant is Sushi King.*
B: *Me, too!*

2 In the real world

What country would you like to visit? What two cities in that country would you like to see? Find information online or in a travel magazine about these cities. Then write about them.

- Which city is more densely populated?
- Which city is slower-paced?
- Which city is cheaper?
- Which city has better weather?

Two Cities in Peru
I'd like to visit Lima and Arequipa in Peru.
Lima is more densely populated than Arequipa.

The way we are

Warm-up

☐ sauce ☐ cheese ☐ spices ☐ meat ☐ other toppings ☐ crust

Pizza and you

CRUST: You are very adventurous. You love to try new things.

SAUCE: You like trendy things. You enjoy the finer things in life.

CHEESE: You don't care for trendy things. You prefer tradition.

SPICES: You enjoy traditional and modern things equally.

MEAT: You are strong and like to be in control of any situation.

OTHER TOPPINGS: You make changes easily. You like everyone and everything.

Source: Adapted from www.blogthings.com/whatsyourpizzapersonalityquiz

A Look at the picture. What is your favorite part of a pizza? Check (✓) the box.

B Read the *Pizza and you* box. What does your answer in Part A show about your personality? Do you agree? Do you think personality tests like this can tell you about your personality?

A Who I am

1 Vocabulary Character traits

A 🔊 Match the adjectives and the descriptions. Then listen and check your answers.

1. competitive _b_
2. energetic _c_
3. idealistic _a_
4. imaginative _f_
5. independent _d_
6. logical _e_
7. loyal _i_   *Lealtiar*
8. rebellious _h_
9. studious _g_

a. You believe you can make good things happen.
b. You want to be better than everyone else.
c. You are active and enthusiastic.
d. You think and act without help from others.
e. You make decisions based on facts.
f. You always think of new and creative ideas.
g. You spend time studying and learning new things.
h. You do not follow other people's rules.
i. You always support people and places you know.

B Pair work Describe people you know with these traits. How do they show these traits?

"My friend is very idealistic. She says she wants to make the world a better place, so she volunteers a lot."

2 Language in context Personality types

A 🔊 Read these personality types. Which personality type best describes someone who studies all the time? likes to have fun? makes decisions quickly?

1. The **Reformer** is logical and idealistic. This type of person wants everything to be perfect.
2. The **Helper** is caring and generous. This type likes to please people. *Lograr*
3. The **Achiever** is a person who wants success. This type of person is studious and ambitious.
4. The **Individualist** is sensitive and often quiet. This type likes to be independent.
5. The **Investigator** is curious and creative. This is a person who is always questioning things.
6. The **Loyalist** is hardworking, responsible, and extremely loyal. This is someone that people can trust.
7. The **Enthusiast** is optimistic and spontaneous. This type of person is cheerful and fun-loving.
8. The **Challenger** makes decisions that other people find difficult to make. This type is confident and powerful.
9. The **Peacemaker** dislikes situations which create conflict. This type is easygoing and agreeable.

Discover Your Type

Source: Adapted from www.enneagraminstitute.com

B What about you? What personality type are you?

The Loyalist

54

3 Grammar ◄)) **Defining relative clauses**

Defining relative clauses supply essential information about a noun. They answer the questions "what kind" or "which one(s)." Use the pronouns who *or* that *for people. Use* which *or* that *for things.*

> The Achiever is a person **who** / **that wants success.**
> The Peacemaker dislikes situations **which** / **that create conflict.**

The relative pronouns are optional when they are the object of the relative clause.

> The Loyalist is someone (**who** / **that**) **people can trust.**
> The Challenger makes decisions (**which** / **that**) **other people find difficult to make.**

→ para personas ~ cosas   *who — that para persona*

A Complete the sentences with *who* or *which.*

1. My sister has a rebellious side ____which____ my parents never see.
2. I like friends ____who____ are easygoing and loyal.
3. I hardly ever do things ____which____ are spontaneous.
4. I have idealistic views ____which____ some people can't understand.
5. I was a studious child → ____who____ was also very energetic.
6. My brother is a person ____who____ other people find competitive.

B Cross out *who, which,* or *that* when it's optional.

1. I'm the kind of person ~~that~~ *who* other people think is very logical about things.
2. I can make decisions ~~that~~ *which* others find difficult to make.
3. Do you think you have any personality traits ~~which~~ people dislike?
4. What would be a good job for someone ~~who~~ is independent and responsible?

C Pair work Compare your answers in Parts A and B. Then complete these sentences with your own information.

I like people who . . .
I like to do things which . . .
I'm someone that other people . . .

4 Speaking Personality and jobs

A Pair work Look at the personality types in Exercise 2. Which personality type(s) would be good for these jobs?

| a businessperson | a musician | a police officer | a politician | a teacher |

B Group work What kind of job do you think would be good for you? What are your character traits that would help you succeed?

"I'm a person who likes to be independent. I'd be good at a job that lets me work at home."

5 Keep talking!

Go to page **136** for more practice.

I can talk about character traits. ☑

1 Interactions   Interruptions

A Do you ever interrupt friends who are talking? What do you say to interrupt them?
When is it OK to interrupt someone, and when is it impolite?

B 🔊 Listen to the conversation. Why does Carol interrupt Kevin?
Then practice the conversation.

Kevin: Did you see that? I can't believe he's safe!

Carol: What a great play! He's one of the most competitive players I've ever seen. Why do you think some people are so competitive?

Kevin: Well, maybe he's the middle child.

Carol: What do you mean?

Kevin: People who have an older and younger brother or sister are often very competitive. I just read something about that. And people who –

Carol: Sorry, but can I ask something?

Kevin: Sure. Go ahead.

Carol: Where did you read that? That's crazy.

Kevin: In a psychology magazine. I can show you. Anyway, as I was saying . . . the youngest person in the family is often the most outgoing and confident.

Carol: That's me! Maybe it's not so crazy.

C 🔊 Read the expressions below. Complete each box with a similar expression from the conversation. Then listen and check your answers.

Interrupting politely	**Agreeing to an interruption**
<u>Sorry but I can ask something.</u>	<u>Sure go ahead.</u>
I'm sorry, but could I ask one thing?	Yeah, of course.
Before you go on, could I ask something?	OK. Sure.

D Pair work Number the sentences from 1 to 6. Then practice with a partner.

   _2_ **A:** What about friends?

   _1_ **A:** Do you think a husband and wife should have similar personalities?

   _5_ **A:** Well, before you go on, could I ask something else?

   _2_ **B:** I think it's different with friends. But husbands and wives have to have some interests in common.

   _1_ **B:** Similar personalities? No, it's better to be different. But I also think . . .

   _3_ **B:** OK. Sure.

2 Pronunciation Stress in thought groups

A 🔊 Listen and repeat. Notice how long sentences are divided into shorter thought groups. The most important word in each thought group receives stronger stress.

Why do you **think** / **some** people / are so **competitive**?

B 🔊 Listen. Mark the stressed word in each thought group. Then practice with a partner.

1. Before you go on / could I ask something?

2. And the youngest person / in the family / is often / very outgoing / and confident.

3 Listening Type A and Type B personalities

A 🔊 Listen to Emily give a presentation on Type A and Type B personalities. How many times do her classmates interrupt?

B 🔊 Listen again. How does Emily describe each personality type? Check (✓) the words.

Type A		Type B	
☐ independent	☑ impatient	☑ easygoing	☑ imaginative
☑ hardworking	☐ energetic	☑ patient	☑ relaxed
☑ ambitious	☑ competitive	☐ logical	☐ idealistic

C Do you know someone who has a Type A personality? Do you know someone who has a Type B personality? How are they different? How are they the same?

4 Speaking Opinions on personality

A Choose a topic and take notes to prepare for a discussion.

Topic	Notes
1. Three qualities of a great friend	hardworking , polite, helpful, discreet smart
2. Three good character traits	handson, honest, loyal, easygoing, Patient , imaginative Logical, ambitious ,smart, idealistic.
3. Three reasons people are competitive	Good Educative Power, independent. Good training ambition, ability, control Talents!

B **Group work** Begin a discussion on your topic. Interrupt one another politely to add to the discussion.

A: *A great friend is someone who is loyal and always ready to help.*
B: *Before you go on, could I ask something?*

I can *interrupt politely.* ☑
I can *agree to an interruption.* ☑

C Wishing for change

1 Vocabulary Tips to manage stress

A 🔊 Match the phrases and the pictures. Then listen and check your answers.

a. balance work and play	c. find time to relax	e. live within a budget
b. be more organized	d. lead a healthier lifestyle	f. manage time better

1. a

2. c

3. b

4.

5. f

6. d

B Pair work Which tips in Part A would help you? Why?

"I want to balance work and play. I work all the time. I don't have time to relax."

2 Conversation Stressed out

A 🔊 Listen to the conversation. Why is Rosa stressed out?

Rosa: How was your weekend?
Chul: Great. I saw a movie, finished a great novel, and went out with friends.
Rosa: Where do you find time to relax like that? I wish I had more free time.
Chul: What's keeping you so busy?
Rosa: Work and school, mostly. I wish there were more hours in the day.
Chul: Listen, I have this book. It's about ways to manage stress. It has great tips on managing your time better.
Rosa: Like what?
Chul: Well, for example, it recommends making a plan of what you want to achieve each day.
Rosa: I wish I could read it now, but it's not part of my plan! I don't have the time.

B 🔊 Listen to the rest of the conversation. What causes Chul stress? What is he doing about it?

He Stress too. because is up budget
Not eating Out
He improvice in better cook

58

3 Grammar ◄)) **Wish**

Use wish + *a past tense verb to talk about present wishes. For wishes with the verb* be, *use* were *with both singular and plural nouns and pronouns.*

I **have to** study.	→	I wish I **didn't have to** study.
I **don't have** enough free time.	→	I wish I **had** more free time.
I **can't** read it now.	→	I wish I **could** read it now.
I **am** so busy.	→	I wish I **weren't** so busy.
I **am not** very organized.	→	I wish I **were** more organized.

Past time

Past tense

A Complete the sentences with the past form of the verbs.

1. I wish I _didn't have to_ *worry so much* (not / worry) so much.
2. I wish I _could find_ (can find) more time to relax.
3. I wish I _did better in school_ (do) better in school. → *was (past tense)*
4. I wish my schedule _was not_ (not / be) so full.
5. I wish I _didn't have todo_ (not / have) to do chores every day.
6. I wish my brother _could visit me_ (can visit) me this week.

B Write sentences with wish and the phrases in the box.

balance work and play	be more organized	lead a healthier lifestyle
be more easygoing	be more studious	manage time better

1. I'm always late for everything. _I wish manage my time better._
2. I get stressed over little things. _I wish I were more easygoing_
3. I don't get enough exercise. _I wish I could lead a healthier lifestyle._
4. I'm not an organized person. _I wish I were more organized._
5. I have trouble concentrating on my studies. _I wish I were more studious._
6. I can't find time to relax. _I wish you balance work and play_
   I could

C Pair work Compare your sentences in Parts A and B. Which sentences are true for you?

4 Speaking Make a wish.

A Do you wish you could change any of these things? Write down three wishes.

my friends and family	my possessions
my personality	my school or job
my clothes	my skills and abilities

B Group work Share your wishes.

A: *I wish I had a car.*
B: *Me, too! I wish I could get a sports car.*
C: *I wish I had a driver's license!*

5 Keep talking!

Go to pages **134–135** for more practice.

I can talk about present wishes. ☑

D Alternative therapies

1 Reading

A Are alternative therapies popular where you live? Have you ever tried one?

B Read the article. Which of these therapies are used in hospitals?

THERAPIES THAT WORK!

Aromatherapy helps calm stress with pleasant smells. Some smells relax people. Others make people more energetic. Popular scents include fruit, grasses, and flowers. In Japan, engineers have created aroma systems in public buildings. They send different scents into the air to create a better environment. For example, customers who are waiting in long lines at some banks might smell fresh flowers to help them relax.

Pet therapy uses animals to help calm and comfort people, especially young patients in hospitals and older people in nursing homes. The animals are brought to the hospitals and homes so that patients can see and touch them. This has an amazingly relaxing effect. Pet therapists usually use dogs and cats, but sometimes rabbits, birds, horses, and even llamas are used.

Color therapy uses colors to change your mood and emotions. Color therapists believe that the colors around you can affect you in different ways. For example, the color blue can relieve pain, and the colors red and orange can make you energetic. Some therapists even believe different parts of the body are influenced by different colors. They believe that having the right colors around you can help you get better when you are sick.

Humor therapy helps you find ways to laugh or smile. Laughter reduces stress and fear and anger. Many hospitals encourage their nurses to laugh with their patients, or put funny pictures on the walls. In India there are "laughing clubs" where people come together in the morning to tell funny stories, just to have a good laugh to start the day. Laughter is often the best medicine.

C Read the article again. What therapies are pictured? Number the pictures from 1 to 4 in the order you read about them.

2   3   1   4

D What do you think of the therapies? Would you like to try any of them? Do you think they work? Do you think they could be harmful in any way?

2 Listening Guided imagery *usar imaginación para relax.*

A 🔊 Listen to a therapist discuss guided imagery. What is guided imagery? Check (✓) the answer.

☐ a way to see new things ☑ a way to reduce stress ☐ a way to practice aromatherapy

B 🔊 Listen again. Check (✓) the true sentences.

1. ☑ Guided imagery uses your imagination.
2. ☐ One of the best things to use it for is to reduce pain.
3. ☐ You can only use the technique with a therapist.
4. ☑ It's important to be in a comfortable place.
5. ☑ Some people think it can help you learn.

C 🔊 Listen to an exercise in guided imagery, just for fun. Follow the directions. How do you feel after listening?

3 Writing About relaxation

A What do you do to relax? Write about it. Use the questions and the model paragraph to help you.

- What techniques have you tried to help you relax?
- What worked?
- What didn't work?
- What do you wish you could try to help you relax?

B **Pair work** Share your writing. Do you do similar things to relax?

> *Relaxing*
>
> *My job is very stressful, so when I have some free time, I try to do things to help me relax. I've tried yoga and baking. Yoga really helps me relax my body and my mind, and I do it twice a week. Baking didn't work for me because I made a big mess in the kitchen, so I got more stressed because of that. I wish I could . . .*

4 Speaking Relaxing creatively

A **Group work** Look at the ways that some people relax. Which do you think would work for you? Which wouldn't? Why not?

watching fish	painting
baking	shopping
cleaning the house	singing in the shower
dancing	watching a horror movie
keeping a journal	watching the stars
keeping a pet	writing poetry
listening to rock music	yelling alone in a forest

A: *I think watching fish would help me relax.*
B: *Me, too. But writing poetry wouldn't. That would be stressful for me.*

B **Class activity** Brainstorm other creative ways to relax. Share them with the class.

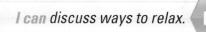

I can discuss ways to relax. ☑

Wrap-up

1 Quick pair review

Lesson A **Find out!** Which two family members do both you and your partner have with these character traits? You and your partner have two minutes.

- A family member who is competitive
- A family member that's very loyal
- A family member who is idealistic and imaginative

A: *I have a brother who is competitive. Do you?*
B: *No, but my aunt is competitive.*
A: *So is my aunt!*

Lesson B **Do you remember?** Check (✓) the expressions that show interrupting politely. You have one minute.

1. ☐ Sorry, but can I ask something?
2. ☐ Oh, really? I'm not sure about that.
3. ☐ Sure. Go ahead.
4. ☐ I'm sorry, but could I ask one thing?
5. ☐ Before you go on, could I ask something?
6. ☐ I'll let someone know right away.

Lesson C **Guess!** Tell your friend about a problem. Can your partner guess what you wish? Take turns. You and your partner have two minutes.

A: *I have a lot of homework. I have three meetings this week. I have to call my mother.*
B: *You wish you weren't so busy.*

Lesson D **Give your opinion!** What things do you and your partner think cause stress? What things do you think reduce stress? Write them in the chart and compare. You have two minutes.

Things that cause stress	Things that reduce stress

2 In the real world

Which therapy are you interested in? Who does it help? Go online and find information about one of these therapies. Then write about it.

adventure therapy
art therapy
light therapy
writing therapy

Light Therapy
Light therapy uses light to make you feel better. It is for people who live in places that don't get a lot of sunlight. They use bright lamps in their homes.

New ways of thinking

Warm-up

A Look at the pictures. What do you see?

B What problem did each of these creations try to solve? Do you think they were successful?

A Inventions

[handwritten: before Prefix, Un in / Suffix end, end —ly]

1 Vocabulary Positive and negative descriptions

A 🔊 Make the words negative. Write them in the chart. Then listen and check your answers.

[handwritten labels: in, un, Adj.]

convenient	uncreative	uneventful	in significant
conventional	ineffective	unimaginative	unsuccessful

un-	in-
unconventional ✓	*inconvenient* ✓ *inconvenient*
uncreative ✓	*ineffective* ✓ *ineffective*
unimaginative ✓	*insignificant* *insignificant*
uneventful —	
✓ *unsuccessful* —	

B Pair work What do you think? Discuss the sentences. Circle the correct word.

1. The first computers were huge. They filled an entire room. They were very
   convenient / **(inconvenient)** for everyday use.

2. Coco Chanel's fashion designs are world famous. They were so **(imaginative)** /
   unimaginative. Many people have copied them.

3. The new hybrid car is **(conventional)** / unconventional. I've never seen one like it. It
   uses air, not gasoline.

4. One day in 1847, Joseph Fry discovered a way to make chocolate bars. What an
   (eventful) / uneventful day that was! What would we do without them?

2 Language in context Early inventions

A 🔊 Read the descriptions of early inventions. What was each invention used for?

The abacus is over 5,000 years old. It was used to count numbers. It was such an effective tool in China and the Middle East that it spread to other parts of the world and is still used in many countries today.

Rubber was first used by the ancient Mayans in Mexico and Central America about 3,500 years ago. They took rubber from trees, boiled it, and made rubber balls, which they used in ancient ball games.

More than 2,000 years ago, the ancient Romans built aqueducts to bring water into their cities from miles away. Some of these aqueducts were so well made that they still carry water today.

B What are some modern examples of these inventions? Do you know any other early inventions?

3 Grammar 🔊 **So and *such***

Use so *and* such *with an adjective to make the adjective stronger.*

so + *adjective* ~very~   such + a / an + *adjective* + singular noun
  It was **so creative**.   It was **such a creative** idea.
  It was **so well made**.   It was **such a well-made** aqueduct.

Use a that *clause with* so *or* such *to show a result.*
  The abacus was **so** effective **that** it spread to other places.
  The abacus was **such an** effective tool **that** it spread to other places.

A Complete the sentences with *so* or *such*. Then compare with a partner.

1. The wheel was ___such___ a significant invention.
2. Her ideas were ___so___ unimaginative.
3. His inventions have been ___so___ successful.
4. His thinking is ___so___ unconventional. ~Adj~
5. She was ___such___ a creative woman. ~Adj~
6. Wireless Internet access is ___so___ convenient. ~Adj~

B Complete the sentences. Use *so . . . that* or *such . . . that*. Then compare with a partner.

1. Downloading music is _____so_____ (popular) CD sales have decreased.
2. I think the Perfect Cake Cutter was _____such_____ (an ineffective invention) no one wanted to buy it.
3. Cell phones are _____so_____ (inexpensive) almost everyone has one.
4. MP3 players were _____such_____ (a big success) they changed the way we listen to music.

4 Pronunciation Emphatic stress

A 🔊 Listen and repeat. Notice the extra stress on *so* and *such* for emphasis.

That is **so** conventional.   That is **such** a conventional thing to say.

B **Pair work** Practice the sentences in Exercise 3A. Pay attention to your pronunciation of *so* and *such*.

5 Speaking Top inventions

Group work Discuss three important inventions in each category. Why are they so important?

| communication | technology | transportation |

6 Keep talking!

Go to page 137 for more practice.

B Got any suggestions?

1 Interactions   Solutions

A Look at the picture in Part B. What problem do the people have?
How can they solve it?

B 🔊 Listen to the conversation. How do they plan to solve the problem?
Then practice the conversation.

Ralph: Here we go . . . almost there.
Carl: This sofa is going to look great in
my living room. Thanks again for
helping me.
Jim: No problem.
Ralph: Wait a minute. It doesn't fit.
Carl: What? Are you kidding?
Jim: Did you measure it before you
bought it?
Carl: Of course. There should be enough
room. I even made a sketch, see?
Ralph: Well, I'm sure there's something we
can do.
Jim: Do you have any ideas?
Ralph: Well, one idea could be to turn the
sofa the other way.
Carl: It's worth a try. If that doesn't
work, I'm not sure what else to do.

C 🔊 Read the expressions below. Complete each box with a similar expression from
the conversation. Then listen and check your answers.

Eliciting an idea

Do you have any idea
Got any ideas?
Got any suggestions?

Suggesting a solution

One idea could be turn the sofa
Something we could try is to _the other way._
One solution might be to . . .

D **Group work** Have conversations like the one in Part B. Use these ideas.

go through the window

remove the legs

2 Listening Sticky situations

A Look at the pictures. What problems do you see?

The truck trapped

The ship stuck crashed or shipwreck

birdcage

Jar *stuck*

B 🔊 Listen to people discuss how to solve the problems in Part A. Number the
pictures in Part A from 1 to 4.

Locksmith

C 🔊 Listen again. Check the solution they decide to try.

1. ☐ Stand on the reef and lift the boat.
   ☑ Wait and let the tide lift the boat.
2. ☑ Take the parrot's cage outside.
   ☐ Give the parrot treats.

3. ☑ Pour oil around the opening.
   ☐ Put the jar under hot running water.
4. ☐ Add weight to push the truck down.
   ☑ Remove all the air from the tires.

3 Speaking Inventive solutions

A **Group work** What could you do in these situations? Discuss your answers.

1. You forgot your wallet and don't have money to pay for the dinner you have just eaten at a restaurant.

2. Your pet cat is sitting at the end of a high tree branch. It's so scared that it won't come down.

3. You realize you made plans with your best friend and your mother for the same night.

4. You discover you locked your keys inside your apartment.

A: *Do you have any ideas about situation 1?*
B: *Well, one idea could be to call a friend for help.*
C: *Or one solution might be to wash the dishes to pay for your meal.*

B **Class activity** Share your solutions. Vote on the best solution for each situation.

Locksmith = person who change Locks

I can *elicit ideas.*
I can *suggest solutions.*

C | Accidental inventions

1 Vocabulary Verb and noun formation
—substantive (handwritten)

A 🔊 Read about the inventions. Complete the chart with the missing form of the words. Then listen and check your answers.

Sometimes a successful **invention** happens by accident: the tea bag, for example. Thomas Sullivan **introduced** tea bags to the world in 1908. He was a New York tea importer. He sent tea to his clients in tin cans. But tin was so heavy and expensive that he needed a more convenient way to send it. So he **designed** inexpensive bags to hold the tea leaves and sent them instead. Thomas's customers were supposed to open the bags and put the leaves in hot water. Instead, they used the entire bag. But this **innovation** worked! Immediately, tea bags **proved** to be a big **success**.

Ruth Wakefield **created** another accidental invention in her Massachusetts hotel in 1930. One day, Ruth didn't have enough chocolate for her usual chocolate cookie recipe. So she cut a chocolate bar into small pieces and made more cookies with less chocolate. The chocolate chips didn't melt completely, but her guests loved them! Ruth **developed** the original chocolate chip cookie. And her recipe has never needed much **improvement**. It's still the world's most popular chocolate chip cookie recipe today.

Verb	Noun	Verb	Noun	Verb	Noun
invented	*invention*	innovated	innovation	created	creation
introduced	introduction	proved	proof	developed	development
designed	design	succeeded	success	improved	improvement

B Pair work Choose four of the words from the chart. Make sentences with these words about something you have done. Tell your partner.

2 Conversation A delicious discovery

A 🔊 Listen to the conversation. Why did the chef get angry?

Dana: Do you know how the potato chip was invented?
Emma: I have no idea.
Dana: Apparently, in 1853, a customer in a restaurant sent his French fries back to the kitchen several times because they weren't thin enough. The chef was so angry that he sliced them even thinner, fried them again, and sent them back to the customer.
Emma: And the customer liked them?
Dana: Yeah, he asked for more! The chef's creation was such a success that they were requested by other customers, too. At that time they were only salted, but since then, lots of different flavors have been developed.
Emma: Fascinating. So, can I have my chips back?

B 🔊 Listen to the rest of the conversation. What three countries do they mention? What flavors of potato chips are mentioned for each country?

Ingla – Garlens chips   Argentina – Onion sour   Roster chicken, french chips (handwritten)

3 Grammar 🔊 The passive

Active	Passive
Simple present: People still **use** her recipe today.	Her recipe **is** still **used** today.
Simple past: A chef **invented** it in 1853.	It **was invented** in 1853.
Present perfect: Companies **have developed** many flavors since 1853.	Many flavors **have been developed** since 1853.

A Rewrite these sentences. Use the passive. Then compare with a partner.

1. Thomas Sullivan introduced tea bags to the world in 1908.
   Tea bags were introduced to the world in 1908.

2. Sullivan designed small bags to hold the tea.
   Small bags were designed to hold the tea.

3. A man produced the first flavored potato chip in the 1950s.
   The first flavored potato chip was produced in the 1950s

4. Potato chip makers have developed many unique flavors.
   Many unique flavors have been developed

B Complete the sentences. Use the passive with the simple present, simple past, or present perfect. Then compare with a partner.

The 3M company _has been known_ (know) for its innovation for a long time. But there have been mistakes along the way. Today employees _are encouraged_ (encourage) to learn from past mistakes. That's how Arthur Fry learned about a special glue. It _was created_ (create) in the 3M lab in 1968. The glue wasn't strong enough, so it _was forgotten_ (forget). But Fry found it in 1974 and used it to develop Post-it Notes. The original Post-it Notes _have been improved_ (improve) since then, and now they _are sold_ (sell) all over the world.

4 Speaking Early innovations

Group work Look at these products. What improvements have been made to the products recently? Have all of the improvements been good ones?

"Tennis shoes have been made lighter. Their design has been improved a lot."

5 Keep talking!

Go to page 138 for more practice.

I can *discuss how things have been improved.*	✓

D Making life easier

1 Reading 🔊

A Look at the picture. What do you think this article is about?

B Read the article. Check (✓) the best title.

☐ Top Innovations in Japan   ☐ Technology Helps Japan's Elderly
☐ The Future of Technology   ☐ Growing Old In Japan

ONCE UPON A TIME, there was a land where robotic bears helped lift the elderly out of bed and into wheelchairs. In this land, robotic seals comforted lonely people and were an **essential** part of elder care. Is this science fiction? Not in Japan. These robots already exist, and you may actually experience them as you get older. These examples of **state-of-the-art** technology are helping to solve a big problem for the Japanese – the problem of taking care of their **senior citizens**.

It is estimated that 40% of the population in Japan will be over 65 by 2055. At the same time, there will be an estimated 16% decrease in the size of the workforce by 2030. This **shortage** of labor presents a serious challenge: Who will look after all the people in their **golden years**? There are simply not enough younger people to care for this older population. And with the breakdown of traditional family responsibilities, a growing number of elderly are living away from their families and the family care they have been given in the past.

Robots to the rescue! Robotic beds that are controlled by voice can change from a bed to a wheelchair on command. The robotic bear nurse can lift patients who weigh up to 135 pounds (61 kilos). And for comfort and friendship, a soft robotic pet seal has been designed to show emotions with facial expressions, movement, and noises, and to respond to touch. These are just a few of the inventions that are so promising. Robots are the future of elder care.

C Find the words in **bold** in the article. Circle the correct meanings.

1. **essential**   a. necessary   b. unnatural
2. **state-of-the-art**   a. the most advanced   b. imaginary
3. **senior citizens**   a. elderly people   b. people who need help
4. **shortage**   a. too much of   b. not enough of
5. **golden years**   a. time before retirement   b. time after retirement

D **Class activity** What is your opinion of using robots and technology to help the elderly? What are some other ways that robots and technology are helping people? Discuss your ideas.

2 **Listening** A robot pet?

A 🔊 Listen to a commercial for i-Cybie, a robot dog. Check (✓) the things
the i-Cybie can do.

- ☐ eat
- ☑ scratch its ear
- ☑ show emotion
- ☐ sing
- ☑ dance
- ☑ sleep
- ☑ play
- ☐ taste
- ☑ respond to commands
- ☑ sit
- ☐ smell
- ☑ do a yoga position

B 🔊 Listen to Jason tell his friend Tina about his new i-Cybie.
Write two things he likes and two things he doesn't like about
his new pet.

What he likes	What he doesn't like
1. _Play Sit dance,_	1. _It expensive,_
2. _stand ot head_	2. _Batterias (No good)_

3 **Writing and speaking** An invention

A **Group work** Brainstorm inventions that would make your life easier. Make a list.

B Choose one of the inventions. Draw a picture of it. Then write a paragraph about it.
Give it a name, explain who it's for, and discuss what it does.

Necktie Cardholder
The Necktie Cardholder is for
businessmen who need to carry
business cards with them all the time.
On the back of this necktie, there's a
secret pocket that holds up to 10
cards. There are also places to hold
pens, keys, paper clips, and other things
someone might need around the office.
From the front, it looks like a regular
tie, but . . .

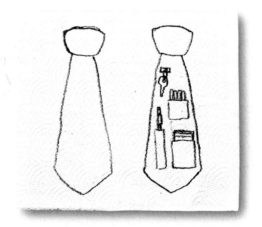

C **Class activity** Walk around the class. Show the picture of your invention to five
people. Describe it and try to convince your classmates that they need your invention.

*"You have to get a Necktie Cardholder. You have a card when you need one, but
you also . . ."*

D As a class, vote on and give these awards for the best inventions.

the best overall invention	the most innovative invention
the greatest improvement to people's lives	the most useful invention

1. It's really fun to play with.   1. It's expensive.
2. It has its own Personality   2. The battery doesn't last long.

I can *describe something I invented.* ☑

Wrap-up

1 Quick pair review

Lesson A **Test your partner!** Say a positive descriptive adjective. Can your partner write the negative adjective correctly? Take turns. You and your partner have one minute.

"Conventional."

1. _____unconventional_____   3. _____   5. _____
2. _____   4. _____   6. _____

Lesson B **Give your opinion!** What are solutions to these problems?
Elicit ideas and suggest solutions. Take turns. You and your partner have two minutes.

- You have only one day to study for a test.
- You can't find your keys.
- You have a broken-down car and need to get to work.
- You have to fit a big piano through a small door.

A: *I have only one day to study for a test. Got any suggestions?*
B: *One idea could be to stay up all night and study.*

Lesson C **Do you remember?** Write A for active and P for passive. You have one minute.

1. The Internet was invented in the 1970s. _P_
2. My mother doesn't like new technology. _A_
3. This cell phone has won an award for best design. _A_
4. That movie has been seen all over the world. _P_

Lesson D **Guess!** Describe an invention, but don't say its name. Can your partner guess what it is? You and your partner have two minutes.

A: *This invention is so useful. It helps you see.*
B: *Glasses?*
A: *No. It goes in a lamp.*

2 In the real world

What's a great invention? Find information online about one of these inventions, or choose your own idea. Then write about it.

| computer mouse   pencil sharpener   Silly Putty   TV remote control |

- What is it?
- Who invented it?
- When was it invented?
- What do you think about the invention?

Silly Putty
Silly Putty is a toy for children. It was
invented by James Wright in the 1940s.

Lessons in life

LESSON **A**	LESSON **B**	LESSON **C**	LESSON **D**
• Prefixes: *mis-*, *dis-*, and *re-* • Past perfect	• Expressing worry • Reassuring someone	• Expressions with *make* and *get* • Third conditional	• Reading: "The Story of My Life" • Writing: About a memorable day

Warm-up

A Describe the pictures. What's happening? How do you think each person feels?

B What would you do if these things happened to you?

A Why did I do that?

1 Vocabulary Prefixes: *mis-*, *dis-*, and *re-*

A Read the sentences. Match the prefixes *mis-*, *dis-*, and *re-* and their meanings.

1. I **mis**spelled your name. Can you correct it?   b ~~a. do something again~~
2. Please **dis**regard my email. It wasn't important.   c ~~b. do something wrong~~
3. Let's **re**consider. There might be a better way.   a   c. don't do something

B 🔊 Add the correct prefixes to the words, and write them in the chart. Then listen and check your answers.

> dis agree dis continue mis judge re make dis regard re think
> re consider re do dis like mis pronounce mis spell mis understand

mis-	dis-	re-
misjudge misspell	disagree dislike	reconsider redo
mispronounce misunderstand discontinue disregard		remake rethink
		redo remade

C Pair work Answer the questions.

- What word do you often misspell? What word do you often mispronounce?
- Do you ever disagree with your friends? Do you disregard their advice? Why?

2 Language in context Awkward situations

A 🔊 Listen to two people describe awkward situations. What was awkward about each situation?

When I was emailing my classmate about a surprise party for my friend Leo, I hit "send" and it went to Leo. I'd sent the email to Leo before I realized my mistake. I called him and asked him to disregard the email. Luckily, he hadn't read it yet.

– John

The other day, my boss mispronounced my name in the elevator. He had done it once before, and I hadn't corrected him. But this time, I reconsidered. Unfortunately, by the time I started to say something, my boss had already left the elevator.

– Angelica

B What do you think? Did John and Angelica do the right thing? Has anything similar ever happened to you?

3 Grammar � Past perfect

Use the past perfect to describe an action that took place before another action in the past.

I'd sent the email to Leo before I realized my mistake.   [handwritten: *had*]   [circled: *before*, 1, 2]

The words *yet* and already *are often used with the past perfect.*

I asked him to disregard the message. Luckily, he **hadn't read** it yet.

By the time I started to say something, my boss **had** already **left**.

Contraction   **I'd** = I **had**

[handwritten: I had gone home before I realize I left my phone at his apartment]   [circled: Simple Past]

Complete the sentences. Use the simple past and past perfect in each sentence. Then compare with a partner.

1. I ___had planed___ (plan) on working all weekend, but then I ___reconsidered___ (reconsider) and went to the beach instead.

2. I was so late this morning. By the time I ___got___ (get) to work, I ___had missed___ (miss) the whole meeting.

3. Alice ___woke up___ (wake up) at 9:30 because she ___had forgotten___ (forget) to set her alarm clock for 8:00.

4. Before Richard and Alex ___met___ (meet), they ___had been___ (be) e-pals for a year.

5. I ___called___ (call) my friend to cancel our plans. Luckily, he ___had not left___ (not / leave) yet.

[handwritten note at right:
Past Perfect
- Describes two actions that happend in the past.]

4 Pronunciation Reduction of *had*

A illustration Listen and repeat. Notice how *had* is pronounced /d/ in the past perfect.

I'd sent the email to Leo.   My boss **ha**d already left the elevator.

B Pair work Practice the sentences in Exercise 3. Pay attention to your pronunciation of the past perfect.

5 Speaking I'd forgotten to . . .

A Choose a situation and prepare to talk about it. Think about the events that happened *before* and *after*.

you disagreed with someone [handwritten: no estar de acuerdo]	you misjudged someone [handwritten: Juzgar mal]	you redid something incorrectly [handwritten: rehiciste]
you forgot something	you misunderstood someone	you were very late

B Group work Tell your classmates what happened. Answer any questions.

A: *I was embarrassed at a job interview once. I'd forgotten to turn off my cell phone.*

B: *Really? Did the job interviewer say anything?*

6 Keep talking!

Go to page **139** for more practice.

[I can describe events in the past.]

B I'm sure you'll do fine.

1 Interactions   Worries and reassurance

A In which of these situations do you feel the most confident? the least confident?

public speaking in English	speaking in front of a large group
public speaking in your own language	speaking in front of a small group

B 🔊 Listen to the conversation. What is Feng worried about?
Then practice the conversation.

Mei: Hi, Feng. How are you?
Feng: Oh, hi, Mei. I'm fine, I guess. But I have to give a presentation in my English class, and I'm kind of worried about it.
Mei: Really? Why?
Feng: Well, I always forget what I'm planning to say. I'm not confident speaking in front of people.
Mei: Can you use notes?
Feng: Yeah, I can, so that will help.
Mei: I'm sure you'll do fine. You're great in front of people.
Feng: Do you really think so?
Mei: I do. Just try to relax.
Feng: Well, thanks. We'll see how it goes.

C 🔊 Read the expressions below. Complete each box with a similar expression from the conversation. Then listen and check your answers.

Expressing worry

I'm kind of worried about it
I'm a little anxious about it.
I'm pretty nervous about it.

Reassuring someone

I'm sure you'll do fine
I'm sure you'll be OK.
Don't worry. Everything will work out.

D Pair work Number the sentences from 1 to 6. Then practice with a partner.

_2_ **A:** When is it?

_1_ **A:** Hi, Bill. How are you?

_3_ **A:** This weekend? Well, I'm sure you'll do OK.

_3_ **B:** Really? I'm not so sure. But thanks anyway.

_2_ **B:** It's this weekend.

_1_ **B:** Fine, I guess. But I'm pretty nervous about my driver's test.

2 **Listening** Feeling anxious

A 🔊 Listen to four friends talk about situations that worry them. Number the pictures from 1 to 4.

2

4

1

3

B 🔊 Listen again. What do their friends say to reassure them? Write the sentences.

1. I'm sure you'll do fine, good work
2. I'm sure you will be OK
3. I'm sure you'll do fine
4. Don't worry everything will work out.

3 **Speaking** Please don't worry.

A Pair work Role-play the situation.

Student A: You have been invited to a party. You are a little anxious about it. You're afraid you won't know anyone. Tell Student B how you feel.

Student B: Student A is a little anxious about going to a party. Find out why. Reassure your friend.

> **A:** *I'm pretty nervous about going to this party.*
> **B:** *Why are you so nervous?*
> **A:** *I won't know anyone there.*
> **B:** *But you can meet new people there. Don't worry. . . .*

B Change roles and role-play the situation.

Student A: You are changing schools. You are worried about it. You're afraid you might not make new friends easily. Tell Student B how you feel.

Student B: Student A is changing schools and is worried about it. Find out why. Reassure your friend.

C Pair work Write a role play about reassuring someone in a difficult situation. Give it to another pair to role-play. Use one of these situations, or use your own ideas.

doing a home-stay abroad	getting a new roommate	traveling alone

I can express worry. ☑
I can reassure someone. ☑

C   *What if . . . ?*

1 **Vocabulary** Expressions with *make* and *get*

A 🔊 Match the statements. Then listen and check your answers.

1. I hate to **make a fool of myself**. __b__   ⌐ a. I sometimes don't even tell anyone.
2. I always **make an effort** to do my best   ⌐ b. I dislike it when people laugh at
   in school. __c__   my mistakes.
3. I often **make mistakes**. __d__   ⌐ c. I try very hard.
4. I never **make a big deal** about my   __d__ d. I am careless.
   birthday. __a__   ⌐ e. It's not difficult for me to decide
5. I **make up my mind** easily. __e__   things.
   (hacer decisiones)
                                                 Ignorar
6. I never **get into trouble**. __g__   ⌐ f. I just disregard it.
7. If someone isn't nice to me, I try to   ⌐ g. I always try to follow the rules.
   get over it quickly. __f__   ⌐ h. I get annoyed when they play loud
   Not Worried   music. *molestar*
8. I always try to **get out of** doing the   ⌐ i. It's my least favorite chore.
   dishes. __i__
9. My friends sometimes **get on my nerves**. __h__   j. I don't like to keep unnecessary
10. I like to **get rid of** things I don't need. __j__   things.
    tirar

B **Pair work** Which statements in Part A are true for you? Discuss your answers.

*"I like to get rid of old newspapers and magazines, but my roommate likes
to save them."*

2 **Conversation** A new boyfriend

A 🔊 Listen to the conversation. What mistake did Alicia make?

Dan: So, how was Aki's party?   *had*

Alicia: Well, the party was fun. But I'd forgotten
it was her birthday, so I was a little
embarrassed.

Dan: Why?

Alicia: I didn't bring a gift. If I'd remembered, I'd
have brought her something really nice.

Dan: Well, I'm sure she didn't mind.

Alicia: Then, I think I made a fool of myself at
the party. We all had to sing, and you
know how bad my voice is.

Dan: Oh, come on.

Alicia: I tried to get out of it, but I couldn't. And
that's when I met Santiago. Just think. If I
hadn't sung at the party, I wouldn't have
met Santiago.

Dan: Santiago? Who's Santiago?

Alicia: He's my new boyfriend.

B 🔊 Listen to the rest of the conversation. What's Santiago like?
What gets on Alicia's nerves?   *talk about himself*
friendly,
Act

3 Grammar 🔊 **Third conditional**

Third conditional sentences describe hypothetical situations in the past.
Use the past perfect in the if *clause and* would have + *past participle in the main clause.*

> If I**'d remembered**, I **would have brought** her something.
> If I **hadn't forgotten**, I **would have brought** her a gift.
> If she **had missed** the party, she **wouldn't have met** Santiago.
> If she **hadn't gone** to the party, she **wouldn't have met** him.

[handwritten annotations: unreal; Past; P P; If I had remember, I would have brought haría; If I had +]

Remember: I**'d** = I **would** *or* I **had**

A Read the conditional sentences. Circle the true statements about them.

1. If Henry had made an effort, he would have passed all of his exams.
   a. Henry made an effort.   (b.) Henry didn't make an effort.

[handwritten: Wouldn't = Habría]

2. If Mike had followed the instructions, he wouldn't have made a mistake.
   (a.) Mike made a mistake.   b. Mike didn't make a mistake.

3. If Luz hadn't become a doctor, she would have become an artist.
   (a.) Luz became a doctor.   b. Luz didn't become a doctor.

4. If Andrea hadn't sold her old books online, she wouldn't have gotten rid of them.
   (a.) Andrea got rid of her books.   b. Andrea didn't get rid of her books.

B Complete the sentences with the third conditional.
Then compare with a partner.

1. If I _had known_ (know) about the party, I _wouldn't have made_ (not / make) such a fool of myself.
2. If you _had come_ (come) home before midnight, you _wouldn't have gotten_ (not / get) into trouble.
3. If I _hadn't gotten_ (not / get) rid of my old cell phone, I _would have let_ (let) you have it.
4. I _wouldn't have made_ (make) up my mind easily if I _hadn't had_ (not / have) so many choices.

4 Speaking If only I hadn't . . .

A Check (✓) the things you've done.

☐ made a mistake   ☐ gotten rid of something important
☐ made an effort to do something   ☐ gotten out of something
☐ made a fool of yourself   ☐ gotten into trouble

B **Pair work** Tell your partner the things you checked in Part A. What would have been different if you hadn't done these things? Share your stories.

5 Keep talking!

Go to page 140 for more practice.

> *I can talk about how things might have been.* ☑

D A day to remember

1 Reading 🔊

A Helen Keller was two years old when she became ill and lost both her sight and hearing.
Read the excerpt from her book, *The Story of My Life*. What made March 3, 1887,
a day to remember?

The Story of My Life

The most important day I remember in all my life is the one on which my teacher, Anne Mansfield Sullivan, came to me. I am filled with wonder when I consider the immeasurable contrast between the two lives which it connects. It was the third of March, 1887, three months before I was seven years old.

The morning after my teacher came, she led me into her room and gave me a doll. When I had played with it a little while, Miss Sullivan slowly spelled into my hand the word "d-o-l-l." I was at once interested in this finger play and tried to imitate it. When I finally succeeded in making the letters correctly, I was filled with childish pleasure and pride. Running downstairs to my mother, I held up my hand and made the letters for "doll." I did not know that I was spelling a word or even that words existed; I simply made my fingers go in monkey-like imitation. In the days that followed, I learned to spell in this uncomprehending way many words, among them, "pin," "hat," "cup," and a few verbs like "sit," "stand," and "walk," but my teacher had been with me several weeks before I understood that everything has a name.

One day while I was playing with my new doll, Miss Sullivan gave me my old doll, too. She then spelled "d-o-l-l" and tried to make me understand that "d-o-l-l" applied to both. Earlier in the day, we had a struggle over two words. "M-u-g" is "mug" and "w-a-t-e-r" is "water," but I persisted in mixing up the two. I became impatient, and seizing the new doll, I dashed it on the floor, breaking it into pieces. I was not sorry after my fit of temper. In the dark, still world, I had no strong sentiment for anything.

My teacher brought me my hat, and I knew we were going out into the warm sunshine. We walked down the path to the well-house. Someone was drawing water, and my teacher placed my hand under the spout. As the cool stream gushed over one hand, she spelled into the other the word "water," first slowly, then rapidly. I stood still; my whole attention was fixed upon the movements of her finger. Suddenly I seemed to remember something I had forgotten – a thrill of returning thought – and the mystery of language was revealed to me. I knew then that the "w-a-t-e-r" meant that wonderful cool something that was flowing over my hand. That living word awakened my soul and set it free.

Source: Adapted from *The Story of My Life* by Helen Keller

B Read the excerpt again. Number the events from 1 to 6.

2 Miss Sullivan began to teach Helen to spell.

5 When Helen felt water on one hand, Miss Sullivan spelled "water" in the other.

6 Helen understood that everything has a name, and her life changed.

1 Helen didn't know that there were words for things.

3 Helen learned how to spell "doll" with her fingers.

4 Helen didn't understand the meaning of the words she spelled.

C What do you think Helen's life was like before this day? after this day?

2 **Listening** Looking back

A 🔊 Listen to four people talk about important days in their lives. Check (✓) which day they're talking about.

Day	What made it a memorable day?
1. ☐ first day of middle school ☑ first day of high school	☐ Her friend was a teacher at the school. ☑ Her friend was going to the same school.
2. ☐ wedding day ☑ birth of a child	☒ Their parents were there. ☑ The announcement appeared in the newspaper.
3. ☐ first day at work ☑ last day at work	☑ His co-workers gave him a party. ☐ He'd traveled on his own in Europe.
4. ☐ first airplane trip ☑ first trip overseas	☐ She could speak Korean with her host family. ☑ Her hosts were so kind and friendly.

B 🔊 Listen again. Check (✓) what made the day memorable.

3 **Writing and speaking** About a memorable day

A Think about a memorable day. Use these ideas or your own ideas.

the day you got accepted to college	your first airplane ride
the day you spoke English to a native speaker	your first day at a new job
the first time you rode a bicycle	your first day of school
a special celebration	

B Write a paragraph about your memorable day. Use the questions and the model paragraph to help you.

- When was it?
- What made the day memorable?
- Did you look forward to this day?
- What did you do that day?
- How did you feel then?

A Memorable Day
One of the best days of my life was when I got accepted to City University. I had always wanted to go there. I'd been pretty worried until I got my official acceptance letter. I remember I called some of my friends to tell them. Then that night, I went out with my family to celebrate. I was so happy that day.

C Group work Share your writing. Ask and answer questions about that day. As a group, decide which day was the most interesting, unusual, or exciting day.

My Memorable day was When, My Son Brandon was born. I was so happy that I didn't remember my own birthday. He was my birthday Present. because My birthday in may 29 and He born on may 26th So Now We Celebration it. Togethers. We like to Celebration eating outside in Restaurents.

I can describe a memorable day. ☑

Wrap-up

1 Quick pair review

Lesson A Do you remember? Cross out the words that don't belong. You have one minute.

1. *mis-*	spell	understand	~~think~~	pronounce	judge
2. *re-*	do	think	consider	make	agree
3. *dis-*	agree	make	continue	regard	like

Lesson B Brainstorm! Make a list of ways to express worry and ways to reassure someone. How many do you remember? You have two minutes.

Lesson C Give your opinion! Imagine these things happened to you. Ask your partner what he or she would have done. Take turns. You and your partner have two minutes.

- You forgot to take your passport to the airport.
- You didn't remember a friend's birthday.
- You didn't go to class on the day of a test.

A: *What would you have done if you had forgotten your passport?*
B: *If I had forgotten my passport, I would have called my friend and asked her to bring it to me. What about you?*

Lesson D Guess! Think about important first days in a person's life. Guess how old your partner was for each of these firsts. You and your partner have two minutes.

first time he or she traveled alone	first time he or she spoke English
first time he or she rode a bicycle	(your own idea)

A: *Were you 18 the first time you traveled alone?*
B: *No, I was younger.*
A: *Were you 13?*
B: *Yes, I was.*

2 In the real world

What was the first day of school like for someone in your family or for a close friend? Interview the person. Then write about it.

> *First Day of School*
> My father was nervous on his first day of school. His father, my grandfather, took him to school. My father met Charlie on the first day of school. Charlie became his best friend.

Can you explain it?

LESSON **A**	LESSON **B**	LESSON **C**	LESSON **D**
• Suffixes: *-ful* and *-less* • Past modals for speculating	• Expressing probability • Expressing improbability	• Mysterious events • Embedded questions	• Reading: A myth • Writing: A story

Warm-up

herd

identical

fraternal - no identicos

A Describe the pictures. What do you see?

B Can you explain the pictures? Think of several possible explanations.

Everyday explanations

1 **Vocabulary** Suffixes: *-ful* and *-less*

A 🔊 Circle the correct words to complete the sentences. Then listen and check your answers.

1. I can't get this old computer to work at all. It's useful / (useless) for me to even try.
2. The storm was so (powerful) / powerless that it destroyed a hundred homes.
3. I read about a man who raised a lion as his pet. He was totally fearful / (fearless.)
4. The police made people leave the building because the bad odor was (harmful) / harmless to their health.
5. Jane was fined $300 for careful / (careless) driving.
6. I couldn't understand his explanations at all. They were so meaningful / (meaningless.)
7. Sara gave me a lovely graduation present. That was very (thoughtful) / thoughtless of her.
8. I'm (hopeful) / hopeless that I'll get a good grade on my exam. I have been studying a lot.

B Pair work Make sentences about your experiences. Use the words you did *not* circle in Part A. Tell your partner.

2 **Language in context** Explainable behavior

A 🔊 Read the online chat between co-workers. Why are they talking about Kenny?

> ⦿ ◯ ◯
>
> **Maria:** Ethan, did you see Kenny yesterday?
>
> **Ethan:** How could I miss him? He was wearing a suit. He looked so impressive in his suit and tie! ☺
>
> **Maria:** Yeah, I know. But it was really hot yesterday, so he couldn't have been comfortable in a suit.
>
> **Ethan:** Did you ask him why he was so dressed up?
>
> **Maria:** Yeah, but it was useless. He wouldn't say a word.
>
> **Ethan:** He might have had a presentation to give.
>
> **Maria:** Yeah, that's possible. Or maybe it wasn't meaningful at all. He could have simply felt like dressing up in a suit.
>
> **James:** Hi, you guys. Did you hear about Kenny?
>
> **Ethan:** Actually, we were just chatting about him.
>
> **James:** Well, he called me earlier today. He said he had interviewed for a new job yesterday. And they offered it to him!
>
> **Maria:** That explains it! He must have gone to his interview after work. He wasn't very careful about it, was he?

B What are some other reasons that people dress up for work?

3 Grammar 🔊   Past modals for speculating

Speculating with more certainty

He **must have gone** to his interview.

It was really hot yesterday, so he **couldn't have been** comfortable in a suit.

Speculating with less certainty

He **might have had** a presentation.

He **could have felt** like dressing up.

[Handwritten notes:]
Modals
Must + √ Debe
Could + √ Podria
Would + √ haria
Should + √ deberia
Might +√ Podria

A Complete the conversations with past modals. Then practice with a partner.

1. **A:** Why hasn't Kate been answering her phone?

   B: Who knows? She could *have turned i* (turn) off the ringer.

2. **A:** Why did Randy quit his job yesterday?

   B: I'm not sure. He might *have gotten* (get) a better one.

3. **A:** Have you seen Nancy?

   B: No, she hasn't come to work yet. She could *have overslept* (oversleep) again.

4. **A:** Is Emma here? She's late for her appointment. That never happens.

   B: Something important must *have delayed* (delay) her.

5. **A:** What's wrong? Did Jack forget your birthday?

   B: He could *haven't forgotten* (not / forget) it. He always remembers.

B Read the questions in Part A. Write different explanations. Then practice with a partner.

1. _____

2. _____

3. _____

4. _____

5. _____

4 Speaking   Possible explanations

Group work Discuss possible explanations for these situations.

1. Your classmate seemed very forgetful today.

2. Your friend is fluent in Russian after only three months of study.

3. Your friend used to be very careless, but suddenly you can depend on her for anything.

4. Your cousin used to be afraid of animals, but now he is fearless.

"My classmate might have had very little sleep. That could have made him forgetful."

5 Keep talking!

Students A and B go to page 141 and Students C and D go to page 142 for more practice.

I can speculate about everyday situations. ☑

85

B *I'm pretty sure that . . .*

1 Interactions — Probability and improbability

A Pair work Try this experiment. Do it ten times and then change roles.

Student A: Think of a number between 1 and 10.
Student B: Try to read your partner's mind by guessing if the number is
even (2, 4, 6, . . .) or *odd* (1, 3, 5, . . .).
Did you guess correctly? Who else in the class guessed correctly? How many times?

B 🔊 Listen to the conversation. How does Daniela explain mind-reading between twins?
Then practice the conversation.

Daniela: I saw a TV show yesterday about twins who read each other's minds. Do you think that's possible?
Jenny: Well, twins spend a lot of time together. It's likely that they can read each other's thoughts.
Daniela: Really?
Jenny: Why not? When they're young, some twins develop a secret language only they understand. That shows that twins can be special.
Daniela: But I doubt that anyone can really read minds. They could have guessed each other's thoughts because they spend a lot of time together. But that's not mind-reading.
Jenny: You are so skeptical. *escéptico*
Daniela: I know. So, should we order now?
Jenny: You just read my mind!

C 🔊 Read the expressions below. Complete each box with a similar expression from the conversation. Then listen and check your answers.

Expressing probability

~~It's very probably~~ It's likely that.
I'm pretty sure that . . .
It's very probable that . . .

Expressing improbability

I doubt that
It's doubtful that .can real minds
It's highly unlikely that . . .

D Group work Check (✓) the sentences you think are probable. Then talk to your group about what is probable and what is improbable.

☑ Twins have a special relationship.   ☑ Twins are more alike than different.
☐ Only some people can read minds.   ☐ All twins can read each other's minds.

86

2 Listening Likely . . . or unlikely?

A Pair work Which of these things can help you know what others are thinking?

| body language | emotions | hairstyles | memory |
| dreams | facial expressions | laughing | tone of voice |

memoria
Latin
riendo

B 🔊 Listen to Karl tell his friend Jenna about an article on mind-reading. How do people read minds? Look at Part A again, and circle the ways that are mentioned in the article.

Pensar
Taught
Thought *Penso*

C 🔊 Listen to the rest of the conversation. Correct the statements.

              20%
1. Strangers can read each other's minds ~~30%~~ of the time.

                      35%
2. Married couples can read each other's minds 45% of the time.

              60%
3. No one can read minds more than 6% of the time.

        no difference
4. There's a big difference in how well men and women can read minds.

        unlikely
5. It's likely that Jenna believes what Karl says about men and women.

3 Speaking Anything's possible.

A Read the statements. Do you think they are probable? Write P (probable) or I (improbable) next to each statement.

___\ People will travel through time someday.

___|___ Some people can remember their past lives.

___\ Some people can predict the weather.

___\ Some people can communicate with animals.

___P___ Some people can predict trends in the stock market.

___|___ Some people can heal themselves with their mind.

B Group work Share your ideas.

A: *I doubt that people will travel through time someday.*
B: *I agree. It's highly unlikely.*
C: *I'm not so sure. I bet it will happen someday because . . .*

I can **express probability and improbability.** ☑

87

1 Vocabulary Mysterious events

A ◁)) Match the words and the stories. Then listen and check your answers.

1. __d__ In 1962, three men broke out of San Francisco's Alcatraz prison. They were never seen again.

2. __e__ In 1908, a huge object from space exploded over Siberia. It destroyed 80 million trees.

3. __b__ In 1937, Amelia Earhart disappeared during a flight over the Pacific Ocean. She was never seen again.

4. __a__ In 1961, Betty and Barney Hill claimed they were taken aboard a UFO by unfriendly aliens.

5. __c__ In 1985, divers found large rocks near Japan that some believe are a lost underwater city.

6. __f__ In 1990, robbers in Boston stole paintings worth $300 million. They have never been recovered.

a. abduction
b. disappearance
c. discovery
d. escape
e. explosion
f. theft

B Pair work Choose three words from Part A. What are other examples of these types of events? Tell your partner.

2 Conversation It remains a mystery.

A ◁)) Listen to the conversation. What does the tourist learn about the Great Pyramid?

Guide: No one really knows how the Egyptian pyramids were built. There are many theories and new discoveries, but it remains a mystery.

Tourist: Do you have any idea how long it took to build them?

Guide: Yes. It took about 20 years to build the tallest one, the Great Pyramid.

Tourist: Can you tell me how tall it is?

Guide: It's more than 450 feet, or about 139 meters. It was the tallest structure in the world for thousands of years.

Tourist: Really?

Guide: Yes. It was the world's tallest structure until the Eiffel Tower was built.

Tourist: That's amazing! Do you know how many pyramids were built in Egypt?

Guide: No one knows. But at least 80 pyramids have survived, and many more are still under the sand.

B ◁)) Listen to the rest of the conversation. Why was the Sphinx built? What happened to its nose?

Larges
face was panting red.

3 Grammar 🔊 [Embedded questions]

An embedded question is a question included in another question.

Wh- questions	Embedded *Wh-* questions
How many pyramids were built?	Do you know **how many pyramids were built?**
How long did it take to build?	Do you have any idea **how long it took to build?**
How tall is the Great Pyramid?	Can you tell me **how tall the Great Pyramid is?**
Yes/no questions	Embedded *yes/no* questions
Was the Sphinx painted?	Do you know **if the Sphinx was painted?**
Are there any chambers?	Can you tell me **if there are any chambers?**
Did its nose fall off?	Do you know **if its nose fell off?**

Rewrite the questions. Use embedded questions. Then compare with a partner.

1. Have there been many thefts from the pyramids?
   A: Do you know _if they have been many thefts from the pyramids?_ ? B: Yes, many.
2. How long was the Great Pyramid the world's tallest structure?
   A: Do you know _how long was it to build was the Great Pyramid the world's tallest structure?_ ? B: For 3,800 years.
3. How many chambers are there in the Great Pyramid?
   A: Can you tell me _How many chambers are there in the Great Pyramid?_ B: There are three.
4. Can tourists climb the Sphinx?
   A: Do you have any idea _how many tourist climb the Sphinix?_ ? B: No, it's not allowed.
5. Did aliens build the pyramids?
   A: Do you know _if the aliens buid the pyramids?_ B: It's highly unlikely.

4 Pronunciation Intonation in embedded questions

A 🔊 Listen and repeat. Notice the falling intonation in embedded questions.

Can you tell me how tall it is?   Do you know if the Sphinx was painted?

B Pair work Practice the embedded questions in Exercise 3. Pay attention to your intonation.

5 Speaking Endless possibilities

Pair work Discuss possible explanations for the mysteries in Exercise 1.

A: *Do you have any idea what happened to Amelia Earhart?*
B: *No one does. But she might have crashed on an island.*

6 Keep talking!

Go to page 143 for more practice.

I can ask and speculate about historical events. ☑

D Explanations from long ago

1 Reading ◀))

A Long ago, people created stories, called myths, to explain the world around them. Read the story. What does it try to explain?

Long ago in Australia, an old **wombat** walked toward a **kangaroo** and her baby. As the wombat came closer, the kangaroo heard him say, "Useless and worthless, worthless and useless. I'm blind. Nobody wants me around." The kangaroo was very kind and said, "I'll be your friend. I'll show you where the best grass grows." She let the wombat hold her tail, and she took him to a green area of grass. The wombat was very happy.

Suddenly the kangaroo remembered her baby! She had told him to stay close, but he had walked off. She ran back to look for him and found him asleep under a tree. She didn't want to wake him.

The kangaroo decided to go back and check on the old wombat. Suddenly, something moved nearby – a man was silently following the wombat! His **boomerang** was raised above his head. The kangaroo wanted to run and escape, but she had to protect the wombat! So she began to jump up and down. The man turned toward her. "Run! Someone wants to kill you!" she screamed. The wombat ran, but now the man wanted the kangaroo!

The kangaroo ran until she came to a **cave**. She stayed inside, afraid to go out. She saw the man walk past the cave. She waited until it was safe, and then she ran back to her baby, who was now awake. Together they went to look for the wombat, but he had disappeared.

The kangaroo didn't know that the wombat wasn't really a wombat. He was the very wise being Byamee, who had come to discover the creature with the kindest heart. Now Byamee knew the kindest creature was the kangaroo. He wanted to give her the gift that would help her most of all. So he went to where the trees grow tall and used the soft wood from the outside of the tree to make an **apron**. He gave it to the kangaroo mother, and told her to tie it around herself.

As soon as the kangaroo tied the apron around herself, it turned into a **pouch**. Now she had a place to carry her baby. Byamee then decided to make pouches for all the kangaroo mothers, and since then, their babies have never gotten lost.

Source: Adapted from *Pacific Island Legends: Tales from Micronesia, Melanesia, Polynesia, and Australia*

B Read the story again. Find the words in **bold** in the story. Match the words and the pictures.

1. wombat _b_
2. kangaroo _a_
3. boomerang _e_
4. cave _f_
5. apron _d_
6. pouch _c_

a.
b.
c.
d.
e.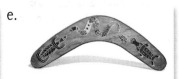
f.

C **Pair work** What is the best title for this story? Discuss your ideas.

2 Listening "The Magpies and the Bell"

A 🔊 Listen to a story from Korea. Number the pictures from 1 to 6.

3

1

2

6

4

5

B 🔊 Listen again. Answer the questions.

1. Where was the man going? _Was for away_
2. Who was the woman that the man met at the house? _the Serpent wife_
3. What did the snake tell the man to do? _three bells sunds_
4. Who saved the man? How? Why? _The magpies saved the man_

C What lesson about life do you think the story tells?

3 Writing and speaking A story

A Think of a story from your culture that explains something. What does it explain? How does the story explain it?

B Write the story, or retell the story in Exercise 2. Use the model paragraph to help you.

C Group work Share your stories. Are there any similarities among your stories? Are there any similarities to other stories you know?

> The Sleep Tree, a Brazilian Myth
> One day, a man in the rain forest saw a huge, old tree he'd never seen before. Its roots went deep into the ground, and its branches spread all across the sky. The man was amazed. He saw a large group of animals sleeping under the old tree. . . .

I can tell a story from my culture. ☑

Wrap-up

1 Quick pair review

Lesson A **Do you remember?** How certain are the sentences?
Write M (more certain) or L (less certain). You have one minute.

_____ 1. Tom might have been sick yesterday.

_____ 2. The glass must have fallen off the table and broken.

_____ 3. Wendy couldn't have had lunch with Michael yesterday.

_____ 4. Lola could have been at the party.

_____ 5. The storm might have started in Florida.

Lesson B **Give your opinion!** What do you think? Use phrases of probability
and improbability. Discuss your answers and give your reasons. You have two minutes.

1. Will cars run on water one day?

2. Will people be able to control the weather?

3. Will we find life on other planets?

A: *Do you think cars will run on water one day?*
B: *It's highly unlikely. There isn't enough energy in water. What do you think?*

Lesson C **Test your partner!** Say four questions. Can your partner write
them as embedded questions? Take turns. You have three minutes.

"Where is Sheila?"

1. *Do you know where Sheila is?*   3. _____

2. _____   4. _____

Lesson D **Brainstorm!** Make up myths about one of the items with a partner.
Be creative! You have three minutes.

| why fish live in the ocean | why snakes don't have legs | why the sky is blue |

A: *A long time ago the sky was white, but a boy found blueberries, and he threw*
   them in the sky. It turned the sky blue.
B: *The sky was black, but when it rained for the first time, it turned blue.*

2 In the real world

Why are these animals unusual? Go online and find information in English about
one of them. Then write about them. What do they look like? Where do they live?
What do they eat?

| tree kangaroos |
| albino snakes |
| magpies |
| wombats |

Tree Kangaroos
Tree kangaroos are unusual because they live in
trees. They have shorter legs than most kangaroos.
They live in Australia and Papua New Guinea.

92

Perspectives

Warm-up

 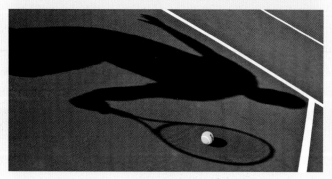

A Look at the pictures. What do you see? What is the most unusual perspective?

B Do you always see things the same way as your friends?

A A traffic accident

1 Vocabulary Three-word phrasal verbs

A 🔊 Match the statements in columns A and B. Then listen and check your answers.

A

1. I like to **catch up with** friends online. _b_
   Ponerse al día con
2. I can **come up with** imaginative ideas. _c_
   Presentar
3. I **look up to** my father. _a_
   admirar a alguien
4. I **get along with** everybody. _e_
   llevarse bien con
5. It's hard to **keep up with** my friends. _f_
   seguir
6. I think that too many people **get away with** speeding. _d_
   escapar con
7. I cannot **put up with** people who lie. _i_
   soportar
8. I try to **take care of** my car. _g_
   cuidado de
9. I always **look forward to** Sunday mornings. _h_
   esperar

B

a. I really respect him.

b. We chat several times a week.

c. I'm a very creative person.

d. The police should give more tickets.

e. People think I'm very friendly.

f. We don't have time to get together.

g. I change the oil every six months.

h. I love to sleep late on weekends.

i. I get very angry when people don't tell the truth.

B **Pair work** Which statements in Part A are true for you? Discuss your answers.

"It's hard to keep up with my friends. I have a lot of friends because I get along with everybody."

2 Language in context Whose fault was it?

A 🔊 Read the traffic accident report that the police officer wrote. What did the witness see?

Traffic Accident Report

Mrs. Fran Perry, 35, hit a traffic light pole on the corner of First and Lexington at 6:45 this evening. She said she had turned quickly to avoid a dog. The pole was not damaged, but her car had a broken light. She said she would take care of it right away.

Mr. Jerry Thomas, 62, told an officer he'd seen the accident from his bedroom window. He saw a man who had taken his dog off its leash. He said the driver had been on her cell phone.

Both the driver and the witness said that they would come in and make a full statement.

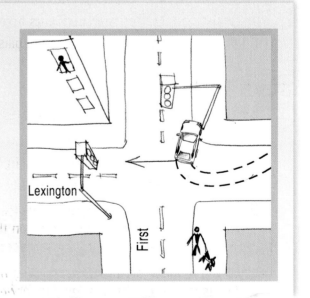

B What about you? Who do you feel is more responsible for the accident – the driver or the dog owner? Why?

3 Grammar 🔊 Reported statements

Use reported speech to tell what a speaker has said without using the person's exact words. When using reported speech, you often have to change pronouns and the tense of the verb.

Direct speech	Reported speech
"I **am** in a hurry."	She **told me** (that) she **was** in a hurry.
"I **am telling** the truth."	She **told me** (that) she **was telling** the truth.
"I **have** an appointment."	She **told me** (that) she **had** an appointment.
"I **saw** the accident."	He **said** (that) he **had seen** the accident.
"The dog **has disappeared**."	He **said** (that) the dog **had disappeared**.
"We **will make** a statement."	They **said** (that) they **would make** a statement.

A Complete the report with *said* or *told*. Then compare with a partner.

~~~~~~

Car Accident on Main St.

Last night, Darren Jones, 18, was riding his bicycle when a car suddenly stopped in front of him. He crashed his bicycle into the car. Darren ___told___ police that he hadn't seen it stop. He ___said___ police he was sorry, but he ___said___ it hadn't been his fault. The driver, Lacey Reed, 45, ___said___ that she had stopped because a man was crossing the road. A witness, James Lee, 68, ___said___ police he had seen everything. Everyone ___said___ they would make a formal report.

~~~~~~

B Rewrite these sentences. Use reported speech. Then compare with a partner.

1. Lacey said, "I want to call my husband." *Lacey said she wanted to call her husband.*
2. Darren told me, "It's not my fault." *Darren told me* It wasn't my fault.
3. James told me, "I heard a loud crash." James told me he heard a loud crash.
4. James said, "I have seen accidents here before." James said I had seen accidents here before
5. Lacey told me, "I'll take care of the bills." Lacey told me. He will take care of the bills

4 Speaking What did he say?

A Choose one question. Write the answer in one sentence.

- What do you do to catch up with your friends?
- What are you looking forward to doing?
- How do you keep up with the news?

B Group work Whisper your sentence to the person on your right. That person whispers your sentence to the person on the right. Continue until the sentence is reported back to you. Was it your sentence, or was it different?

A: *I'm looking forward to graduating next year.*
B: *Jason told me he was looking forward to graduating next year.*
C: *Maria said that Jason was looking forward to . . .*

5 Keep talking!

Student A go to page 144 and Student B go to page 146 for more practice.

I can *report what people say.* ☑

B As I was saying, . . .

1 Interactions — Changing and returning to the topic

A Do you enjoy sports? Which do you prefer, watching sports live or on TV? Why? Have you ever disagreed with a referee's call?

B ◀)) Listen to the conversation. What topics are they discussing? Then practice the conversation.

Maria: I don't believe it!
Kate: What?
Maria: He used his hands. That goal shouldn't have counted.
Kate: Are you sure he used his hands?
Maria: He did. I saw it clearly.
Kate: That reminds me, did you see the game last weekend? I didn't see it, but my brother told me that the same player had scored the winning goal. They won 1-0.
Maria: No, I missed it. But as I was saying, I don't think that was a real goal.
Kate: Maybe the referee just didn't see it. I know it happens sometimes.
Maria: That's possible. Referees are only human, after all.

C ◀)) Read the expressions below. Complete each box with a similar expression from the conversation. Then listen and check your answers.

Changing the topic

~~that reminds me.~~
~~Did you see the game last weeken~~
By the way, . . .
I just thought of something.

Returning to a topic

~~But as I was saying.~~
~~I don't thing~~
To finish what I was saying, . . .
To get back to what I was saying, . . .

D Number the sentences from 1 to 6. Then practice with a partner.

_3_ **A:** I know. It was. I wish I could go to the game next Sunday, but I don't have tickets. And I have to –

_5_ **A:** I can't. Because to finish what I was saying, I have to study all weekend.

_1_ **A:** Did you see the soccer game last night?

_2_ **B:** I did. I watched it on TV. It was awesome.

_6_ **B:** That's too bad. But I have tickets for the game the following weekend, too. Want to go then?

_4_ **B:** Hang on. I just thought of something. I have two tickets! Want to go?

2 Pronunciation Linked vowel sounds with /w/ and /y/

A 🔊 Listen and repeat. Notice how vowel sounds at the beginning and end of words are linked with a /w/ sound or a /y/ sound.

/w/	/w/	/w/	/y/	/y/	/y/
know if	do it	go over	say anything	see it	I am

B 🔊 Listen. Write /w/ or /y/ over the linked sounds. Then practice with a partner.

/y/	/w/	/y/	/w/	/w/	/y/
pay any	how exactly	be in	too old	no one	who is

3 Listening Sports talk

A 🔊 Listen to three conversations between Alex and Celia. What do they begin to discuss in each conversation? Check (✓) the answers.

What do they begin to discuss?	What is the topic changed to?
1. ✓ extreme sports ☐ the dangers of sports	Snow is going to rain in weekend, weather, forecast
2. ☐ sports on TV ✓ the Olympics	She is late for work.
3. ☐ sports fads ✓ sports fans	live soccer games.

B 🔊 Listen again. What is the topic changed to in each conversation? Write the topics in the chart.

4 Speaking Stick to the topic.

A Choose one of these topics or another topic related to sports. Prepare to talk about it for at least a minute.

extreme sports *anuncios* ads in sports benefits of sports a great athlete	a great team sports equipment sports fads *modas en los deportes* sports fans

B **Group work** Take turns. Discuss your topic. The other students keep trying to change the topic. Return to your topic each time.

> **A:** *I think snowboarding is an amazing extreme sport.*
> **B:** *I agree. You know, that reminds me, did you see the ice skating at the Olympics this year?*
> **A:** *Um, no. I couldn't watch the games. But as I was saying, snowboarding is really . . .*

I can change and return to the topic. ✓

C There's always an explanation.

1 Vocabulary Verbs + prepositions

A 🔊 Match the verbs and the prepositions. Add the verbs to the chart. Then listen and check your answers.

| believe ~~creer~~ | depend ~~depender~~ | forget ~~olvidar~~ | participate | rely ~~confiar~~ |
| decide ~~decidir~~ | dream ~~sueño~~ | hear ~~oir~~ | plan ~~plan~~ | worry ~~preocupación~~ |

about		**on**		**in**
dream ✓	heard ✓	decide	plan participate	believe
forget ✓	worry	depende	rely	participate

B Pair work Complete these questions with the correct prepositions. Ask and answer the questions. Do you see things the same way?

1. Do you believe ____in____ UFOs?
2. Who do you rely ____on____ the most?
3. What do you plan ____on____ doing in the future?
4. What's the most important news event you have heard ____about____ recently?
5. What did you dream ____about____ last night?
6. Do you participate ____in____ any community organizations?

2 Conversation Strange behavior

A 🔊 Listen to the conversation. Who do you think Chad is?

Gina: I'm worried. Chad's been acting strangely.
Marissa: What do you mean?
Gina: Well, I asked him if he wanted to see a movie on Friday. He told me he couldn't, but he wouldn't say why.
Marissa: That's odd.
Gina: Then last night he asked me if I was free for dinner on Saturday and if I'd ever been to Michel's.
Marissa: I've heard about Michel's. It's one of the nicest places in town.
Gina: I know. We never go to places like that. We usually just get a pizza and sodas as takeout.
Marissa: Well, I wouldn't worry about it. Just enjoy your dinner.

B 🔊 Listen to a phone conversation between Marissa and Chad. What did Chad do on Friday night? What's he planning on doing on Saturday night?

98

3 Grammar 🔊 Reported *yes/no* questions

Use reported yes / no questions to tell what a speaker has asked without using the person's exact words. When using reported yes / no questions, you often have to change pronouns and the tense of the verb.

Direct questions	Reported questions
"**Are** you free for dinner?"	He asked me if I **was** free for dinner.
"**Are** you **having** a good day?"	He asked me if I **was having** a good day.
"**Do** you **want** to see a movie?"	He asked me if I **wanted** to see a movie.
"**Did** you **speak** to your mother?"	He asked me if I **had spoken** to my mother.
"**Have** you **been** to Michel's?"	He asked me if I **had been** to Michel's.
"**Will** you **marry** me?"	He asked me if I **would marry** him.

(handwritten note: Past Do you speak → had spoken)

Rewrite the questions. Use reported questions. Then compare with a partner.

1. Marissa asked Chad, "Have you spoken to Gina yet?"
   Marissa asked Chad if he had spoken to Gina yet.

2. Marissa asked Chad, "Are you planning on asking Gina to marry you?"
   Marissa asked chad, if He was planning on asking Gina

3. Marissa asked Chad, "Are you worried about Gina's answer?"
   Marissa asked Chad, if He was worried about Gina's answer

4. Chad asked Marissa, "Will Gina say yes?"
   Chad asked Marissa if Gina would say yes?

5. Gina asked Marissa, "Do you believe in love at first sight?"
   Gina aske Marissa if she believedve in love at first sight?

6. Marissa asked Gina, "Did you dream about the perfect wedding as a child?"
   Marissa asked Gina if she had dream about the

7. Marissa asked Gina, "Have you already decided on a wedding date?"
   Marissa asked Gina if she had already deaded on weddling date?

4 Speaking Ask me anything!

A Class activity Imagine you are someone famous. Walk around the class. Find out who your classmates are. Ask and answer *yes/no* questions.

> A: *Hello. I'm Prince William.*
> B: *Can I ask you a question? Do you participate in any charities?*

B Group work Report the most interesting questions and answers.

"Francesca asked me if I participated in any charities. I told her I participated in a lot of charities – especially ones that work with world hunger."

5 Keep talking!

Go to page 145 for more practice.

| I can report what people ask. ✓ |

1 Reading

A What questions do you ask to get to know someone?

B Read the questionnaire. Which answers tell you that Allie is a friendly person?

THE PROUST QUESTIONNAIRE

The Proust Questionnaire is based on a game created in the early 1890s. Marcel Proust, a French writer, believed that the answers could show a lot about people's thoughts, values, and experiences.

We asked 15-year-old Allie Davis to answer our questions. What do you think the answers tell us about Allie and teenagers today?

What is your idea of perfect happiness?
Doing what you want with your life.

What is your greatest fear? Snakes.

What trait do you most dislike in others?
When people steal all the attention.

What is your favorite journey?
The one where you don't know the destination.

Which word do you most overuse?
I use "SRSLY" too much when I text my friends.

What is your greatest regret? 4
Not taking more risks.

What or who is the greatest love of your life?
My friends.

When and where are you happiest? 1
When I'm with people that I love, and when I'm getting something done in time.

What talent would you most like to have?
Being an amazing dancer.

What is your current state of mind?
Can't wait till summer! 3

What do you consider your greatest achievement? Meeting my friends.

What is your most valued possession?
My cell phone.

What is your most noticeable characteristic?
My height.

What is the quality you most admire in a man?
Being a quick thinker.

What is the quality you most admire in a woman?
Confidence.

What do you most value in your friends?
The fact that they know me really well and always try to make me have a great time.

Who is your favorite hero of fiction?
Scout from *To Kill a Mockingbird*.

Who are your heroes in real life?
Oprah Winfrey, Audrey Hepburn, and Sofia Coppola.   Lema

What is your motto?
Live for yourself.

C Read the questionnaire again. Find this information about Allie. Complete the chart.

1. three women she admires — 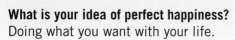 Oprah Winfrey, Audrey Hepburn and Sofia Coppola.
2. a talent she'd like to have — Being an amazing dancer
3. something she's looking forward to — Being an amazin' dancer
4. what would make her happy — When I'm people, that I Love, and when
5. an answer that shows she texts a lot — She uses, SRLY too much when she text

D **Pair work** Is Allie a typical teenager? How is she the same or different from teenagers that you know? Discuss your ideas.

2 Listening Justin's turn

A 🔊 Listen to Allie ask her friend Justin some of the questions from Exercise 1.
Number them from 1 to 5 in the order she asks them.

Questions	Answers
4 What is your greatest fear?	beeng along *fear to* ①
2 What is your idea of perfect happiness?	ride a biclcle
1 What word do you most overuse?	Welrever
3 What is your current state of mind?	Thoughtful.
5 What is your greatest regret?	Not taking more risck

No learning to play Instrument

B 🔊 Listen again. Write Justin's answers.

3 Writing Questionnaire results

A Choose any two questions from Exercise 1, and write them in the chart. Think about
your answers. Then ask each question to two classmates and write their answers.

Questions	Name: Rogalia	Name: Luis *Sofia*
1. No finish the colleger	⑤	①
2. No Swimm		

B Write about the questionnaire results in Part A. Use the model to help you.

> ### Questionnaire Results
> *The three of us have very different regrets. Eun-ju said her greatest regret was
> quitting piano lessons. Antonio said that his was not listening to his grandfather's
> advice. I think my greatest regret is something I said to my brother once. . . .*

C Group work Share your writing with your classmates.

4 Speaking Imagine that!

A Look at the questionnaire below. Think about your own answers.

- If you could have one superpower, what would it be? *resolve people family problems. No longer slave.* *fairy godmother*
- What famous person do you think you look like?
- What song title best describes your feelings about life? *when the sun rises in the morning.*
- If you could be any animal for a day, what would you be? *bird.* *ego.* *again*
- If a movie were made about your life, what would the title be?

B Pair work Ask your partner the questions in Part A. Write the answers.

C Group work Report the most interesting information you found out.

> I can discuss thoughts and values. ✓

Wrap-up

1 Quick pair review

Lesson A **Test your partner!** Say four sentences to your partner using direct speech. Can your partner say the sentences using reported speech? Take turns. You and your partner have one minute.

A: *My sister will take good care of my dog.*
B: *You told me that your sister would take good care of your dog.*

Lesson B **Do you remember?** Complete the expressions for changing a topic and returning to a topic. Circle the correct words. You have one minute.

1. I **back / just** thought of something.
2. By the **way / what**, I saw a concert on Friday.
3. That **says / reminds** me, are you driving to work tomorrow?
4. As I was **saying / finishing**, I look up to my teachers. They work very hard.
5. To finish **way / what** I was saying, let's have Chinese food.
6. To get **me / back** to what I was saying, Carly gets along with everybody.

Lesson C **Find out!** Who is one person both you and your partner depend on? worry about a lot? have heard about recently in the news? plan on visiting soon? You and your partner have two minutes.

A: *I depend on my brother. He's older and knows a lot of things. What about you?*
B: *I don't have a brother. But I depend on my father. Do you?*
A: *Yes, I do.*

Lesson D **Give your opinion!** Who are people that you could describe using these phrases? You have two minutes.

a talented athlete	_____	an amazing singer	_____
a hardworking actor	_____	a quick thinker	_____
a friendly teacher	_____	a confident woman	_____

2 In the real world

Whose side are you on? Go online and find information in English about one of these topics. Then write about it. What do people think about it? What do you think?

art made from recycled trash
extreme sports
hybrid cars
reality shows

Trash Art
Many people think art made from recycled trash is good for the environment. Other people think it's ugly. I agree with both opinions. It is good for the environment, but it's usually ugly!

The real world

Warm-up

A Match the jobs and the pictures.

1. animal trainer	4. fashion designer	7. singer / songwriter
2. archaeologist	5. hairstylist	8. tour guide
3. DJ	6. race-car driver	9. video-game designer

B What three jobs do you think would be the most interesting? What would you like about them? Why?

A *Getting it done*

1 **Vocabulary** Word partners

A 🔊 Cross out the words that do *not* go together. Then listen and check your answers.

1. accept — a job offer / ~~a job ad~~
2. apply for — ~~a letter~~ / a job *formato*
3. format — ~~an interview~~ / a résumé
4. prepare for — ~~a business card~~ / an interview
5. print — an email / ~~a job~~
6. proofread — a résumé / ~~a job offer~~ *corregir*
7. provide — ~~a company~~ / references
8. research — a job / ~~a résumé~~
9. send — a thank-you note / ~~a phone call~~
10. translate — ~~a job~~ / a letter

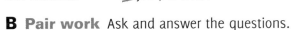

B **Pair work** Ask and answer the questions.

1. If you were looking for a job, what things in Part A would you do?
2. Have you ever applied for a job? What was it?
3. What would you include on your résumé?

2 **Language in context** Tips from a recruiter

A 🔊 Read the tips from a recruiter to job hunters. Which tip should you do after the interview?

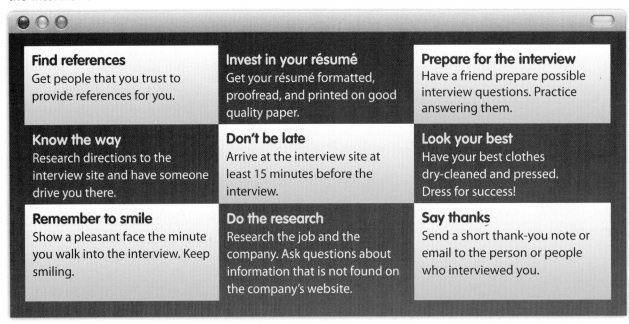

Find references
Get people that you trust to provide references for you.

Invest in your résumé
Get your résumé formatted, proofread, and printed on good quality paper.

Prepare for the interview
Have a friend prepare possible interview questions. Practice answering them.

Know the way
Research directions to the interview site and have someone drive you there.

Don't be late
Arrive at the interview site at least 15 minutes before the interview.

Look your best
Have your best clothes dry-cleaned and pressed. Dress for success!

Remember to smile
Show a pleasant face the minute you walk into the interview. Keep smiling.

Do the research
Research the job and the company. Ask questions about information that is not found on the company's website.

Say thanks
Send a short thank-you note or email to the person or people who interviewed you.

B What about you? Are all the tips appropriate in your culture? What other tips can you add?

3 Grammar — Causative *get* and *have*

get + someone + to + verb
Get people **to provide** references for you.

get + something + *past participle*
Where can I **get** my résumé **printed**?

have + someone + verb
I plan to **have** a friend **practice** with me.

have + something + *past participle*
I need to **have** my clothes **dry-cleaned**.

A Circle the correct words. Then compare with a partner.

1. My company is trying to get Greg **accept** / **to accept** / **accepted** our job offer.
2. I need to have someone **translate** / **to translate** / **translated** my résumé into English.
3. I'd like to get my former boss **provide** / **to provide** / **provided** a reference letter.
4. You should have your suit **dry-clean** / **to dry-clean** / **dry-cleaned** before the interview.
5. Where can I get some business cards **print** / **to print** / **printed**?

B Put the words in order. Then compare with a partner.

1. Paul / his brother / gets / his hair / cut / to — Paul _gets his brother to cut his hair_ .
2. I / to / a reference letter / got / write / my boss — I _____ .
3. Where / have / proofread / I / can / my résumé — Where _____ ?
4. Jay / his house / on Saturday / had / cleaned — Jay _____ .
5. Liz / to get / proofread / her presentation / needs — Liz _____ .

4 Listening — So much to do!

A Listen to three busy people talk about their plans. Write what they are going to do themselves.

	Do themselves	Have or get done
1.		
2.		
3.		

B Listen again. Write one thing each person is going to have or get done.

5 Speaking — Do it yourself?

Group work Imagine you are preparing for an interview. Look at the "to do" list. What would you do yourself? What would you have or get done? Share your ideas.

cut my hair	iron my shirt	proofread my résumé
dry-clean my suit	photocopy my résumé	take photos
format my résumé	print business cards	translate my résumé

A: *I'd format my résumé, but I'd get someone else to proofread it.*
B: *Me, too. I'd have my résumé translated, and then I'd photocopy it myself.*

6 Keep talking!

Go to page 147 for more practice.

I can talk about getting things done.

B | *Let me see . . .*

1 Interactions — Interviewing

A Imagine you've applied for a job at a company and are preparing for an interview. What topics do you think you would discuss in the interview?

benefits	hours	salary	your education
break times	retirement plan	travel opportunities	your skills and abilities

B 🔊 Listen to the conversation. How does Mr. Reed describe himself? Practice the conversation.

Interviewer: I just have a few more questions, Mr. Reed. Why do you want to work here?

Mr. Reed: I'd like to get some experience in this field and put my skills to work.

Interviewer: And what are your best skills?

Mr. Reed: Oh, let's see. . . . I'm responsible, hardworking, and can work independently.

Interviewer: That's good. Can you work weekends?

Mr. Reed: Sure. That's not a problem.

Interviewer: Can you provide references?

Mr. Reed: Of course.

Interviewer: Well, it's been nice meeting you. I want to thank you for coming in for this interview.

Mr. Reed: Thank you very much.

C 🔊 Read the expressions below. Complete each box with a similar expression from the conversation. Then listen and check your answers.

Taking time to think

_____

Um, let me see. . . .
Hmm, let me think. . . .

Closing an interview

_____

Well, it's been great talking to you.
Well, I've really enjoyed talking to you.

D Number the sentences from 1 to 8. Then practice with a partner.

____ **A:** You're welcome. We'll be in touch.	____ **B:** Thank you for the interview.
_1_ **A:** So, what skills do you have?	____ **B:** Good-bye. Thank you again.
____ **A:** Good. Well, it's been nice meeting you.	____ **B:** Um, let me see. I could start in a week.
____ **A:** That's good. What's the earliest you can start?	____ **B:** I'm good with people, and I can use all of the latest office software.

2 Listening Getting the job?

A ◀)) Listen to the last part of a job interview. Check (✓) the job the man is most likely applying for.

☐ TV host   ☐ soccer coach   ☐ radio DJ   ☐ translator   ☐ scientist

B ◀)) Listen again. How does the man answer the interviewer's questions? Complete the interviewer's notes.

1. What skills do you have?   _____ and asking questions
2. What would you like about the job? the _____ _____
3. What is your greatest strength?   _____ skills
4. What is your greatest weakness?   doesn't _____ some current _____
5. What is your career goal?   host TV _____ _____
6. Can you work weekends?   can work _____ but not _____

C Pair work Did the man interview well? Why or why not?

3 Speaking Help wanted

A Prepare for a job interview. Choose one of the jobs. Think of answers to the questions below.

JOBS

MAGAZINE COLUMNIST

Trendy magazine seeks outgoing person to write weekly column on what's hot around town. Latest knowledge of music, food, movies, and fashion required. Must be able to write quickly under pressure. Pay per word.

ASSISTANT COACH

Energetic and patient person needed to work as part-time assistant to head coach at local high school. No experience necessary. Strong ability in several sports desired. Applicant must be a team player. Pay negotiable.

ONLINE TUTOR

Work from home! Reliable tutor needed to teach English and / or math to high school students online. Must have own phone and computer and be able to work independently. Flexible hours. Hourly pay. Perfect for college students.

- Can you tell me a little about yourself?
- What skills do you have?
- What is your greatest strength?
- What is your greatest weakness?
- What is your career goal?
- Can you work weekends?
- How would your friends describe you?
- How do you cope with stress?

B Pair work Role-play the job interview for a job in Part A. Then change roles.

Student A: Tell your partner which job you have chosen. Answer Student B's questions. Take time to think when you need to.

Student B: Interview Student A. Ask the questions in Part A and questions of your own. Then close the interview.

> *I can* take time to think in an interview. ☑
>
> *I can* close an interview. ☑

Future goals

1 **Vocabulary** Setting goals

A 🔊 Match the words and the pictures. Then listen and check your answers.

a. be financially independent	c. have a big wedding	e. prepare for my exams	g. work as a journalist
b. do volunteer work	d. live in the countryside	f. study abroad	h. write travel books

1.

2. e

3.

4. b

5. c

6. d

7.

8. h

B **Pair work** Do you have any of these goals? Which ones? Have you already reached any of these goals? Tell your partner.

2 **Conversation** Planning ahead

A 🔊 Listen to the conversation. Who will Zac marry in five years?

Zac: Guess what! I've decided to study abroad next year. At this time next year, I'll be studying in Paris!

Lucy: Really? That sounds wonderful.

Zac: I've been thinking a lot lately about what I want to achieve in my life. In five years, I'll be working as a journalist. In seven years, I'll be living in the countryside. In twenty years –

Lucy: But what about family? Will you get married?

Zac: Oh, yes. I'll have a big wedding in five years.

Lucy: OK . . . and who will you marry?

Zac: I have no idea. But I'm sure I'll meet someone.

B 🔊 Listen to the rest of the conversation. What two things is Lucy doing these days? What job does she think she'll have in five years?

3 Grammar Future continuous vs. future with *will*

Use the future continuous to describe actions in progress at a specific time in the future.
Where will you be studying next year?
I'll be studying in Paris. I won't be working as a journalist then.

Use the future with will *with verbs that are not usually used in the continuous form.*
What will you achieve in twenty years? Will you be financially independent?
Yes, I will. But I'll have to work really hard.

Complete the conversations with the future continuous or future with *will*. Then practice with a partner.

1. **A:** What ___are___ you ___doing___ (do) a year from now?
   B: I ___will be study___ (study) abroad.
2. **A:** What ___will happen___ (happen) to your friends after graduation?
   B: Sam and Ann ___will have___ (have) a big wedding. Jacob ___will work___ (work) in the city.
3. **A:** Where ___are___ you ___living___ (live) in ten years?
   B: I don't know, but I probably ___won't live___ (not / live) here.
4. **A:** What ___are___ your life ___bing___ (be) like in the future?
   B: I ___won't work___ (not / work) for a large company. I _____ (write) travel books.
5. **A:** _____ you _____ (go) on vacation in July?
   B: Yes, I _____ (go) to Rome. I _____ (see) the Colosseum and the Trevi Fountain.

4 Pronunciation Reduction of *will*

A Listen and repeat. Notice how *will* often gets reduced to *'ll* after *Wh-* question words and nouns.

When will your friends finish this class? What will they be doing afterwards?

John will still be studying, and Beth will be looking for a job.

B Pair work Practice the questions and answers in Exercise 3A. Pay attention to the reduction of *will*.

5 Speaking My own goals

A What goals do you have? When do you hope to reach those goals?

B Group work Share your goals. Ask and answer questions to get more information.

A: *I'll be married in five years. I think I'll be working for a large company.*
B: *What kind of large company will you be working for?*

6 Keep talking!

Go to page 148 for more practice.

I can ask and talk about future goals.

1 Reading ◀))

A The jobs of today may not be the jobs of the future. Which of these jobs do you think will exist in the future? Will they be different in any way? Which will disappear? Why?

| cashier | doctor | farmer | pilot | reporter | soldier | teacher | travel agent |

B Read the article. What is it about? Check (✓) the main idea.

☐ jobs that will appear   *futuro Aparecer*   ☐ jobs that will disappear   ☐ current jobs that will stay the same

JOBS OF THE FUTURE

Drowned-city specialist – What will happen if the climate continues to change so quickly? One problem will be an increase in flooding and drowned cities. Someone will have to rescue people and their possessions, and move houses to higher ground. That person will be the drowned-city specialist.

Dirigible pilot – Dirigibles may revolutionize life in much of the world. They're relatively cheap to operate and don't require expensive airplane runways. They can stop in midair to drop off passengers or deliver goods. Skilled dirigible pilots will be in high demand.

Robot mechanic – The robots available now mostly clean carpets or mow lawns. Someday these machines will become cheaper, and middle-class families everywhere will be able to buy robotic personal assistants or companions. Robot mechanics will be needed to take care of the mechanical problems that these companion robots will certainly have.

Space tour guide – More and more people will be taking leisure trips to space, and they will need tour guides. One company has already begun a space program with trips costing about $200,000. In the future, these high prices should become more affordable, and more space guides will be needed.

Teleport specialist – Imagine walking onto a teleport station. Immediately you disappear, and then suddenly you reappear at your destination. There will be no more cars and no more auto mechanics. Instead, the teleport specialist will help you move from place to place. A whole new economy based on the teleporter will appear.

Source: Adapted from "New Jobs" slideshow, Forbes.com, 5/23/2006

C Check (✓) the true sentences. Then correct the false ones.

☑ 1. A drowned-city specialist may be a needed job in the future. *above* T _____

☑ 2. Dirigibles are very expensive to operate. F _____

☐ 3. There are no home robots available now. F _____

☑ 4. Space travel for tourists has already begun. T _____

☑ 5. Teleporting may replace commuting by car. T _____

D **Pair work** Which of the jobs in the article do you think is most likely to happen? What qualifications would someone need for these jobs? Discuss your ideas.

2 **Writing and speaking** A letter of interest

A Read these job ads for positions at Carolina Industries. Then read the letter below.
What job is Teresa interested in?

Tech Support Officer
Maintain and ensure smooth running of computer systems and internal network. Must be familiar with latest hardware and software. Flexible hours.

Recruiter
Find, interview, and test applicants to locate qualified employees for job openings. Must be organized and able to travel to colleges and job fairs.

Marketing Assistant
Entry-level job ideal for recent graduate. Assist staff in Marketing Department. Duties include filing, research, and working with new customers.

Your address	Portal Bravo #19D 37529 Leon, Mexico
Date	June 7, 2012
Name, title, company, and address of the person you're writing to	Ms. Susan Dodd Personnel Manager Carolina Industries 662 Beacon Road Salt Lake City, Utah 84110
Try to use the name of the person.	To Whom It May Concern. Dear Ms. Dodd:
State why you are writing.	I would like to express my interest in the marketing assistant job recently advertised on your website.
Briefly state your education and any experience or skills.	I will be graduating next month with a B.A. in Marketing from Monterrey University. I am fluent in English and Spanish, with a basic knowledge of Japanese. Enclosed is my résumé, which contains detailed information on my education and experience.
Say how you can be contacted.	I would appreciate the opportunity to discuss this position with you. I can be reached by cell phone at 319-555-8116 or by email at teresasanchez@cup.org.
Thank the person.	Thank you very much for your time and consideration.
Use a formal closing.	Sincerely,
Sign your name.	*Teresa Sanchez* Teresa Sanchez

B Choose a job from this lesson or use your own idea. Write a letter of interest.

C **Group work** Share your letters. What kinds of jobs are your classmates interested in? What do you think they will be doing in five years?

A: *Jean is interested in the tech support job.*
B: *Really? I think Jean will be working as a space tour guide in the future, not a tech support officer. She's so friendly and outgoing.*

I can discuss future careers. ✓

Wrap-up

1 Quick pair review

Lesson A Find out! What are two things both you and your partner usually have done or get done? You and your partner have two minutes.

A: *I get my photos printed at the drugstore.*
B: *Really? I print my pictures on my computer. I usually have my nice clothes dry-cleaned. What about you?*
A: *Yes, I do, too.*

Lesson B Do you remember? What can you say when you need time to think? Check (✓) the correct answers. You have one minute.

_____ 1. Oh, let's see.

_____ 2. Well, it's been great talking to you.

_____ 3. I'm not sure that's really true.

_____ 4. Oh, really?

_____ 5. Um, let me see.

_____ 6. Hmm, let me think.

Lesson C Guess! Describe something you will be doing in the future, but don't say where it will be. Can your partner guess the place? You have two minutes.

A: *I'll be sitting in the sun in two months, and I'll be swimming in the ocean.*
B: *Will you be on vacation? Will you be going to the beach?*
A: *Yes, I will.*

Lesson D Give your opinion! How important will these jobs be in 50 years? Rank them from 1 (the most important) to 8 (the least important). Compare your answers. You have three minutes.

_____ computer programmer	_____ lawyer
_____ librarian	_____ TV host
_____ English teacher	_____ flight attendant
_____ art teacher	_____ chef

2 In the real world

How can you prepare for jobs of the future? Go to a university website. See what classes they offer, such as video-game design, robotics, or solar energy. Then write about a job of the future.

Preparing for Jobs of the Future
In the future, most jobs will be high-tech. Everyone will have to study math and science to get a good job. I want to design video games, so I will . . .

Finding solutions

Warm-up

"It's just their little way of saying, 'Sorry we wrecked the planet.'"

A Describe the cartoons. What are the problems in each cartoon?

B How do you feel about the problems?

Environmental concerns

1 Vocabulary Preventing pollution

A 🔊 Match the **bold** words and their meanings. Then listen and check your answers.

Ways of preventing air pollution

1. **Combine** ~~tareas~~ tasks if you drive. _c_
2. **Commute** by bicycle if possible. _b_
3. **Maintain** your car so that it's more efficient. _d_
4. **Avoid** products that come in spray cans. _a_

a. don't use
b. go to work
c. do together
d. keep in good condition

Ways of preventing water pollution

5. **Store** paint and chemicals in safe containers. _f_
6. **Limit** your use of harmful cleaning products. _h_
7. **Discard** paint and batteries properly. _g_
8. **Conserve** water whenever possible. _e_

e. save
f. put or keep
g. throw away
h. control the amount

Ways of preventing land pollution

9. **Purchase** products with little packaging. _l_
10. **Recycle** any item you can. _i_
11. **Identify** where trash cans are. _j_
12. Never **dump** motor oil on the ground. _k_

i. use again
j. find or locate
k. put carelessly
l. buy

B **Pair work** Which things in Part A do you think you could do? Which do you already do? Tell your partner.

2 Language in context Promoting "green" travel

A 🔊 Read about a high-tech solution to traveling "green." What problem did it solve?

Bicycles are being parked in a whole new way in Tokyo. Commuters used to leave their bicycles on the sidewalks outside train stations, but people couldn't move around them and something clearly had to be done. Now, at Kasai Station, commuters can leave their bikes in a 10-level underground parking garage that is controlled by robots. Robots store nearly 10,000 bicycles a day. When commuters want their bicycles, they use cards to identify them. Within seconds, a robot finds and brings it to them. The Tokyo garage is so successful that more "green" garages are being considered.

B How does the underground parking garage help "green" travel? Could Tokyo's solution work for you?

3 **Grammar** 🔊 Present continuous passive; infinitive passive

Use the present continuous passive to describe an action in progress when you want
to focus on the receiver of the action instead of on the doer of the action.

Active	*Passive*
Commuters **are parking** bicycles in a new way.	Bicycles **are being parked** in a new way.

Use the infinitive passive after verbs like have *and* need *when you want to focus on*
the receiver of the action instead of on the doer of the action.

Active	*Passive*
Somebody **had to do** something.	Something **had to be done**.
People **needed to put** the bikes somewhere.	The bikes **needed to be put** somewhere.

A Rewrite these sentences in the passive. Then compare with a partner.

1. People are reusing more items every day. _____
2. People need to maintain cars for safety. _____
3. Guests are conserving water in hotels. _____
4. You have to discard old batteries properly. _____
5. Homeowners need to store chemicals safely. _____

B Complete the sentences with the present continuous passive or the infinite passive.
Then compare with a partner.

The Billabong clothing company has found an unusual way to
make clothes. Plastic soda bottles and discarded clothing
_____ (combine) to make "eco-friendly"
shorts. The company says that with this new material,
environmental pollution _____ (limit). For
example, ten recycled bottles have _____
(use) to make one pair of Billabong shorts; that means ten fewer
bottles in landfills. Currently, the shorts _____
(sell) for about $50.

4 **Speaking** Environmental trends

A Which trends are happening in your town, city, or country? Check (✓)
your answers.

- ☐ More products are being reused.
- ☐ More water is being conserved.
- ☐ The air is becoming less polluted.
- ☐ More hybrid cars are being purchased.
- ☐ Money is being spent on "green" technology.
- ☐ More solar energy is being produced.

B **Group work** Compare your answers. What do you think is causing each trend?
Choose one trend that is not happening. What do you think needs to be done about it?

5 **Keep talking!**

Go to page 149 for more practice.

I can *discuss environmental trends.* ☑

B That's a good point.

1 Interactions Opinions

A Do you do any of these activities when you travel? How could these activities affect the environment?

> bicycling   camping   hiking   kayaking   snorkeling   viewing wildlife

B ◀)) Listen to the conversation. Where does Daniela want to stay on vacation? Then practice the conversation.

> **Elena:** Where are you going on vacation?
> **Daniela:** Maybe to this eco-friendly resort.
> **Elena:** What do you mean, "eco-friendly"?
> **Daniela:** Well, it combines eco-tourism and helping the local community. It's important to be responsible when you travel, don't you think?
> **Elena:** That's a good point.
> **Daniela:** So, this place looks good. They're trying to conserve water. And they want you to purchase handmade objects from the local businesses.
> **Elena:** Do you know who owns it?
> **Daniela:** I have no idea. Why do you ask?
> **Elena:** Well, some eco-resorts are owned by big companies, so the money they make doesn't help the local community very much.
> **Daniela:** I don't see it that way. Eco-resorts give jobs to local people and help raise environmental awareness, no matter who owns them.

C ◀)) Read the expressions below. Complete each box with a similar expression from the conversation. Then listen and check your answers.

Supporting an opinion

_____

I see what you mean.
You make a very good point.

Not supporting an opinion

_____

I see it a little differently.
Actually, I have a different opinion.

D **Pair work** Share your opinions about eco-tourism. Use the ideas below or your own idea. Support or don't support one another's opinions.

> builds environmental awareness   helps locals more than it hurts them
> can actually damage the environment   is only a trendy marketing word

2 Listening A case for tap water?

A 🔊 Listen to the conversation between Eric and Mandy about bottled water.
Number the pictures from 1 to 4.

B 🔊 Listen again. Complete the sentences with the correct numbers.

1. People in the U.S. spend more than _____ billion dollars a year on bottled water.
2. More than _____ % of bottled water is just tap water.
3. People are drinking _____ % more bottled water every year.
4. Manufacturing bottles uses _____ times the amount of water in the bottle.
5. The energy used to make plastic bottles can drive _____ million cars a year.
6. People in the U.S. buy _____ billion bottles of water a year.
7. Only _____ % of the bottles are being recycled.
8. It only costs _____ cents a gallon to get tap water in your home.

C Does Eric approve of buying bottled water? How do you feel about buying bottled water?

3 Speaking Seeing both sides

Group work Check (✓) the opinions you agree with. Then compare and discuss your opinions.

☑ Schools should be required to serve only healthy food.
☐ Kids at school should be free to eat whatever food they want.
☑ Rich countries have to pay more to fight climate change.
☐ Every country has to pay more to fight climate change.
☑ The worst kind of pollution is air pollution.
☐ The worst kind of pollution is water pollution.
☐ The worst kind of pollution is land pollution.

A: *I think the worst kind of pollution is air pollution. If the air is dirty, people can't breathe.*
B: *I see it a little differently. Water pollution is worse because . . .*

I can support and not support an opinion. ☑

C My community

1 Vocabulary Community improvement

A ◀)) Complete the sentences. Then listen and check your answers.

1. A **beautification project** makes a community _a_ .
   a. more attractive   b. less expensive
2. At a **community garden**, people _b_ .
   a. can go camping   b. grow vegetables or flowers
3. At an **employment center**, people can get _a_ .
   a. job information   b. marriage advice
4. At a **health clinic**, people can get medical _b_ .
   a. problems   b. help
5. With a **neighborhood watch**, neighbors try to limit _a_ .
   a. crime   b. pollution
6. A **public library** is used by _b_ .
   a. members only   b. everyone
7. A **recreation center** is a place to _b_ .
   a. help build homes   b. play sports or games
8. A **recycling center** is a place to _a_ .
   a. take used materials   b. get housing advice

B Pair work Which services in Part A do you have in your community? What other services do you have in your community? Who do these services help?

A: *I know we have a public library, a health clinic, and a recreation center.*
B: *But I don't think there's a community garden.*

2 Conversation A better place to live

A ◀)) Listen to the conversation. Who will a recreation center help?

Interviewer: Hi. I'm with the community improvement board. tablero

Mr. Brown: Great. You guys are doing a fantastic job.

Interviewer: Thank you. As you know, we no longer have a community garden because of a lack of interest. Would you want to build a recreation center instead?

Mr. Brown: That's a good idea. We should build one so teens have a place to go.

Interviewer: OK. Now, although we have a neighborhood watch, there's still crime. So we're planning on putting video cameras on streetlights –

Mr. Brown: Great. There goes our privacy.

Interviewer: So you wouldn't support these cameras?

B ◀)) Listen to the rest of the conversation. Which community improvement would Mr. Brown support? Which one wouldn't he support?

3 Grammar 🔊 | Linking words

Reason: We no longer have a community garden **because of** a lack of interest.
Result: There's still crime, **so** we're planning to install video cameras.
Contrast: **Although** we have a neighborhood watch, there's still crime.
Condition: Teens will have a place to go **if** we build a recreation center.
Purpose: We should build a recreation center **so (that)** teens have a place to go.

A Circle the correct words. Then compare with a partner.

1. The city stopped all beautification projects **because of** / so that a lack of money.
2. Why don't you visit the employment center **if** / so that you need a job?
3. Let's go to the public library because of / **so that** we can borrow some books.
4. I'm not feeling well, although / **so** I'm going to go to the health clinic.
5. **Although** / So we have a community garden, few people know about it.
6. Crime in our community is down **because of** / so that the neighborhood watch.

B Pair work Complete these sentences with your own ideas.

Although our town is safe, . . .	If you want a place to relax, . . .
I have a bag of empty cans, so . . .	We need to make changes because of . . .

4 Pronunciation Rise-falling and low falling tones

🔊 Listen and repeat. Notice the rise-falling and low falling tones in the responses. A rise-falling tone means you really mean what you're saying. A low falling tone can mean that you don't mean what you're saying.

A: I'm with the community board.   B: Great. You guys are doing a fantastic job.

A: We're putting in video cameras.   B: Great. There goes our privacy.

5 Speaking Quality of life

Group work How can you improve the quality of life for these people in your community? Share your ideas.

children	families	teenagers
the elderly	new arrivals	unemployed people

"Although there's playground equipment in the park, it's old. So I think we should raise money for new equipment."

6 Keep talking!

Go to page 150 for more practice.

I can discuss ways to improve my community.

D Getting involved

1 Reading 🔊

A What are some of the challenges young people face today?

B Read the article. According to Reginald Caster and Robert Harris, what risk do boys from their old neighborhood face today?

THE ELEPHANT MEN

The Elephant Men program is the creation of Reginald Caster and Robert Harris, two friends who grew up together in a poor neighborhood in Memphis, Tennessee. They grew up, moved away, and became successful. They remained friends and shared a goal. The goal was to help boys ages 9 to 13 in their old neighborhood. They wanted to act as role models, or good examples, for young boys and to stop them from getting into trouble as they got older.

They called their program The Elephant Men after reading how elephant families in Africa surround and protect their young when they are in danger. Reginald and Robert's program supports the young men in inner cities who are at risk of losing their lives to drugs and crime. Their slogan is, "Protecting our youth with the strength and conviction of the elephant."

They look for different ways for the young men to build respect for themselves and others. One way is to use sports, especially basketball, to bring the boys together. Another successful project is a four-week summer work program that includes more than 100 young boys. The boys pick up

litter across the city in exchange for a $200 gift certificate to purchase clothes for school. To be part of the program, the boys have to get a reference letter from an adult at their school who is willing to write something positive about them. This gives the boys a reason to do well in school.

"We know our program works," says Reginald. "We have some kids in college now, and the best day of the year for us is the weekend before school starts, when we see our boys in the malls buying their clothes and books for school."

Source: www.grass-roots.org/usa/elephant.shtml

C Read the article again. Answer the questions.

1. Who does The Elephant Men program help? *Protect their young boys who are at risk of losing their lives to drugs and crime.*
2. Why did they choose the name The Elephant Men? *after reading how elephant families in Africa surround and protect youngs save their lives to drugs and crime*
3. What qualities do they hope to build in the young men?
4. What do the boys need to do to be part of the summer work program? *a reference letter from an adult at their school who is willing to write something positive about them*
5. What do the boys receive at the end of the summer work program? *$200 gift certificate to purchase clothes for school.*

D Pair work How might this program change the adults and kids who participate in it? Discuss your ideas.

2 **Writing** A letter to a community leader

A Write a letter to a community leader about an issue that you feel needs to be addressed. Use these questions and the model to help you.

- Who are you?
- What is the issue? *problema*
- What is currently being done?
- What needs to be done?

B Pair work Exchange letters with a partner. Do you agree?

> Dear Councilman Perez,
>   I am a third-year student at Union University. I am writing to express my concern about how difficult it is for people in wheelchairs to enter many buildings on campus. Although some public buildings have wheelchair ramps, most do not. The city needs to require that all buildings have ramps. . . .

3 **Listening** Helping out

A 🔊 Listen to three people talk about issues. Check (✓) the issue they're involved in.

	Issue	What they're doing to help
Fernando *Fortaleza, Brazil*	☐ translating ☐ job training	
Aicha *Casablanca, Morocco*	☐ beautification projects ☐ parking issues	
Ingrid *Düsseldorf, Germany*	☐ helping new arrivals ☐ recreation centers	

B 🔊 Listen again. What are they doing to help? Write one example in the chart.

C Which issue in Part A are you concerned about? What other ways can people help?

4 **Speaking** Raising awareness

A Work with a partner. Agree on a charity, a cause, or an organization you would like people to be aware of. Then plan a way to raise awareness of the problem or its solution. Consider these ideas and ideas of your own.

organize a community event
create a social networking group
give presentations at schools
have a contest to raise money
pass out information on the street
put up informational posters around town
run public-service announcements on the radio
set up an information table on the sidewalk

B Class activity Share your ideas with the class. Ask and answer questions for more information.

I can discuss ways to raise awareness. ☑

Wrap-up

1 Quick pair review

Lesson A Do you remember? Match the active and passive sentences. You have one minute.

1. You need to limit your use of running water. _b_

2. Our building is limiting our use of running water. ____

3. The office store is discarding printer ink. ____

4. You need to discard your printer ink at an office store. ____

5. You have to purchase "green" items online. ____

a. Your printer ink needs to be discarded at an office store.

b. Our use of running water is being limited.

c. "Green" items have to be purchased online.

d. Printer ink is being discarded by the office store.

e. Your use of running water needs to be limited.

Lesson B Give your opinion! What do you think about these eco-friendly activities? Use expressions to support or not support your partner's opinion. You and your partner have two minutes.

Avoid using plastic bags.	Don't purchase a new cell phone every year.
Buy energy-saving lightbulbs.	Take your own bags to a store.
Don't dump paint.	Walk to work.

A: *Don't dump paint.*
B: *That's a good point. Recycle it. For example, give it to a friend to use.*

Lesson C Brainstorm! Make a list of community improvement ideas. How many can you remember? You have two minutes.

Lesson D Find out! Who are two people that both you and your partner think are role models? You and your partner have two minutes.

2 In the real world

What is a problem in your community? Go online and find information about one of these problems, or choose your own idea. Find out about possible solutions. Then write about it.

parking
pollution
traffic
trash

Trash
People dump trash everywhere. There aren't enough trash cans for people to throw things away in. Trash cans need to be put on every corner in every city.

Keep talking!

News survey

A Pair work Interview your partner. Check (✓) his or her answers.

ARE YOU A NEWS LOVER?

Do you always like to be up-to-date on the latest news? Are you a news lover? Complete this survey and find out.

1. Do you share interesting news stories with friends or family?
   ☐ yes   ☑ no

2. Did you read or listen to a news story yesterday?
   ☑ yes   ☐ no

3. Have you read or listened to a news story today?
   ☑ yes   ☐ no

4. What area of news are you interested in? You can check (✓) as many as you want.
   ☑ world news   ☑ national news   ☐ local news

5. What types of news are you interested in? You can check (✓) as many as you want.
   ☐ business   ☑ entertainment   ☐ travel
   ☐ technology   ☐ sports   ☑ lifestyle
   ☑ health   ☑ weather   ☐ other: _____

6. Where do you get your news? You can check (✓) as many as you want.
   ☐ newspapers   ☑ radio   ☑ the Internet
   ☐ magazines   ☑ TV   ☐ other: _____

7. How much time do you spend learning about the news every day?
   ☐ 0–5 minutes   ☐ 6–15 minutes   ☑ 16 minutes or more

B Pair work Score your partner's answers. Add up his or her points to find the results.

Questions 1–3	Questions 4–6	Question 7
no = 0 points	each ✓ = 2 points	0–5 minutes = 0 points
yes = 2 points		6–15 minutes = 4 points
		16+ minutes = 8 points

More than 20 points ★
You're definitely a news lover. You always want to know what's happening in the news.

11–19 points
You're a well-informed person. You balance your interest in the news with other interests.

0–10 points
You don't follow the news every day. You may not know what's going on in the world.

C Group work Share the results. Do the results in Part B describe you well? What do you think the results say about your personality and interests?

What's the question?

A Read the sentences. Write a *Wh-* or *yes/no* question.

1. _When He likes to be outdoor?_
   He likes to be outdoors when the weather is nice.

2. _When are you planning?_
   I'm planning my next outdoor adventure.

3. _When you made a small fire?_
   We made a small fire when it got dark.

4. _Where they was walking when they heard a loud car crash_
   They were walking down the street when they heard a loud car crash.

5. _Who seen seen snakes?_
   He's seen snakes on a hiking trail.

6. _When do you go camping?_
   I'll go camping next weekend.

B Pair work Compare your questions. How many of your questions are the same? What other questions can you make?

C Pair work Write three sentences using words from the box and your own ideas. Then read the sentences to your partner. How many *Wh-* or *yes/no* questions can your partner make?

attack	camping	crash	miss	rescue
bear	car	experiences	mountain	survive
boat	chase	fire	news	

1. Sentence: _____
2. Sentence: _____
3. Sentence: _____

Finding out more

A Add two more topics to the chart.

Find someone who's been . . . lately.	Name	Extra information
listening to songs in English		
saving money to buy something		
skipping breakfast		
planning a vacation		
spending a lot of time at the mall		
studying for an important exam		
getting up early		
chatting online in English		
playing sports on the weekend		
watching online videos		

B **Class activity** Find classmates who have been doing the things in Part A. Write their names and ask questions for more information. Write the extra information.

> **A:** *José, have you been listening to songs in English lately?*
> **B:** *Yes, I have.*
> **A:** *Really? What kinds of music have you been listening to?*

C **Class activity** Share the most interesting information.

Communication with body language

A Match each common North American gesture with its meaning.

Be quiet.	Come here.	Hello.	Stop.	What time is it?
Call me.	Go ahead.	Speak louder.	Wait a moment.	

1. Call me <u>louder</u>
2. Wait a moment
3. Come here
4. Wha time Is it?
5. Go ahead
6. Hello
7. Stop
8. Speak louder
9. Be quiet

B Group work Act out a gesture from Part A. Your classmates guess what you're doing. Use these words when guessing.

ask	have	help	invite	let	make	remind	tell

A: *You're asking someone to stop.*
B: *Actually, I think you're making someone stop.*

C Group work What other gestures do you know? Act them out. Your classmates guess what you're doing.

Festival food

A Pair work Look at these popular festival foods. Which do you want to try? Which would you not want to try? Why? Tell your partner.

Shaved ice
Ice is first shaved, and then a choice of different fruit syrups is added.

Elephant ear
Dough is pressed flat, fried in a pan, and then covered with sugar and cinnamon.

Turkey leg
A turkey leg is covered with sugar, salt, and spices and then roasted slowly.

Meatballs on a stick
Meatballs are baked, put on a stick, and then covered with tomato sauce.

Corn on the cob
An ear of corn is roasted and buttered. Salt, pepper, or hot sauce is then added.

Fried candy bar
A whole chocolate candy bar is covered in batter and then fried. Whipped cream is sometimes added on top.

B Pair work Close your books. Take turns. Describe one of the festival foods. Your partner guesses the food.

C Group work Discuss these questions.

- Which foods in Part A are healthy? Which aren't? In what way?
- Which foods and drinks are popular at festivals in your country?
- How are they made? Who usually eats them?
- Are these foods different from street foods? If so, how?
- How does food vary in your country from region to region?
- Think about your hometown. Is it known for a particular food?

Fun food facts

A **Pair work** Interview your partner. Circle his or her answers. Do you agree?

Secrets of the chefs

How many food tricks do you know? Try this quiz to find out.

1. Sometimes salt gets sticky in a salt shaker. What can you put in the salt shaker to fix the problem?
   a. a coin   b. rice   c. tea leaves

2. What can you put on fruit as soon as you cut it so that it doesn't become brown?
   a. milk   b. sugar   c. lemon juice

3. After you have used your microwave, what can you boil in it to clean it?
   a. water and vinegar   b. milk and butter   c. coffee and sugar

4. Where can you put a green banana to make it become yellow?
   a. in the fridge   b. in the sun   c. in a paper bag

5. When you put an egg into salty water, it floats. What does this mean?
   a. It's fresh.   b. It's not fresh.   c. It's from a duck.

6. After you boil an egg, where can you put it so that you can peel it easily?
   a. in cold water   b. in salty water   c. in the microwave

7. What can you put in a cookie jar to make cookies stay soft and chewy?
   a. noodles   b. sticky candy   c. a piece of bread

8. Cutting onions makes people cry. What can you do to prevent this?
   a. Chew gum.   b. Add salt to them.   c. Hold your breath.

B **Pair work** Check your guesses. How many food tricks did you know?

5. b   6. a   7. c   8. a
1. b   2. c   3. a   4. c

Dilemmas

A Read the questions. Circle your answers, or add your own ideas.

1 What would you do if you found a lost pet in the street?

a. Tell someone.

b. Follow it.

c. Feed it.

d. Take it home.

e. other: have a add with picture

4 What would you do if you didn't have enough money to pay for dinner?

a. Call someone.

b. Go to an ATM.

c. Let my friend pay.

d. Leave without paying.

e. other: _____

2 What would you do if you accidentally hit a parked car?

a. Call the police.

b. Wait for the owner.

c. Leave a note.

d. Drive away.

e. other: _____

5 What would you do if you saw someone take something from a store?

a. Talk to the person.

b. Tell the manager.

c. Call the police.

d. Look the other way.

e. other: _____

3 What would you do if you found a cell phone on the subway?

a. Wait for someone to call.

b. Call the last number dialed.

c. Give it to a ticket agent.

d. Keep it.

e. other: _____

6 What would you do if you accidentally broke a cup at your friend's house?

a. Try to fix it.

b. Offer to pay for it.

c. Apologize.

d. Hide it.

e. other: _____

B **Group work** Discuss your answers. Do you agree?

A: *What would you do if you found a lost pet in the street?*
B: *I'd probably tell someone. What would you do?*
C: *I'd look for a name tag. If it didn't have one, I'd call the police.*

Right and wrong

A **Pair work** Read the situations. Answer the questions. Discuss your answers.

- Did the people do the right thing?
- If not, what should or shouldn't they have done?
- What could they have done differently?
- Would you have done anything differently? Why?

Jill and her husband Frank were flying to Thailand on vacation. The flight attendant offered one empty seat in business class to them. Because he's tall, Frank took the seat. Jill also wanted it, but Frank didn't ask her opinion. Now she's angry.

Steven invited Chuck and his wife Maria to his wedding. They accepted the invitation. Later Steven changed the wedding date, but Maria had a business trip then. So Chuck called Steven, offered an apology, and said they had to turn down his invitation. Steven was disappointed.

Tim borrowed his brother Mike's jacket without asking. Tim's girlfriend Allison accidentally spilled grape juice on the jacket. Mike saw the jacket the next day and asked for an explanation. Tim told the truth. Mike made Tim buy him a new jacket.

Lisa came home late and couldn't find her key. Her roommate Sue was sleeping. So Lisa broke a window to get inside. A neighbor heard the noise and called the police. Lisa offered a good explanation, and the police let her go. But Sue was very angry.

A: *I don't think that Frank did the right thing.*
B: *I agree. He shouldn't have moved up to business class. He could have . . .*

B **Group work** Did any of your partner's answers surprise you? Do you and your partner agree on the people's behavior? Share your opinions.

Travel adventures game

Group work Work in a group of three. Play the game.

Rules of the game

Student A: Choose a pair of pictures and compare them.
Student B: Make another comparison about the same pictures.
Student C: Make a different comparison about the same pictures.

A: *New York is more exciting than Miami.*
B: *Maybe, but Miami is more relaxing.*
C: *Miami is sunnier, too.*

Continue making comparisons. If someone can't make a comparison, he or she is "out." The last person to make a comparison about the pair of pictures "wins."

The winner chooses a new pair of pictures, and the game begins with another comparison.

Cities

New York

Miami

Countries

Canada

Singapore

Transportation

train

plane

Places to stay

campground

youth hostel

Natural wonders

the Amazon
rain forest

the Sahara
desert

Landmarks

the Eiffel Tower

the Parthenon

What to do?

A Imagine a friend has these travel problems. Write your advice.

1. Your friend reserved a city tour online, but the tour guide can't find his reservation.

   My advice: *Buy a new ticket.*

   My partner's advice: Wait for resolution
   irafueru del contry

2. Your friend's checking in for his overseas flight, but he finds out his passport is expired.

   My advice: Cancel You flight Ticket

   My partner's advice: remove you flight for later.

3. Your friend's been traveling all day, and he now finds out his hotel is overbooked. — No rooms
   She told me

   My advice: get you money

   My partner's advice: Look for other and ask you money back.

4. Your friend's train is going to be delayed an hour. He doesn't know why, and he's already late for an appointment.

   My advice: Call your friend

   My partner's advice: Call and cancel the appoiment.

5. Your friend's been waiting at the baggage claim for his luggage, but his luggage is missing.

   My advice: Report to the manager

   My partner's advice: Calm dow.

6. Your friend expected nice weather for his beach vacation, but it's been raining for two days.

   My advice: do other activity

   My partner's advice: study English.

B **Pair work** Interview your partner. Write your partner's advice.

C **Group work** Report your advice and your partner's advice. What are the advantages and disadvantages of each person's advice?

   A: *I told my friend to buy a new ticket. Mario told him not to get upset.*
   B: *I reminded him to show his reservation number. Christina advised him to talk to the owner.*

The wishing game

Group work Play the game. Put a small object on *Start*. Toss a coin.

 Move 1 space.   Move 2 spaces.

Heads   **Tails**

Read aloud the question and answer it. Then answer a follow-up question from each person in your group. If you land on *Ask your own question*, make up a question to ask someone else in your group.

A: *"What do you wish you could spend less time doing?"* I wish I could spend less time doing chores.
B: *What is your least favorite chore?*

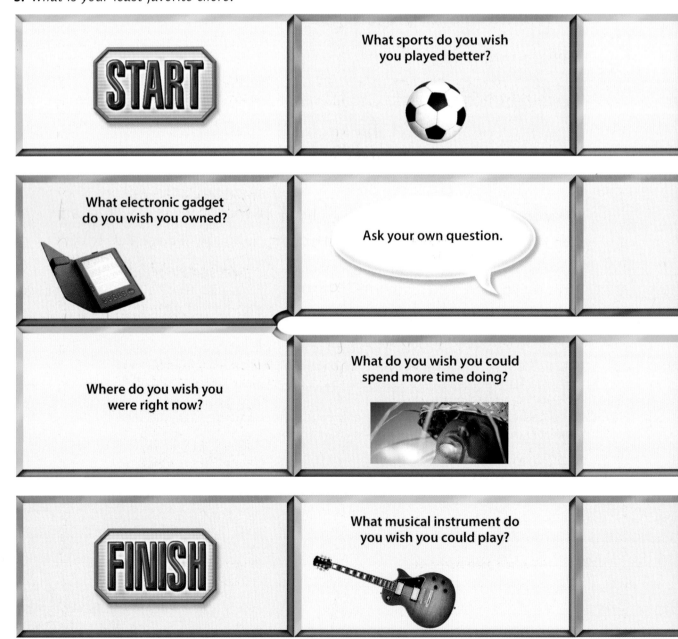

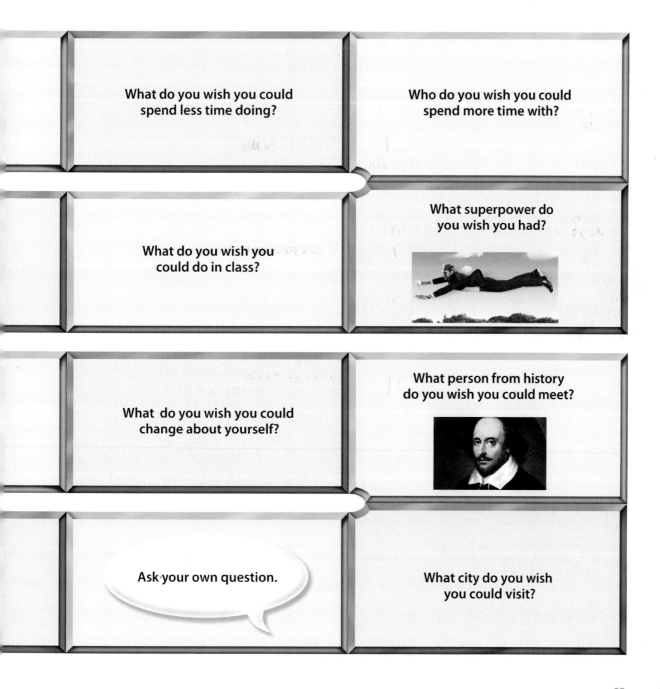

What do you wish you could
spend less time doing?

Who do you wish you could
spend more time with?

What do you wish you
could do in class?

What superpower do
you wish you had?

What do you wish you could
change about yourself?

What person from history
do you wish you could meet?

Ask your own question.

What city do you wish
you could visit?

Birth order and personality

A Class activity Find and write the names of two classmates who are:

The first born (the oldest) in their family:

_____ _____

The middle child:

_____ _____

The last born (the youngest):

_____ _____

An only child (no brothers or sisters):

_____ _____

B Read about your birth order. What does it show about your personality?

Birth order	Personality	Careers	Fun fact
First-born children	First-born children are often ambitious, confident, logical, studious, and very organized.	First-born children are often people who become lawyers, doctors, and scientists.	Of the first 23 astronauts, 21 were first-born children.
Middle-born children	Rebellious, competitive, independent, loyal, and imaginative are traits that often describe middle-born children.	Diplomats, artists, and designers are jobs that middle-born children are good at.	Middle-born children often make opposite decisions from first-borns.
Last-born children	Last-born children like to take risks. They are often hardworking, idealistic, outgoing, and very confident.	Firefighters, inventors, and actors are jobs that often attract last-born children.	Last-born children are often "the life of the party."
Only children	Only children are good problem-solvers. They're mature, responsible, energetic, and often very ambitious.	Similar to first-borns, only children are often lawyers, doctors, and scientists.	Elvis Presley, Indira Gandhi, and Frank Sinatra were all only children.

C Pair work Talk to a classmate from Part A with the same birth order as you. What kind of person are you? Do you agree with your personality description? Do you think the other descriptions are accurate for people you know?

> **A:** *I don't agree with the description. I'm the first born in my family, but I'm a person who likes to take risks.*
> **B:** *Really? I agree with the description. I'm the kind of person who is very organized.*

You've got to have this!

A Read the ads below. Choose one. Make a list of reasons to buy the product. Use these ideas and your own ideas.

It's so creative that . . .   It's such a convenient product that . . .
It's so unconventional that . . .   It's such an effective item that . . .
It's so useful that . . .   It's such an imaginative product that . . .

Flying alarm clock
Can't get up in the morning? When this alarm clock goes off, it flies around the room. You have to get out of bed to turn it off.

Keyboard waffle maker
Say good-bye to boring old waffles. This waffle maker makes the tasty breakfast treat in the shape of computer keyboards.

Bakery flash drives
Flash drives are such a great way to carry data. But why not make yours a little more interesting with these bakery items?

Gel ant house
Ants can be a little boring to watch – but not when they live in this world of green gel. When the ants move, the gel changes colors.

Mini motorcycle
Motorcycles have one wheel in front of the other, but this one has two side by side. Just turn it on, lean forward, and go!

Umbrella light
No more walking home in the dark. This umbrella has a light inside. Just turn it on and you have a light – and a safe walk home.

B Pair work Take turns. Describe your product from Part A. Try to convince your partner to buy the product.

"The umbrella light is such a convenient product that all of your friends will want one. You can keep it in your bag. It's so useful that you will never leave home without it."

C Pair work Would you buy your partner's product? Would you buy any of the products? Why or why not? Share your ideas.

Product improvements

A Pair work Choose a product. What is it used for? What features does it have? Brainstorm all the things the product does.

car	coffeemaker	hair dryer	refrigerator
cell phone	computer	headphones	TV

A: *A cell phone is used to call people.*
B: *They're used to check the time, text people, and . . .*

B Pair work Re-design your product. What words describe your product? What improvements have you made to your product? How is it used now?

C Group work Present your product to another pair.

A: *We have developed a creative and useful product.*
B: *It is a flying car. It is terrific in traffic, and it will be very successful someday.*

Lucky Larry

A Pair work Make a story. Number the pictures from 1 to 9.

Some people were moving a piano into the upstairs apartment, but they hadn't gotten it inside yet.

It took a long time to get home. Earlier, a police officer had stopped him for speeding.

He was very thankful that he hadn't been in the car at the time.

He went to the concert with Gail because she'd given him the tickets for his birthday.

He then realized he hadn't taken his umbrella from his apartment.

By the time he parked his car in front of his apartment, it had started to rain.

After he'd locked his car, he ran to the front door in the rain.

1

Larry drove home one evening. He'd been at a piano concert with his friend Gail.

He heard a very loud noise, so he turned around. The piano had fallen on his car!

B Group work Join another pair. Take turns. Tell your stories. Are they the same?

C Group work Close your books. Tell the story in your own words from memory.

A different path?

A Read the topics in each box. Check (✓) three that were important moments in your life. Write an example of each and why these moments were important.

"If I hadn't gone to summer camp, I wouldn't have met my best friend."

"I bought a new computer last summer, and now I can work from home."

Important moments in life	Examples and explanations
☐ a job you got ☐ a job you didn't get	
☐ someone you met who changed your life ☐ someone you wish you hadn't met	
☐ something you said to a friend ☐ something you didn't say to a friend	
☐ a place you visited ☐ a place you didn't visit	
☐ something you bought ☐ something you didn't buy	
☐ an exam you passed ☐ an exam you didn't pass	
☐ something you learned to do ☐ something you didn't learn to do	
☐ other: (your own idea)	

B **Group work** Take turns. Talk about the important moments in your chart. Ask each other questions for more details. Then find out: How would things have been different without these moments?

A: *One time, I missed my plane to Los Angeles.*

B: *Why were you going to Los Angeles?*

A: *I had an interview for a job.*

C: *Why did you miss your plane?*

A: *I made a mistake and turned off my alarm. If I hadn't turned off the alarm, I wouldn't have missed my plane. I would have had the interview. And I would have gotten the job, I'm sure.*

B: *Too bad.*

A logical explanation?

Students A and B

A Pair work You have a picture of a home office AFTER something happened. What do you think might have happened? Think of as many explanations as you can.

AFTER

B Group work Join classmates who have a BEFORE picture. Their picture shows the office five minutes before. Tell them what you think might have happened. Then find out what really happened.

> **A:** *We think that someone might have . . .*
> **B:** *Or someone could have . . .*
> **C:** *Actually, here's what really happened. . . .*

C Pair work Now you have a BEFORE picture of a restaurant. Describe the scene. What has happened? What's happening?

BEFORE

D Group work Join classmates who have an AFTER picture. Their picture shows the restaurant five minutes after your picture. Listen to their ideas about what might have happened. Then tell them what really happened.

A logical explanation?

Students C and D

A **Pair work** You have a BEFORE picture of a home office. Describe the scene. What has happened? What's happening?

BEFORE

B **Group work** Join classmates who have an AFTER picture. Their picture shows the office five minutes after your picture. Listen to their ideas about what might have happened. Then tell them what really happened.

> **A:** *We think that someone might have . . .*
> **B:** *Or someone could have . . .*
> **C:** *Actually, here's what really happened. . . .*

C **Pair work** Now you have a picture of a restaurant AFTER something has happened. What do you think might have happened? Think of as many explanations as you can.

AFTER

D **Group work** Join classmates who have a BEFORE picture. Their picture shows the restaurant five minutes before. Tell them what you think might have happened. Then find out what really happened.

Unsolved mysteries

A **Group work** Choose a different picture from others in your group. Read about the picture. How can you explain the unsolved mystery? Take turns. Describe the mystery and answer questions.

> **A:** *There is a manuscript that no one can read.*
> **B:** *Do you know where it's from?*
> **A:** *Yes, it's from Italy, but the manuscript isn't in Italian.*
> **C:** *Do you have any idea if . . . ?* How

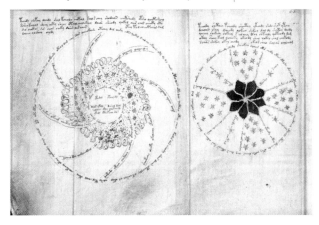

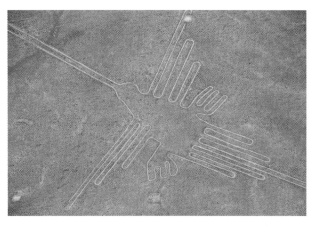

The Voynich manuscript is a book that was written in the 15th or 16th century. The author and alphabet are unknown. The book was discovered in Italy, but the language isn't like any European language. Even modern computers haven't "cracked" the code. Who wrote it, and why?

The Nazca lines are hundreds of "pictures" that were created in the Nazca Desert of Peru. They include birds, fish, spiders, monkeys, llamas, and lizards. How were they made? And why would anyone create such complicated pictures that you can only see from the air?

In the 1930s, workers in the Costa Rican jungle discovered mysterious stone balls that were perfectly round. Some were as small as a tennis ball, but others were larger – very large! They are human-made, but who made them, and how? What were they used for?

In 1947, something crashed near Roswell, New Mexico. At first the U.S. military said it was a "flying disc," but later changed its story and said it was a secret weather balloon. Others believe it was an alien spaceship. They think the government is hiding the truth. What crashed at Roswell?

B **Class activity** Describe other unexplained mysteries that you know about. Answer your classmates' questions.

Find the differences.

Student A

A Pair work You and your partner have a picture of the same accident. Tell your partner what the witnesses said in your picture. Your partner will report what other witnesses said. Find four differences in their reports.

> The driver didn't stop at the light.
> I saw the light turn red.
> The driver wasn't on his cell phone.
> It's the driver's fault.

> I heard a loud scream.
> There have been other accidents at this corner.
> The accident happened at 10:30.

> The bicyclist waved to someone on the sidewalk.
> She had a large pizza in one hand.
> It's the bicyclist's fault.

A: *Peter told the police officer that the driver hadn't stopped at the light.*
B: *Jan also said he hadn't stopped at the light. She said that she'd seen the light turn yellow.*
A: *But Peter told the police officer he'd seen the light turn red. So that's different.*

B Pair work Who do you think are the most reliable witnesses? the least reliable? Why? Whose fault was it – the driver's, the bicyclist's, or both? Why?

Who said what?

A Write a *yes* / *no* question for each topic.

Topics	Questions	Notes: Who said what?
Work or school		
Entertainment	*How*	
Relationships		
Sports		
Past experiences		
Future goals		
Other: (your own idea)		

B **Class activity** Ask different classmates your questions. Write their names. Take notes on the most interesting answers.

    A: *Claudia, have you ever gotten in trouble at school?*
    B: *I have. I arrived an hour late once, and my teacher was really angry.*

C **Group work** Report your most interesting questions and answers.

"I asked Claudia if she'd ever gotten in trouble at school. She told me that she had. . . ."

Find the differences.

Student B

A **Pair work** You and your partner have a picture of the same accident. Tell your partner what the witnesses said in your picture. Your partner will report what other witnesses said. Find four differences in their reports.

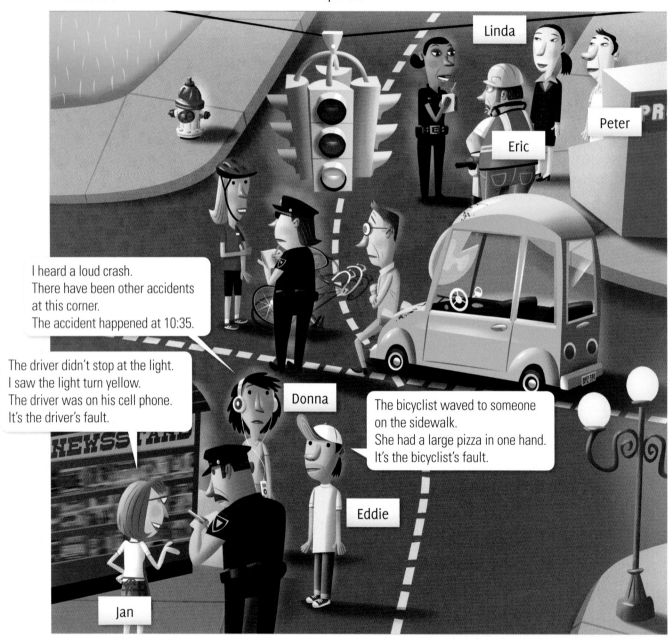

> I heard a loud crash.
> There have been other accidents at this corner.
> The accident happened at 10:35.

> The driver didn't stop at the light.
> I saw the light turn yellow.
> The driver was on his cell phone.
> It's the driver's fault.

> The bicyclist waved to someone on the sidewalk.
> She had a large pizza in one hand.
> It's the bicyclist's fault.

A: *Peter told the police officer that the driver hadn't stopped at the light.*
B: *Jan also said he hadn't stopped at the light. She said that she'd seen the light turn yellow.*
A: *But Peter told the police officer he'd seen the light turn red. So that's different.*

B **Pair work** Who do you think are the most reliable witnesses? the least reliable? Why? Whose fault was it – the driver's, the bicyclist's, or both? Why?

Convenient services

A **Pair work** Look at the picture of the shopping mall. Where can you have or get these things done?

get a doctor's prescription filled	have a résumé photocopied
get a passport photo taken	have a skirt made
get photos printed	have a suit cleaned
get your hair cut	have a watch repaired
get your nails done	have your eyes checked
have a computer virus removed	have your glasses fixed

A: *You can get a passport photo taken at Picture It.*
B: *And maybe at Office Works.*

B **Pair work** What else can you get or have done at the places in the picture? Tell your partner.

C **Class activity** Where do you get or have things done near you? Use the ideas in Part A and ideas of your own.

"I get my hair cut at Hair and Now. It's on Main Street, near my house."

Will that really happen?

A Add three more question topics to the chart about life in the future.

Find someone who believes . . . in the future.	Name
students will be finishing college in just three years	
most people will be eating only organic food	*Organic food is expensive.*
women will be leading most countries in the world	
ocean levels will rise to dangerous levels	
the world's population will reach 10 billion	*7 billion*
there will be computers in every classroom	
people will be working a 20-hour workweek	
most people will be working until age 70	
most people will be speaking English as a native language	

B **Class activity** Ask questions and find classmates who believe the possibilities in Part A will be happening in the future. Write their names. Ask questions for more information.

A: *In your opinion, will students be finishing college in just three years in the future?*
B: *Yes, they will.*
A: *Why do you think that will happen?*
B: *College will be even more expensive, so students will try to finish college faster.*

C **Group work** Share your opinions about the possibilities in the chart. Do you agree with your classmates?

The environmental game

Pair work Play the game. Put a small object on *Start*. Toss a coin.

 Move 1 space.

Heads

 Move 2 spaces.

Tails

Answer the question: "What is being done in the picture?" Use the pictures and the words.
If your answer describes something that helps the environment, move forward one square.
If your answer describes something that hurts the environment, say what needs to be
done and stay on the square.

A: *Heads. Conserve. Water is being conserved. That helps the environment.*
B: *Tails. Waste. Energy is being wasted. That doesn't help the environment.*
   The lights need to be turned off.

Beautification project

A Group work Plan a community improvement project. Decide together on a project, and complete the information.

What you'll make more beautiful:

☐ a park ☐ a road ☐ a playground ☐ a wall
☐ a river ☐ a sidewalk ☐ a building ☐ other: _____

What you'll do:

☐ paint ☐ clean up ☐ rebuild ☐ plant ☐ other: _____

What you'll need:

☐ trash bags ☐ shovels ☐ brooms ☐ paint
☐ flowers / plants ☐ trees ☐ gloves ☐ other: _____

How long it will take: **Who will benefit:**

_____   _____

Who will do which jobs: **What else you'll need to decide:**

_____   _____

A: *I think the front of the school needs to be more beautiful.*
B: *I agree. It looks old, so maybe we could paint it and plant flowers.*
C: *And if everyone helps, it will be a real school community project.*
D: *That's a good idea, although we would need to get permission first.*

B Class activity Share your ideas. Decide on one project. How could you work together to complete the project?

Irregular verbs

Base form	Simple past	Past participle
be	was, were	been
become	became	become
begin	began	begun
bite	bit	bitten
break	broke	broken
bring	brought	brought
build	built	built
buy	bought	bought
catch	caught	caught
choose	chose	chosen
come	came	come
cost	cost	cost
cut	cut	cut
do	did	done
draw	drew	drawn
drink	drank	drunk
drive	drove	driven
eat	ate	eaten
fall	fell	fallen
feel	felt	felt
find	found	found
forget	forgot	forgotten
get	got	gotten
give	gave	given
go	went	gone
grow	grew	grown
hang	hung	hung
have	had	had
hear	heard	heard
hold	held	held
hurt	hurt	hurt
keep	kept	kept

Base form	Simple past	Past participle
know	knew	known
leave	left	left
lend	lent	lent
lose	lost	lost
make	made	made
meet	met	met
pay	paid	paid
put	put	put
read	read	read
ride	rode	ridden
run	ran	run
say	said	said
see	saw	seen
sell	sold	sold
send	sent	sent
show	showed	shown
sing	sang	sung
sit	sat	sat
sleep	slept	slept
speak	spoke	spoken
spend	spent	spent
stand	stood	stood
stick	stuck	stuck
swim	swam	swum
take	took	taken
teach	taught	taught
tell	told	told
think	thought	thought
wake	woke	woken
wear	wore	worn
win	won	won
write	wrote	written

Credits

Illustration credits

CartoonStock: 113; Tom Garrett: 13, 73, 141, 142; Kveta Jelinek: 8 *(top)*, 30; Kim Johnson: 2, 18 *(bottom)*, 28, 37, 38, 48, 68, 108 *(bottom)*, 126, 127, 131, 140; Bill Ledger: 15, 35, 74, 85, 117, 133; Dean MacAdam: 8 *(bottom)*, 18 *(top)*, 33, 41, 58 *(bottom)*, 78, 98, 118, 138, 144, 146; Garry Parsons: 34, 66, 79, 108 *(top)*, 139; Maria Rabinky: 47, 94, 147; Cristina Sampaio: 58 *(top)*, 67, 87; Rob Schuster: 29, 46, 124, 136, 149; Belgin Wedman: 91

Photography credits

3 *(clockwise from top left)* ©BAE/Alamy; ©David J. Green/Alamy; ©Amana Images, Inc./Alamy; ©Shutterstock; ©Agencja Free/Alamy; ©Image Source/Getty Images; 4 *(clockwise from top left)* ©Age Fotostock; ©Craig Lovell/Alamy; ©NASA; ©Age Fotostock; ©Media Bakery; ©Tetra Images/Alamy; 6 ©Frank Veronsky; 7 *(clockwise from top left)* ©White Packert/Getty Images; ©Insadco Photography/Alamy; ©NASA; ©Archangelo Entertainment/Kobal Collection; 9 ©Media Bakery; 11 *(clockwise from top left)* ©Dan Kitwood/Getty Images; ©Courtesy of Robert Bohlke; ©Ryouchin/Getty Images; ©AP Wide World Photo; 16 *(clockwise from top left)* ©Frank Veronsky; 21 ©Media Bakery; 23 *(clockwise from top left)* ©Miguel Sobreira/Alamy; ©Newell Nussbaumer; ©JG Photography/Alamy; ©Istock Photos; 24 *(top row, left to right)* ©Istock Photos; ©Media Bakery; ©Istock Photos; *(middle row, left to right)* ©Davide Piras/Alamy; ©Media Bakery; ©Media Bakery; ©Michael Neelon/Alamy; *(bottom row, left to right)* ©Danita Delimont/Getty Images; ©Mitch Diamond/Alamy; ©Istock Photos; 25 *(top to bottom)* ©Media Bakery; ©Istock Photos; ©J Marshall/Tribaleye Images/Alamy; 26 *(top)* ©Frank Veronsky; *(bottom, left to right)* ©Jupiter/Getty Images; ©Food Collection/Getty Images; 28 *(peach, cereal, gumdrops)* ©Dreamstime; *(all others)* ©Istock Photos; 29 ©Media Bakery; 31 *(both)* ©Shutterstock; 36 ©Frank Veronsky; 43 *(clockwise from top left)* ©PhotoStock-Israel/Alamy; ©Frans Lemmens/Getty Images; ©Iconotec/Alamy; ©Ashley Simmons/Alamy; ©Paul Lovichi/Alamy; ©Alexs Photos/Getty Images; 45 ©Marion Kaplan/Alamy; 46 *(both)* ©Media Bakery; 51 ©Matt Cardy/Getty Images; 53 ©Brian Leatart/Getty Images; 54 ©Alan Kearney/Getty Images; 56 ©Media Bakery; 59 ©Shutterstock; 60 *(left to right)* ©Frank Siteman – Rainbow/Getty Images; ©Corbis/Alamy; ©Media Bakery; ©Spencer Grant/Alamy; 61 ©Martin Sundberg/Getty Images; 63 *(clockwise from top left)* ©Getty Images; ©Richard Levine/Alamy; ©David R. Frazier/Alamy; ©Lukas Miglinas/Alamy; 64 *(top to bottom)* ©The Image Works; ©National Geographic; ©Istock Photos; 65 ©Digifoto Silver/Alamy; 66 ©Frank Veronsky; 68 *(top to bottom)* ©Denkou Images/Alamy; ©Alamy; 69 *(top)* ©Dreamstime; *(bottom, left to right)* ©Dreamstime; ©The Image Works; ©Alamy; ©The Image Works; ©Pierrette Guertin/Alamy; 70 ©Newscom; 71 ©AP Wide World Photo; 76 ©Alamy; 77 *(clockwise from top left)* ©Image Source/Alamy; ©MBI/Alamy; ©Media Bakery; ©Media Bakery; 80 ©Reprinted Courtesy of the Thaxter P. Spencer Collection; R. Stanton Avery Special Collections/New England Historical Genealogical Society; 83 *(clockwise from top left)* ©Image 100/Alamy; ©Istock Photos; ©Ilene MacDonald/Alamy; ©David Noton/Alamy; 86 ©Frank Veronsky; 88 ©De Agostini/Getty Images; 89 ©Pictorial Press Ltd./Alamy; 90 *(clockwise from top left)* ©Image Broker/Alamy; ©Ern Mainka/Alamy; ©Creative Studios/Alamy; ©Istock Photos; ©Nearby/Alamy; ©Media Bakery; 93 *(clockwise from top left)* ©Tito Atchaa/Getty Images; ©Media Bakery; ©Kip Evans/Alamy; ©Bill Dabney/Getty Images; ©Robert Daly/Getty Images; ©Media Bakery; 96 ©Jupiter Images; 97 ©AP Wide World Photo; 99 ©Ferdaus Shamim/Getty Images; 100 ©Courtesy of Allison Bohlke; 103 *(top row, left to right)* ©AP Wide World Photo; ©AP Wide World Photo; ©Media Bakery; *(middle row, left to right)* ©The Image Works; ©Vehbi Koca/Alamy; ©Photo Library; *(bottom row, left to right)* ©Photo Library; ©Photos India/Alamy; ©Joel Saget/Getty Images; 104 ©Insadco Photography/Alamy; 106 ©Stephen Derr/Getty Images; 110 *(top to bottom)* ©Nigel Sawtell/Alamy; ©Justin Sullivan/Getty Images; ©AP Wide World Photo; ©Tim Flach/Getty Images; ©Paramount/Everett Collection; 114 *(top to bottom)* ©Age Fotostock; ©Spencer Platt/Getty Images; ©Istock Photos; ©Age Fotostock; 115 ©Istock Photos; 116 ©Frank Veronsky; 117 *(left to right)* ©Photo Library; ©Shutterstock; ©Age Fotostock; ©Photo Library; 118 ©Media Bakery; 119 ©Shutterstock; 120 ©Photo Library; 121 ©AP Wide World Photo; 124 *(top to bottom)* ©Inmagine; ©Inmagine; ©Shutterstock; ©Shutterstock; ©Istock Photos; 125 ©Media Bakery; 128 *(clockwise from top left)* ©Linda Ching/Getty Images; ©Kreg Holt/Getty Images; ©Shutterstock; ©David Wei/Alamy; ©Hasan Doganturk/Alamy; ©Shutterstock; 129 *(top to bottom)* ©Shutterstock; ©Photo Alto/Alamy; ©Art Directors & TRIP/Alamy; ©Shutterstock; ©Howard Shooter/Getty Images; ©Dave King/Getty Images; ©Shutterstock; ©Shutterstock; 130 *(clockwise from top left)* ©Inmagine; ©Shutterstock; ©Shutterstock; ©Shutterstock; 132 *(top row, left to right)* ©Shutterstock; ©Shutterstock; ©Stéphane Groleau/Alamy; ©Veer; *(middle row, left to right)* ©Bloomberg/Getty Images; ©Courtesy of Dassault Falcon; ©B2M Productions/Getty Images; ©Holger Leue/Lonely Planet; *(bottom row, left to right)* ©Veer; ©Age Fotostock; ©DAJ/Getty Images; ©Age Fotostock; 134 *(top to bottom)* ©Shutterstock; ©Hugh Threlfall/Alamy; ©Chris Williams/Getty Images; ©North Wind Picture Archives/Alamy; 135 *(top to bottom)* ©Upper Cut Images/Getty Images; ©North Wind Picture Archives/Alamy; 136 ©Image Source/Getty Images; 137 *(clockwise from top left)* ©Courtesy of Think Geek; ©Chris Dimino; ©Bupkes Bakery; ©Clever Care; ©Motorcycle Mojo Magazine; ©Ant Works; 143 *(clockwise from top left)* ©Courtesy of Yale University; ©Inmagine; ©Aurora; ©Age Fotostock; 145 ©Superstock; 148 *(left to right)* ©Barry Austin/Getty Images; ©Jupiter Images; ©Jupiter/Getty Images; 149 *(top row, left to right)* ©Chesh/Alamy; ©JG Photography/Alamy; ©Image Source/Alamy; *(middle row, left to right)* ©Age Fotostock; ©Shutterstock; ©Media Bakery; Veer; *(bottom row, left to right)* ©Bernhard Classen/Alamy; ©Photo Library; ©Manor Photography/Alamy; 150 ©Photo Edit

Four Corners

Jack C. Richards · David Bohlke

4

Video Activity Sheets

News

Before you watch

A Pair work Make a list of all of the different ways people can get the news and find out about current events.

> ### Ways People Get the News
> 1. newspapers _____
> 2. _____
> 3. _____
> 4. _____
> 5. _____
> 6. _____
> 7. _____

B Class activity Combine your lists into one class list. Raise your hand for each way you get the news. Which ways are the most popular?

While you watch

A How do they get their news? Complete the sentences with the correct words.

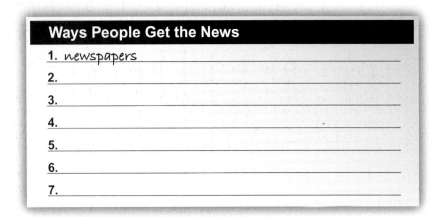

| Emi | Christine | Tony | Ben |

1. Emi gets her news from _____.

2. Christine gets her news from the _____.

3. Tony gets his news from the _____.

4. Ben gets his news from his _____.

B Check (✓) the correct answers.

	Emi	Christine	Tony	Ben
1. Who likes lifestyle and entertainment news?	☐	☐	☐	☐
2. Who doesn't read business news?	☐	☐	☐	☐
3. Who reads headlines during the interview?	☐	☐	☐	☐
4. Who likes to get traffic news every ten minutes?	☐	☐	☐	☐
5. Who likes to read the world and travel sections of the news?	☐	☐	☐	☐
6. Who doesn't read the paper or watch the news on TV anymore?	☐	☐	☐	☐

C Match the phrases.

1. Emi gets all of her news from _____.
2. Christine is relaxing with the paper because _____.
3. Christine can't check the news online at work because _____.
4. Tony doesn't want to talk to Emi because _____.
5. Ben thinks TV news is boring because _____.
6. Ben thinks people are chasing a local rock star because _____.

a. people on the news talk too much

b. his last song was terrible

c. he's in a hurry

d. it's her day off

e. Cool TV

f. the company only allows employees to use the Internet for business

After you watch

Group work Discuss the questions.

- Do you get your news the same ways as Emi, Christine, Tony, or Ben? If not, how do you get your news?
- Why do you get your news the way that you do? What do you like about it? What don't you like about it?
- What are your favorite and least favorite sections of the news? Why?

2 *Communication*

Before you watch

A Label the pictures with the correct forms of communication. Then compare with a partner.

| email   face-to-face   letter   phone   social networking   texting |

1. _____

2. _____

3. _____

4. _____

5. _____

6. _____

B Pair work Which methods of communication in Part A do *you* use? When do you use them? How often do you use each of them? Tell your partner.

C Group work Read the list of situations below. Which method of communication would you use in each situation, and why? Discuss your ideas.

- to communicate with many people
- when you don't want someone to see you
- to tell a friend that you'll be late for a movie
- to tell the doctor that you'll be late for an appointment

- to discuss a serious problem
- when you want to hear the other person's voice
- at 3:00 a.m.
- to set a time for a date
- to catch up on news with an old friend

While you watch

A Which methods of communication do people mention or use in the video? Check (✓) the correct answers.

- ☐ blogs
- ☐ mail
- ☐ face-to-face
- ☐ greeting cards
- ☐ letters
- ☐ phones
- ☐ social networking
- ☐ texting
- ☐ video

B Match the people and their preferred methods of communication.

1. texting _____   a. Alicia
2. face-to-face _____   b. April
3. email _____   c. Ben
4. social networking _____ d. Danielle
5. phone _____   e. Nick

C Circle the correct answers.

1. Danielle explains that she can use more words in a(n) _____ than in a(n) _____.

   a. text . . . email   b. conversation . . . email   c. email . . . text

2. Ben thinks it's easier to explain things on the phone or _____ than in an email.

   a. in person   b. in a text   c. in writing

3. April thinks the phone is _____.

   a. boring and old-fashioned

   b. easy, fast, and personal

   c. convenient but impersonal

4. Ben thinks the phone is more personal than _____ but not as personal as _____.

   a. face-to-face communication . . . texting

   b. email . . . social networking

   c. texting . . . face-to-face communication

5. Ben says Alicia "is really into" social networking. This means Alicia _____.

   a. works for a social networking business

   b. has a page on a social networking site

   c. likes social networking very much

After you watch

A Pair work Make a list of the advantages and disadvantages of these methods of communication: texting, face-to-face conversation, and social networking.

Method of Communication	Advantages	Disadvantages
texting		
face-to-face conversation		
social networking		

B Group work Share your list with another pair. Do you agree or disagree on the advantages and disadvantages of each method of communication?

Before you watch

A Match the words and the pictures. Then compare with a partner.

a. flour	c. muffin pan	e. whisk
b. mixer	d. oven	f. wooden spoon

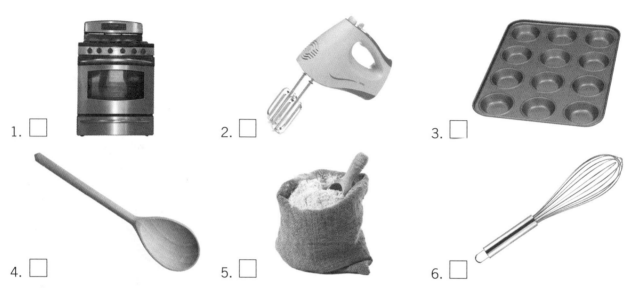

1. ☐   2. ☐   3. ☐

4. ☐   5. ☐   6. ☐

B Complete the sentences with the correct words. Then compare with a partner.

crispy	moist	sweet

1. When you add eggs to dry ingredients, they become _____.

2. When you add sugar to food, it becomes _____.

3. When you bake food in the oven, the outside may become _____, like the outside of fried foods.

While you watch

A Number the steps from 1 to 8.

_____ Mix the ingredients in the second bowl.

_____ Put the flour, baking powder, and salt in a large bowl.

_____ Put the milk, eggs, sugar, vanilla, and butter in another bowl.

_____ Bake for 15 minutes.

_____ Pour everything from the small bowl into the other bowl and whisk it a little bit.

_____ Whisk together the flour, baking powder, and salt.

_____ Taste some chocolate chips before pouring them in.

_____ Once the batter is mixed, pour it into the muffin pan.

B Circle the correct answers.

1. Irma teaches Danielle how to _____ the muffins.

    a. roast   b. microwave   c. bake

2. Danielle says her grandmother's muffins are _____, chewy, and moist.

    a. sweet   b. crispy   c. bland

3. Irma tells Danielle to mix the flour, baking powder, and salt with a

    _____.

    a. spoon   b. fork   c. whisk

4. Danielle makes mistakes with _____.

    a. the sugar and flour

    b. an egg and the vanilla

    c. the milk and the salt

5. Danielle says that her muffins are crispy on the outside and _____ on the inside.

    a. chewy   b. creamy   c. crunchy

6. Irma says Danielle's muffins are _____.

    a. delicious   b. chewy   c. crunchy

C What recipe information is *not* given in the video? Check (✓) the correct answers.

☐ how many eggs to use
☐ how much flour you need
☐ the amount of salt
☐ how many chocolate chips to add
☐ the tools to use to mix ingredients

☐ the temperature of the oven
☐ the amount of vanilla
☐ how much butter to add
☐ the cooking time in the oven
☐ the amount of milk

After you watch

Pair work Discuss the questions.

- In the end, why can Irma "really taste the vanilla"? Why are the muffins "crunchy"?
- Have you ever made or tasted muffins? What were they like? Did you like them?
- Are you considered to be a good cook? Why or why not? Who does most of the cooking in your home?
- Was there a time when someone taught you how to cook something – or you taught someone else how to cook something? What was it? Tell your partner about it.

4 *Acts of kindness*

Before you watch

A Pair work Interview your partner. Ask and answer questions for more information. Take notes.

Have you ever . . .	Yes	No	Extra information
given someone your seat?			
helped someone carry heavy bags?			
given a compliment to a stranger?			
helped a tourist who looked lost?			
helped a stranger fix a flat tire?			
helped a neighbor find a lost pet?			
given someone a gift for no reason?			
held a door open for another person?			
let someone go before you in a supermarket line?			
helped a stranger whose car had broken down?			

B Pair work Look at the random acts of kindness in Part A again. Has anyone ever done those things for you? Tell your partner.

While you watch

A Look at the pictures from the video. What random act of kindness does Ben do for each person? Check (✓) the correct answers.

1. ☐ Ben offers her a seat on the park bench.
   ☐ Ben gives her another bag to carry all of her things in.
   ☐ Ben carries the bags for her.

2. ☐ Ben helps him read the map.
   ☐ Ben takes the man to the place he's looking for.
   ☐ Ben buys him a new map.

3. ☐ Ben pushes her car to the gas station.
   ☐ Ben gives her directions.
   ☐ Ben gets gas for her car.

B Circle the correct answers.

1. Ben offers to help the woman because _____.

    a. she can't carry all of the bags   b. her bags look heavy   c. she's lost

2. The woman lives _____ blocks from where they are in the park.

    a. five   b. six   c. nine

3. When Ben first sees the tourist, Ben _____.

    a. says hello   b. asks if he needs directions   c. walks past him

4. The tourist asks Ben to _____.

    a. recommend a restaurant   b. help him with his bags   c. look at the map

5. The woman in the car needs _____

    a. directions   b. a new part for her car   c. gas

C Write T (true) or F (false).

1. In this video, Ben and Nick investigate uncommon situations in which people can be kind to each other. _____

2. At some point, Ben seems to regret, a little, his offer to help each person. _____

3. Nick thinks Ben did the right thing when he walked by the lost tourist. _____

4. To show their appreciation, each person Ben helps gives him a gift. _____

5. By the end of the video, Ben wishes he had never helped the three people. _____

After you watch

Group work Discuss the questions.

- In what situations might a person be uncomfortable when a stranger offers to help?
- Have you ever offered to help a stranger and then regretted your offer?
- Have you ever regretted *not* offering help to a stranger?
- Has a stranger ever been especially grateful when you offered to help?

Travel and tourism

Before you watch

A Pair work Look at the pictures of different places in New York City. What can you do in each place? Would you like to go to each place? Why or why not?

5th Avenue

Broadway

Little Italy

SoHo

B Pair work What do you know or think about New York City? Have you ever been there, or do you know someone who has? How does it compare to other places you know? Tell your partner.

While you watch

A Complete the sentences with the correct names.

Emi

Elena

Lauren

Diego

Paul

Kathy

1. _____ advises tourists to buy Broadway tickets just minutes before the show.

2. _____ describes New York City as fast-paced, culturally diverse, and fun-loving.

3. _____ and _____ ate at an Italian restaurant.

4. _____ tells tourists to go to SoHo.

5. _____ says everything in SoHo is overpriced.

6. _____ reminds everyone that you get what you pay for.

7. _____ and _____ bought the same bag at Canal Street.

8. _____'s co-workers warned him not to go to museums on Sundays or Mondays.

B Circle the correct answers.

1. Lauren says to shop on Canal Street because _____.

    a. it's cheaper and more culturally diverse than SoHo

    b. it has trendy restaurants and glamorous people

    c. the products are high-quality there

2. Diego says to ask for directions because _____.

    a. New York can be confusing

    b. New Yorkers are friendlier than people think

    c. it's easy to get lost in New York City

3. Paul and Kathy's friends told them to go to a restaurant in Little Italy for _____.

    a. really good pizza

    b. the best spaghetti

    c. the best Italian food in New York City

4. Paul's co-workers said museums are really busy _____.

    a. on Sunday

    b. on Monday

    c. every day

C Write T (true) or F (false).

1. Elena and Lauren suggest that tourists go to SoHo. _____

2. Lauren's handbag isn't a real Giorgio Giorgio bag. _____

3. Diego says tourists should see a Broadway show. _____

4. It's not possible to get an inexpensive ticket to a Broadway show. _____

5. Kathy bought an expensive Giorgio Giorgio handbag. _____

After you watch

Pair work Discuss the questions.

- In the video, from whom do you think Kathy got "a great shopping tip"?
- In your opinion, was it a good tip? Why or why not?
- Which do you think are better – real, but very expensive, products or not real, but cheap, products? Why?

The laugh club

Before you watch

A Who or what makes you laugh? Make a list.

People who make me laugh	Things that make me laugh
1.	
2.	
3.	
4.	
5.	
6.	

B Pair work Share your lists. Ask and answer questions for more information.

A: Mike Myers always makes me laugh. I love his movies!

B: Really? I don't think he's very funny. I think he's silly. Which movie of his is your favorite?

A: Well, it's hard to pick only one, but I'd say . . .

C Class activity Ask your classmates if the people or things on your list make them laugh, too. How many people agree or disagree with you? Which people or things are the most popular?

While you watch

A Read the sentences about Emi. Write T (true) or F (false).

1. Emi's busy and often stressed out. _____

2. She's competitive. _____

3. She's good at managing stress. _____

4. She wishes she could relax. _____

5. She wishes she were busier. _____

B Check (✓) the correct answers. (More than one answer is possible.)

1. What do the people in the video say about laughing?

☐ It's a good form of exercise.

☐ It can help protect your heart from disease.

☐ It's a way to relieve stress.

☐ It can help you think more clearly.

☐ It can reduce pain.

☐ It's helpful even when the laughter isn't real.

2. What do they do in the laugh club?

☐ They just laugh.

☐ They look at funny pictures.

☐ They tell jokes.

☐ They watch funny movies.

C Circle the correct answers.

1. Emi is doing a video about _____.

   a. humor   b. clubs at the college   c. laugh therapy

2. The members of the laugh club _____.

   a. welcome her to the meeting

   b. ask her a lot of questions before letting her join the group

   c. don't want to be in the video

3. At first, Emi _____.

   a. is excited about meeting new people

   b. is uncertain about laughing at nothing

   c. thinks laugh clubs don't help anyone

4. In the end, Emi _____.

   a. promises to come to the next meeting

   b. feels tired from all that laughing

   c. feels great

After you watch

Group work Discuss the questions.

• Do you think Emi will go back to the laugh club? Why or why not?

• Would you ever go to a laugh club? Why or why not?

• What are some things you do when you're stressed out?

The amazing, transportable office necktie!

Before you watch

A Match the words and the pictures. Then compare with a partner.

a. breath spray	c. necktie	e. pockets
b. business cards	d. paper clips	f. sticky notes

 1. ☐

 2. ☐

 3. ☐

 4. ☐

 5. ☐

 6. ☐

B Complete the sentences with the correct words. Then compare with a partner.

improvement	ineffective	innovation	inventor	secret	transportable

1. If something is _____, it means that it doesn't work well, or it doesn't do what it was intended to do.

2. A(n) _____ is a person who makes new things based on creative ideas.

3. If something is _____, it means that it can move from place to place.

4. A(n) _____ is a new product or idea that has been put into use.

5. If something is a(n) _____ over something else, it means that it is better than what came before it.

6. A(n) _____ is a piece of information that is unknown to most people.

While you watch

A For which items did Peter add pockets to his necktie? Check (✓) the correct answers.

☐ breath spray   ☐ a credit card
☐ business cards   ☐ paper clips
☐ car key   ☐ a pen
☐ a comb   ☐ sticky notes

B Circle the correct answers.

1. Peter Jones is a _____.

   a. car salesman   b. necktie salesman   c. full-time inventor

2. Peter used _____ to make the necktie.

   a. a stapler   b. a needle and thread   c. his wife's sewing machine

3. Peter says, "This is just a prototype." A prototype is a thing that is _____.

   a. not well made   b. convenient   c. an example; the first one

4. Wendy saw a similar necktie _____

   a. in a store   b. online   c. on a colleague

5. The "amazing transportable pen holder" is _____.

   a. a pocket on the tie   b. his shirt pocket   c. his ear

C Check (✓) the correct answers.

	Peter	Danielle	Wendy
1. Who thinks the amazing transportable office necktie is such an improvement over the conventional necktie?	☐	☐	☐
2. Who says it's inconvenient that the necktie doesn't have a pocket for a pen?	☐	☐	☐
3. Who thinks a shirt pocket is a good place for business cards?	☐	☐	☐
4. Who thinks the necktie will be a big success?	☐	☐	☐
5. Who says such a necktie has already been invented?	☐	☐	☐
6. Who says the idea is unoriginal?	☐	☐	☐

After you watch

A Consider the things that *you* carry with you – or would like to. Answer the questions.

1. What things do you carry with you most days?

_____

2. Where do you put these things?

_____

3. What things would you *like* to carry with you if it weren't inconvenient?

_____

B Group work Compare your answers. Are any of your items the same?

8 I'll always remember

Before you watch

A Match the words and the pictures. Then compare with a partner.

a. airfield	**c.** gallery	**e.** parachute
b. canal	**d.** manual transmission	**f.** reflection

1. ☐ 2. ☐ 3. ☐ 4. ☐ 5. ☐ 6. ☐

B Complete the sentences with the words from Part A.

1. If you look in a mirror, you'll see your _____.

2. The scariest part about jumping out of a plane is not knowing whether or not the _____ will open!

3. The private jet took off from a small _____ outside of the city.

4. It's difficult for artists to get their work shown in a _____.

5. The boat traveled through the _____.

6. My first car had a _____, not an automatic one.

While you watch

A Check (✓) the correct answers. (More than one answer is possible.)

	Jasmine	Charlie	Reina
1. Who will always remember learning a new skill?			
2. Who will always remember a special vacation?			
3. Who will always remember trying an extreme sport for the first time?			
4. Who was nervous?			
5. Who talks about a friend?			
6. Who talks about a birthday present?			
7. Who became an artist?			

B Circle the correct answers.

1. Jasmine's favorite city in Italy is _____.

   a. Rome   b. Florence   c. Venice

2. Jasmine was inspired by that city's _____.

   a. ancient buildings   b. art galleries   c. light and reflections

3. Charlie was _____ when he went skydiving.

   a. 20   b. 21   c. 22

4. Charlie never would have gone skydiving if it hadn't been for _____.

   a. the instructor   b. his friend Steve   c. the other guys in the training session

5. Reina had never driven a car before her friend William _____.

   a. gave her a lesson   b. bought her a car   c. gave her his old car

6. Reina was afraid she was going to _____.

   a. get lost   b. damage the car   c. make a mistake

C Write T (true) or F (false).

1. According to Jasmine, photos can really show the light in Venice. _____

2. If Jasmine hadn't gone to Venice, she wouldn't have become an artist. _____

3. Charlie didn't enjoy Steve's gift. _____

4. Charlie probably won't go skydiving anymore. _____

5. According to Reina, a car with an automatic transmission is easier to drive than a car with manual transmission. _____

6. It took Reina three days to learn to drive. _____

After you watch

A Think about a memorable experience from your life. Use one of the ideas below or your own idea. Take notes to prepare to talk about it.

- a time when you received wonderful (or terrible) news
- something that changed your life
- an "aha!" moment (when you suddenly understood something)

B Pair work Tell your partner about your memorable experience from Part A. Ask and answer questions for more information.

The six blind men and the elephant

Before you watch

A Label the picture with the correct words. Then compare with a partner.

ear	leg	side	tail	trunk	tusks

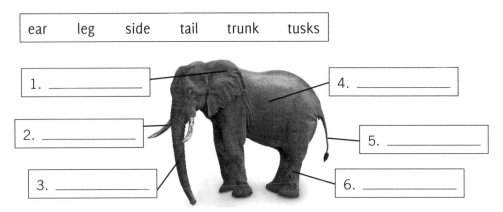

1. _____

2. _____

3. _____

4. _____

5. _____

6. _____

B **Pair work** What does each of these six parts of the elephant remind you of? What do you think they'd feel like? Share your opinions and ideas.

> **A:** In my opinion, the elephant's ear looks a little bit like an umbrella. It'd probably feel soft and smooth like the top of an umbrella if I touched it, too.

> **B:** Really? An umbrella? I don't think the elephant's ear looks like an umbrella at all! If you ask me, it looks kind of like a . . .

While you watch

A Circle the correct answers.

1. The wise man tells the six blind men to use their sense of _____ to describe the elephant.

    a. smell

    b. hearing

    c. touch

2. Each of the six men was _____ about the elephant.

    a. wrong

    b. partly right

    c. unable to describe anything

3. The main idea of the story is that _____.

    a. it's important to communicate with other people

    b. each of us sees only a small part of what is true

    c. people don't have patience to hear others' opinions

B What do the six blind men say each part of the elephant is like? Complete the sentences with the correct objects.

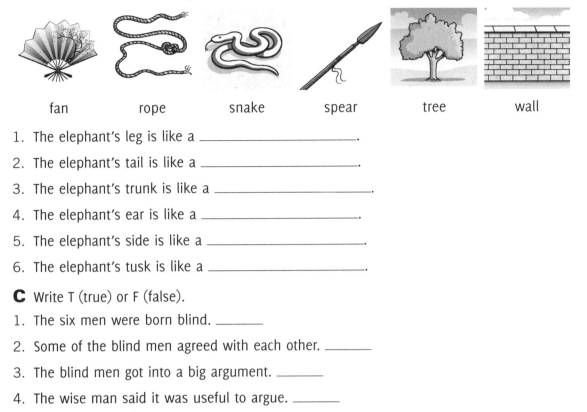

fan   rope   snake   spear   tree   wall

1. The elephant's leg is like a _____.

2. The elephant's tail is like a _____.

3. The elephant's trunk is like a _____.

4. The elephant's ear is like a _____.

5. The elephant's side is like a _____.

6. The elephant's tusk is like a _____.

C Write T (true) or F (false).

1. The six men were born blind. _____

2. Some of the blind men agreed with each other. _____

3. The blind men got into a big argument. _____

4. The wise man said it was useful to argue. _____

5. At the end of the video, the blind men touch the whole elephant. _____

After you watch

A Pair work In the story, the fifth blind man says, "Actually, an elephant is like a wall!" The word *actually* means "in fact" or "in reality." We most often use it in one of these ways: 1) to correct a mistake; 2) to express surprise; or 3) to express a change of mind. Discuss what you think it means in each sentence below.

1. An elephant isn't like a fan at all. Actually, an elephant is like a wall!

2. I ordered a green salad, but I think I actually want a fruit salad, instead.

3. She actually survived the shipwreck and returned to her country.

4. It wasn't an abduction. He actually just quietly left the city without telling anyone.

5. The Amazing Gregory can't actually read minds in his stage act. He's just very good at reading body language and facial expressions.

6. I know you'll think I'm crazy, but I actually liked that movie!

B Think of a time when you had an opinion but later changed it when you learned more. What was your original opinion? What changed your mind? Take notes.

_____

_____

C Group work Tell your group about your experience in Part B. Try to use the word *actually* as you discuss your change of opinion. Ask and answer questions for more information.

A grandmother's perspective

Before you watch

A Complete the sentences with the correct forms of the phrases below.

come up with	get away with	look forward to
get along with	keep up with	put up with

1. Jasmine forgot her homework in class, so she _____ an excuse. The teacher didn't believe her.

2. Cindy didn't study for the test, but she still did well. I couldn't _____ that!

3. Everyone is _____ summer vacation.

4. Diego walks so fast! It's hard for me to _____ him!

5. As a teenager I complained a lot about having to _____ my little brother, but, truthfully, he was a good kid.

6. Surprisingly, my brother and I _____ each other really well when we were kids. We didn't fight like a lot of my friends and their siblings.

B Pair work Ask questions with each of the phrases from Part A. Answer with your own information or ideas. Be creative!

    A: *Can you come up with a title for an action-adventure movie right now?*

    B: *Sure! How about . . . The Last Boy Standing?*

    A: *Sounds interesting!*

While you watch

A Circle the correct answers.

1. Irma's idea of perfect happiness is _____.

    a. skydiving

    b. playing video games

    c. walking on the beach

2. Irma's greatest fear is _____.

    a. recording a hip-hop album

    b. nothing

    c. not having a chance to do everything she wants

3. Irma's greatest regret is _____.

    a. not getting past Level 17 on the video game

    b. never seeing Bob Marley in concert

    c. marrying a short man

4. Irma's greatest achievement is _____.

    a. finally being able to reach Level 17 on the video game

    b. winning awards in journalism

    c. having a good relationship with Danielle

B Write T (true) or F (false).

1. Irma jumped out of a plane as a journalist during the war. _____

2. Irma wants to record a hip-hop album. _____

3. The quality Irma admires most in a man is height. _____

4. Irma's husband couldn't keep up with her in a game of basketball. _____

5. Danielle thinks Irma is like many other grandmothers. _____

C Answer the questions.

1. What time was the interview supposed to begin?

    _____

2. How long has Irma been playing the video game?

    _____

3. For which class is Danielle making this video?

    _____

4. For how many years did Danielle's grandparents get along?

    _____

5. What level of the video game does Irma reach by the end of the interview?

    _____

After you watch

A Pair work Why does Danielle think Irma is an unusual grandmother? Do you agree with her? Share your ideas.

B Group work Discuss the questions Danielle asks Irma. Answer with your own information and ideas. What is your idea of perfect happiness?

- What is your greatest fear?
- What is your greatest regret?
- What quality do you most admire in a person?
- What is your greatest achievement?

unit 11 *The time of your life: Finding a job*

Before you watch

A Match the words and the definitions. Then compare with a partner.

1. apply _____
2. business card _____
3. interview _____
4. format _____
5. proofread _____
6. work experience _____

a. to read a document carefully and correct any mistakes

b. previous jobs that contribute to a person's knowledge and skills

c. to request something in an official way, usually by filling out a form

d. a meeting in which someone answers questions to try to get a job

e. to organize a written document a certain way

f. a small, thick piece of paper with someone's name, company, job title, and contact information printed on it

B Pair work Ask and answer questions with each word in Part A.

While you watch

A Complete the sentences with the correct names of the characters from the video.

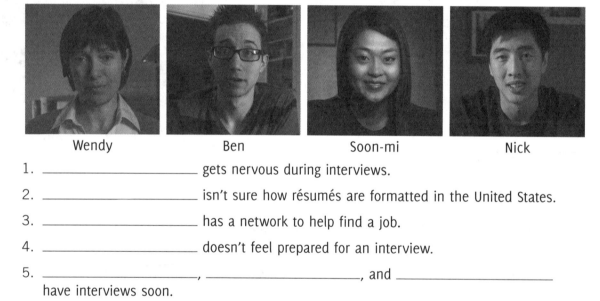

Wendy   Ben   Soon-mi   Nick

1. _____ gets nervous during interviews.

2. _____ isn't sure how résumés are formatted in the United States.

3. _____ has a network to help find a job.

4. _____ doesn't feel prepared for an interview.

5. _____, _____, and _____ have interviews soon.

B Check (✓) the correct answers. (More than one answer is possible.)

1. What does Ben tell Wendy he's already done?

☐ had his clothes dry-cleaned ☐ graduated from college

☐ gotten his résumé printed ☐ practiced answering interview questions

2. What does Wendy tell Soon-mi to include on her résumé?

☐ the colleges she has attended ☐ how long she worked at each job

☐ her date of birth ☐ the name of her junior high school

☐ the degrees she has received ☐ the name of her high school

☐ the jobs she has had ☐ a photo of herself

3. What is Wendy's advice to Nick?

☐ dress well ☐ look very serious ☐ relax ☐ smile

C Circle the correct answers.

1. According to Wendy, what's a network?

a. an online community of co-workers

b. people who can help in your career

c. a television station

2. What do people in your network probably *not* do?

a. have the kind of job you want to get

b. practice interviewing with you

c. know about jobs that are available

3. If you have trouble thinking of an answer to an interview question, what should you say?

a. the first thing that comes into your head

b. "I'm sorry, but I don't know."

c. "That's a good question. Let me think."

4. What does Wendy *not* mention as one of the most important things to do when you're preparing a résumé?

a. Write clearly and simply.

b. Get your résumé proofread.

c. Keep your résumé short (no more than one page).

After you watch

A Pair work What do you think about Wendy's advice to Nick? What situations make *you* nervous? What do you do when you're nervous and don't want to be? Tell your partner.

B Group work Discuss the questions.

• Who is in your network, and why? How can you build your network to help with your career goals?

• Have you ever gone on a job interview? What was the experience like? What did you learn from it?

• Will you be going on an interview soon? If so, how will you prepare for it?

12 *Finding solutions*

Before you watch

A Match the words and the pictures. Then compare with a partner.

a. bike lane	c. collision	e. parking space	g. pollution
b. car exhaust	d. commuters	f. pedestrian	h. traffic

1.

2.

3.

4.

5.

6.

7.

8.

B Pair work What do you think about the special lanes for bicyclists that are found in many cities? What are some advantages and some problems with them? Discuss your ideas.

While you watch

A Who would agree with each statement? Check (✓) the correct answers.

	Commuter	Store owner	Sonia	Diego
1. Bike lanes are bad for business.	☐	☐	☐	☐
2. A lot more people are getting hit by bikes.	☐	☐	☐	☐
3. Bike lanes reduce traffic and therefore pollution.	☐	☐	☐	☐
4. Bike lanes make it possible to avoid traffic and go faster.	☐	☐	☐	☐
5. Bike lanes reduce the number of parking spaces.	☐	☐	☐	☐
6. People don't hear bikes and don't step out of the way.	☐	☐	☐	☐

B Circle the correct answers.

1. What is Danielle reporting on?

   a. traffic accidents   b. bike lanes in Brooklyn   c. air pollution

2. How often does the commuter use bike lanes?

   a. once in a while   b. every other day   c. most days

3. When does the commuter *not* ride his bike to work?

   a. on Mondays   b. when it rains   c. in the winter

4. What does the store owner sell?

   a. refrigerators   b. cars   c. bicycles

5. According to Diego, collisions are increasing between whom?

   a. bicyclists and pedestrians   b. drivers and pedestrians   c. bicyclists and drivers

C Write T (true) or F (false).

1. The store owner thinks that she'll get new customers who ride bikes. _____

2. Sonia Green wants more bike lanes. _____

3. Sonia says one problem with bikes is that they can be expensive. _____

4. Sonia and Diego have the same opinion about bike lanes. _____

5. Danielle was surprised to find out that bike lanes are making some streets more dangerous for pedestrians. _____

After you watch

A Complete the paragraph with the correct words. Then compare with a partner.

| collisions | fit | lanes | pedestrians |
| exhaust | issue | owners | spaces |

Danielle discovers that there are two sides to the _____ of bike _____. On the one hand, because of bike lanes, there are fewer cars in city traffic. This means less _____ from cars and therefore less air pollution. Also, bicycling is good exercise and keeps bike riders _____. On the other hand, some store _____ complain that there are fewer parking _____ for their customers. In addition, there are sometimes _____ between bicyclists and _____.

B Group work Discuss the questions.

• Do you ride a bike? If so, where do you ride? Do you do this for pleasure or for transportation?

• In your city, do a lot of people ride bikes? Are there special bike lanes for them?

• Which side of the issue do you agree with – that there are more advantages or more problems with bike lanes?

• What solutions can you think of for the problems that are mentioned in the video?

Credits

Four Corners

Jack C. Richards · David Bohlke
with Kathryn O'Dell

4

Workbook

Contents

The news

Stories in the news

1 Match the news sections to the headlines.

1. **New Cell Phones in Stores Today** __d__
2. **Singer Wins Music Award** __b__
3. **BIG STORM COMING TO NEW YORK** __f__
4. **Food Can Make You Sick** __e__
5. **Big Company Closes** __g__
6. **Soccer Player Makes Six Goals** __c__
7. **Cheap Vacations in Australia** __a__

a. Travel
b. Entertainment
c. Sports
d. Technology / Science
e. Health
f. Weather
g. Business

2 Circle TWO stories that would be in each news section.

1. Lifestyle
   (a.) a story about a new restaurant that people are going to
   b. a story about a new cell phone and how it works
   c. a story about what people like to do on weekends

2. Local
   a. a story about a school and its students
   (b.) a story about problems in a small town
   c. a story about a singer's tour around the world

3. World
   a. a story about a storm in seven countries
   (b) a story about companies around the world
   c. a weather report for San Diego, California

3 Look at the chart. Then write sentences about the people. Use the past continuous and the present continuous.

Name	When the storm started	Right now
Melvin	work on his computer	watch the storm
Tim	read a good book	finish the book
Susana	drive to Austin	visit her friends there
Emma	shop	take the bus home
Mr. and Mrs. Lee	walk to the park	sit at home
Shelly and Frank	ride their bikes	eat at a restaurant

1. When the storm started, Melvin *was working on his computer* . Now *he is watching the storm* .

2. Tim _____ . Now _____ .

3. Susana _____ . Now _____ .

4. Emma _____ . Now _____ .

5. Mr. and Mrs. Lee _____ . Now _____ .

6. Shelly and Frank _____ . Now _____ .

4 Circle the correct verb forms to complete the conversation.

Jay: Did you hear about what happened last night?
Jorge Morena **makes** / ⟨**made**⟩ six goals in the game!
₁

Becky: Wow! Did you see it on TV?

Jay: No, but I **read** / **'m reading** about it in the
₂
paper today.

Becky: But wait. Morena **hasn't played** / **didn't play** since
₃
he hurt his leg last year.

Jay: Well, he **played** / **has played** last night, and I'm sure he
₄
won / **will win** MVP this year.
₅

Becky: MVP? What's that?

Jay: It **means** / **is meaning** Most Valuable Player. It's the award for the best player
₆
on the team.

Becky: Hmm . . . MVP after only one good game?

Jay: No, he **is** / **was** a great player before he hurt his leg. He **has had** / **had** a great
₇ ₈
career for more than ten years, and he's still great!

Becky: I can't believe I **haven't heard** / **will hear** more about him. I **will watch** / **watch**
₉ ₁₀
him in the future!

5 Complete the text with the correct form of the verbs in parentheses. Use the simple present, the simple past, or the future with *will*.

KSmart: Personal Tech Review
by Justin Wilson

The new cell phone, KSmart by SMT, _____*is*_____ (be) in
stores today. I _____ (think) it's a pretty good
phone for the money. The KSmart _____ (have) a
lot of great features, like its very small camera. The older version of
the phone, the JSmart, _____ (not have) a
camera. The KSmart _____ (come) with many
great applications, and the company _____ (offer)
classes in the future on how to use all of them.

SMT _____ (give) me a phone to test last week.
Right now, there _____ (be) a few problems. For example, the
Internet _____ (not work) in all areas. The company has said they
_____ (fix) the problem soon.
Even with a few problems, I think the KSmart _____ (be) SMT's
most popular phone this year. The JSmart _____ (not be) a great
phone, but the KSmart _____ (be) fantastic!

6 Answer the questions with your own information. Use complete sentences.

Example: *My favorite restaurant is Taco King.*

1. What's your favorite restaurant? _____

2. Is it popular? When is it the busiest? _____

3. What kind of food does the restaurant serve? _____

4. How many times have you been there? _____

5. Who do you usually go there with? _____

6. When was the last time you went? What did you eat? _____

7. What other foods have you eaten there? _____

8. Will you eat there again soon? _____

B │ *I totally agree.*

1 Complete each conversation with the correct sentence from the box.

I couldn't agree with you more.	I'm not sure about that.

1. **Diana:** Hey, Joe. Did you hear about the water problem in Clinton?

   Joe: I read about it yesterday. I don't think it's a big problem.

   Diana: _____ .

   It seems pretty awful to me.

I'm not sure that's really true.	I totally agree.

2. **Yawen:** This radio program is great. I think the radio is the best way to get news.

   Vicky: _____ .

   Yawen: Really?

   Vicky: I think getting news on the Internet is better. You can listen to it or read it.

I don't know about that.	I feel exactly the same way.

3. **Henry:** Look at this, Laura. Josh Grobin will be at the Music Center on Friday.

   Laura: Let's go hear him! He's a great singer.

   Henry: _____ . I love his music.

2 Complete the conversations with your own ideas. Use some of the expressions from the boxes in Exercise 1.

Example: *I couldn't agree with you more.*

1. **Friend:** I think pollution is the biggest problem in our city.

   You: _____

2. **Friend:** I think the best way to get the news is on TV.

   You: _____

3. **Friend:** Let's go to a Lady Gaga concert. She's the best singer!

   You: _____

C Survival stories

1 Complete the puzzle with the correct verbs that complete the headlines.
What's the mystery word?

1. Man _____ Three Days in Ocean

2. Plane _____ into Zoo – No Animals Hurt

3. Mountain Lion _____ Hiker – Hiker Survives

4. Dog _____ Boy Up Tree

5. Car _____ – No One Hurt

6. Storm Coming – _____ Local Beach

7. Lightning Hits House But _____ New Library

```
        1 S  U  R  V  I  V  E  S
     2 [ ][ ][ ]  [ ]
   3 [ ][ ][ ]    [ ]
                  4 [ ][ ][ ][ ][ ]
   5 [ ][ ][ ]    [ ]
        6 [ ][ ][ ][ ]
        7 [ ][ ][ ][ ][ ]
```

2 Write the correct headline from Exercise **1** under each picture.

1. _Storm Coming – Threatens Local Beach_

2. _____

3. _____

4. _____

3 Complete the conversation with the correct form of the verb in parentheses. Use the simple past, the past continuous, the present perfect, or the future with *will*.

Reporter: Today, I'm speaking with Brandon Nelson. He survived three days in the ocean without food. Brandon, what happened?

Brandon: Well, I was on my boat alone, and there was a storm.

Reporter: Where _____**were**_____ you _____**going**_____ (go)?
                                    1   1

Brandon: I was sailing from California to Australia.

Reporter: That's a big trip. You must have experience. How long _____ _____ you _____ (be) a sailor?
                                                                    2   2

Brandon: I've sailed since I was a child.

Reporter: What _____ you _____ (do) when the storm hit?
                   3   3

Brandon: I was preparing the boat for the storm, but it was too late. Suddenly a big wave overturned the boat. The boat broke into pieces, and I was in the water.

Reporter: How _____ you _____ (survive)?
                  4   4

Brandon: At first, I didn't think I would survive. But I found a piece of my boat in the ocean, and I held onto it.

Reporter: What _____ you _____ (eat)?
                   5   5

Brandon: I didn't eat! I found some bottles of water in the ocean that came off the boat in the storm.

Reporter: Wow! You drank only water for three days! So finally some other sailors found you. How _____ you _____ (feel) then?
                                                                                                     6   6

Brandon: Well, of course, I was very, very happy!

Reporter: _____ you ever _____ (go) on a boat again?
              7   7

Brandon: Oh, yes. I hurt my arm, but as soon as it's better, I'll go sailing again.

Reporter: What _____ you _____ (do) differently?
                   8   8

Brandon: Well, I probably won't go alone again.

Reporter: That's a good idea! Well, Brandon, thank you for telling us your story.

4 Complete the conversation by writing Ms. Rivera's questions with the words in parentheses. Use Ms. Hill's answers to help you.

Ms. Rivera: So, _have you been here before_ ?
(you / be / here before)

Ms. Hill: No, I haven't. It's my first time here.

Ms. Rivera: Well, _____
_____ ?
(how / you / hear / about us)

Ms. Hill: My friend Sandra Bern told me about you.

Ms. Rivera: Wonderful. So, _____
_____ ? (how / you / feel / today)

Ms. Hill: I'm feeling sick to my stomach.

Ms. Rivera: I'm sorry. _____ ?
(when / you / get / sick)

Ms. Hill: I got sick last week.

Ms. Rivera: _____ ?
(you / be / to another doctor before today)

Ms. Hill: No, I haven't.

Ms. Rivera: _____ ?
(you / take / any medication)

Ms. Hill: No, I'm not taking anything.

Ms. Rivera: OK, thank you. The doctor will see you soon. Oh,
_____ ?
(how / you / pay / today)

Ms. Hill: I'll pay with a credit card if that's OK.

5 Read the situations. Then answer the questions with your own ideas.

Example: _I close the windows, and I turn on the radio._

1. There is a big storm and you are at home. What do you do? _____

2. A bear is chasing you. What are you doing? _____

3. You have been lost in the mountains for two days. You have a little water and a sandwich.
   How will you survive? _____

4. A shark threatened a beach last week. You are at the beach today. Do you swim
   in the ocean? Why or why not? _____

D Creating news

1 Read the article. Write what the letters mean.

1. JNW _____   2. SMS _____

SMS NEWS

JASMINE NEWS (JNW) gives people in Sri Lanka, an island country south of India, a new way to get news. It sends news headlines to people in text messages on their cell phones. The text messages are short and give people information about important events. JNW is getting news to people faster than radio, television, and even the Internet.

SMS stands for "Short Message Service," and it's the system used for text messages. JNW started in 2006, and then in 2007, JNW started working with a phone company to send SMS news. It was the first company in Sri Lanka, and one of the first companies in Asia, to use SMS news. JNW is using new technology and working with phone services so that people can get the news with any type of phone. Although SMS news is shorter than other types of news stories, JNW has high standards. They want all of their headlines to be correct and neutral. They check all information with at least three sources, like different people and newspapers. If they make a mistake, they quickly send a text with the correct information.

Breaking news: Storm Threatens Beaches

JNW feels the most important part of their service is sharing the news, opinions, and experiences of Sri Lanka's citizens. They report news about what citizens want and need. They have journalists who report the news in three languages – Sinhala and Tamil, two of the languages spoken in Sri Lanka, and English. JNW also uses citizen journalists and gets some news from everyday citizens.

It does cost money to get SMS news, but JNW thinks it's important that anyone who wants it can get it. They have a pay-what-you-can program for people who can't afford the regular price.

2 Read the text again. Then answer the questions.

1. How do people get news from JNW?   *on their cell phones / in text messages*

2. When did JNW start sending SMS news?   _____

3. What does JNW do to make sure headlines are correct? _____

4. What does JNW do if they make a mistake?   _____

5. In what languages does JNW report the news? _____

Communicating

A Language learning

1 Put the letters in the correct order to make sentences.

1. h a t w c / i o n e l n / d e v i o / p c l s i /.   _Watch online video clips._

2. l k t a / o t / e r s y l u o f / u o t / d l o u /.   _____

3. p e e k / a / a r v c a l o y u b / n b e k o o o t /.   _____

4. h w t a c / s m v e o i / t i w h / t s s l i u t b e /.   _____

5. l k t a / t w h i / e a v t n i / a p s e r s e k /.   _____

6. e m k a / h l s f a / d s c a r /.   _____

2 Look at the pictures. Write sentences with language-learning tips.

1. _She watches online video clips._

2. _____

3. _____

4. _____

5. _____

6. _____

3 Check (✓) the correct sentences. Then change the sentences that are NOT correct to the present perfect.

1. ☐ I've been knowing Tom for ten years. _*I've known Tom for ten years.*_ _____

2. ☑ Jill has been keeping a vocabulary notebook recently. _____

3. ☐ We've been driving this car for about two years. _____

4. ☐ Lola has been owning her bicycle for a long time. _____

5. ☐ Su Ho hasn't been belonging to our club very long. _____

6. ☐ I've been watching online video clips all day. _____

7. ☐ They have never been believing my story. _____

8. ☐ How long have you been waiting here? _____

4 Complete the email with the present perfect continuous. Use the words in parentheses.

Hi Rafa,

*Have you been having* _____ (you / have) a good time in summer school? Which classes are
                     1
you taking? I'm not taking summer classes this year, but _____ (I / practice)
                                                                        2
my English a lot lately. _____ (I / live) in Toronto, Canada, this
                                   3
summer, and _____ (I / talk) with native speakers every day.
                    4
_____ (I / watch) a lot of movies recently, but
         5
_____ (I / not watch) them with subtitles. My English
         6
is improving, so I can understand the movies without the subtitles!

Do you have Mr. Payton for English again? _____ (he / use) flash
                                                              7
cards in class? _____ (the class / watch) any online video clips? If
                          8
yes, please send me the websites. _____ (I / not use) my computer
                                              9
because it isn't working. I came to an Internet café to send you this email. I hope you're having a

good summer.

Your friend,

Carla

P.S. _____ (I / take) a lot of pictures.
              10
    Look at the streetcar!

5 Look at the chart. Then answer the questions.

	Talks with native speakers	Watches online video clips in English	Keeps a vocabulary notebook
Tina	✓	✓	✓
Caroline		✓	✓
Marcos	✓		✓
Andrew	✓		

1. Has Tina been watching online videos in English? _Yes, she has._

2. Have Tina and Marcos been keeping vocabulary notebooks? _____

3. Has Caroline been talking with native speakers? _____

4. Has Marcos been talking with native speakers? _____

5. Have Marcos and Andrew been watching online videos in English? _____

6. Has Andrew been keeping a vocabulary notebook? _____

6 Look at the answers. Write the questions. Use the underlined words to help you.

1. **A:** _What have you been studying?_ _____

   B: I've been studying <u>English</u>.

2. **A:** _____

   B: I've been studying English <u>for five years</u>.

3. **A:** _____

   B: I've been taking classes <u>at Monroe Language School</u>.

4. **A:** _____

   B: I've been practicing English <u>by reading in English</u>.

5. **A:** _____

   B: I've been reading <u>magazines</u> lately.

7 Answer the questions with your own information. Use complete sentences.

Example: _Yes, I have. I've been studying English for three years._

1. Have you been studying English for very long? How long?

   _____

2. Have you been reading in English? What have you been reading recently?

   _____

3. Has your teacher been giving you homework lately? How much?

   _____

B *One possibility is . . .*

1 **Read each sentence. Then write E (expressing interest) or O (offering options).**

1. One possibility is reading a lot of books and magazines. __O__

2. How about watching movies with subtitles? _____

3. I'm trying to find a way to improve my vocabulary. _____

4. I'm interested in improving my listening comprehension. _____

5. You might want to consider a local newspaper or the Internet. _____

6. I'm looking for a conversation group. _____

2 **Complete the conversations with the sentences from Exercise 1.**

A. **Albert:** What are you doing, Julia?

    Julia: *I'm looking for a conversation group* .
                             ₁
              I thought there might be information in this magazine.

    Albert: Hmm . . . I don't know if you'll find information

              on a conversation group in a magazine.

              _____ .
                            2

    Julia: I'll try the Internet! Thanks.

B. **Ji Ah:** Excuse me, Dana. Can you help me?

    Dana: Sure, Ji Ah.

    Ji Ah: I wrote the word *very* in my paper too many times.

              _____ .
                          1

    Dana: _____ . You can learn
                          2
              new words and write them in a notebook.

    Ji Ah: Hey, that's a great idea.

C. **Mr. Wei:** So, Atakan, how can I help you today?

    Atakan: Well, _____ . I listen to
                          1
             English music, but my listening skills aren't getting better.

    Mr. Wei: I'm not surprised. Music is difficult to understand.

              _____ ? Try to listen
                         2
             first, and then read the subtitles if you still don't understand what you heard.

    Atakan: That's a good idea, Mr. Wei. Thank you.

C   *Have her text me.*

1 Complete the conversations with the phrases from the box.

answer the phone	left her a voice message	screen my calls
call my mother back	✓let the call go to voice mail	turn off my phone
don't check voice mail	respond to an email	update your status online
ignored my text		

A. **Kim:** Well, if you think the job interview went well, you . . .

   Doug: Sorry, Kim. My phone is ringing.

   Kim: Could you please _let the call go to voice mail_ ?

                   1

     You can call the person back after dinner.

   Doug: No! I really have to _____ !

                       2

     It might be about the job.

B. **Hiro:** Is Wendy coming to the party on Friday?

   Eric: I don't know. She _____ .

                      1

   Hiro: Hmm . . . Well, maybe she would _____ .

                          2

   Eric: Yeah. I'll email her tonight.

C. **Jen:** I'll be right back, Mike. I have to _____ .

                        1

   Mike: OK. Tell your mom "hi."

     . . .

   Mike: That was fast.

   Jen: She didn't answer the phone, so I _____ .

                         2

D. **Lilly:** I could never work at home. How do you get so much work done, Kyle?

   Kyle: Well, I _____ , and I only answer calls about work.

                      1

     And I _____ until the end of the day.

                      2

   Lilly: Really? I check mine every five minutes!

   Kyle: Not me. And if I'm really busy, I _____ .

                          3

     I also don't use the Internet. I mean, I only use it for work!

   Lilly: Wow. You're really dedicated. When do you _____ ?

                            4

   Kyle: I usually update it in the evening.

2 Answer the questions with your own information. Use complete sentences.

Example: _People should turn off their cell phones in restaurants because other_
people don't want to hear them talking.

1. Do you think people should turn off their cell phones in restaurants? Why or why not?

_____

2. How often do you check your voice mail?

_____

3. What else can you do on your cell phone?

_____

4. Do you screen your calls on your cell phone? When?

_____

5. Have you answered your phone in class recently? What happened?

_____

6. Do you think there is ever a good reason to ignore a text? If yes, when?

_____

3 Put the words in the correct order to make sentences.

1. have / Would / Jenny / call me / tomorrow / you / ?

Would you have Jenny call me tomorrow?

2. them / to the party / ask / you / come / Did / to / ?

_____

3. vocabulary / learn / me / help / new / you / Will / ?

_____

4. phone / her / let / use / me / today / Mindy / .

_____

5. his / to / soccer game / go / invited us / to / Dan / .

_____

6. going / take the bus / Are / make / to / you / them / ?

_____

7. be / tell / to / Don't / quiet / me / !

_____

8. next week / remind / I'll / to / the information / email / you / .

_____

4 Complete the sentences with the correct form of the verb in parentheses.

Paula,

Thanks for staying with Lisa and Mark. Here are a few reminders:

- Remind Lisa _to take out_ (take out) the garbage.
- Help Mark _____ (do) his homework every night.
- You can let Lisa and Mark _____ (have) friends at the house, but only on the weekends.
- Mark invited his soccer coach _____ (come) for dinner on Friday. You can order Chinese food.
- Have Lisa or Mark _____ (call) me every night!
- Make them _____ (go) to bed by 10:00 p.m.
- If you can't find something, ask Lisa _____ (help) you.
- Oh, and tell them _____ (clean) the house before I get home.

☺ Yasmin

5 Circle the correct word to complete each sentence.

1. Could you **ask** / **have** Tom to respond to my email?

2. Larry won't **invite** / **let** me help him with his homework.

3. Have they been **helping** / **asking** you make flash cards?

4. Mary **made** / **invited** me to join her conversation group.

5. Please **let** / **tell** Jenna to update her online status.

6. Mr. Kent has been **making** / **telling** his students keep vocabulary notebooks.

7. Did the teachers **remind** / **have** the students turn off their cell phones?

6 Answer the questions with your own information. Use a verb followed by an object and another base verb or infinitive.

Example: _Yes, I have. I helped my grandfather respond to an email._

1. Have you ever helped someone with a computer problem? Who?

   _____

2. Have you ever let someone help you with a problem? What problem?

   _____

3. Have you ever told someone not to call you? Who?

   _____

D Modern communication

1 Read the article. What is the text capital of the world?

TEXT IT TO ME!

The first text message was sent in 1992, and texting has become extremely popular since that time. There are about 6.7 billion people in the world, and in 2009, about 6.8 billion text messages were sent every day. It's a popular way to communicate around the world.

The United States
Text messaging is getting more popular in the United States. In the past, it was popular with people ages 13 to 22, but today, many older people are sending texts, too. People use it to communicate with friends, and it's being used for business, too. Some airlines are sending text messages to people to remind them to check in for their flights.

Japan, China, and South Korea
Japan was one of the first countries to use text messages as a way to communicate. People still use it, but now sending email on phones is more popular. In China, sending text messages is the most popular way to communicate. It's cheaper than talking on the phone. There's a problem in China with "spam" texts. These are unwanted messages sent to a lot of people at the same time. It has been a problem with email in many countries for a long time, but in China, it's now a problem with text messages, too. Many South Koreans use text messaging, and some of the fastest texters are from South Korea. In 2010, Yeong-Ho Bae and Mok-Min Ha won a contest in New York for the world's fastest texters.

Finland
In Finland, there are text-messaging game shows on TV. People watch TV and get quiz questions. They send the answers to the TV station by text. The person who texts the most correct answers wins!

The Philippines
Some people call the Philippines the text capital of the world. Over 67 million people in the Philippines have cell phones, and texting is very popular because it is cheap and reliable. People even use text messaging for sharing their opinions about politics and the news.

2 Read the text again. Then write the country.

1. Yeong-Ho is one of the fastest texters in the world. _____South Korea_____

2. Texting is used for quiz shows. _____

3. People text each other about politics. _____

4. You can get a text with flight information. _____

5. This country was one of the first to use text messages to communicate. _____

6. Getting spam texts is a problem. _____

Food

A Street food

1 Complete the recipes with the correct verbs for food preparation.

EASY DUMPLINGS

Fill the dough with chicken or beef.
Bo*il*_____ the dumplings for
1
10 minutes or s_____ them for
2
about 20 minutes. Serve them right away
with a good soup.

Fantastic Chicken

Put chicken, small potatoes, and carrots
in a pan. Ba_____ or
3
r_____ them for about one
4
hour and 30 minutes. Serve with a
green salad.

SIMPLE STIR-FRY

Cut up the chicken and put it with
vegetables and soy sauce in a hot pan.
F_____ them for 10 to 12
5
minutes. To enjoy the stir-fry the next
day, m_____ it for one minute
6
on high.

Super Burgers

For a fast meal, make Super Burgers.
G_____ hamburgers for about
7
8 to 10 minutes, turning once.
M_____ cheese on the burgers
8
for the last minute. Serve on a bun with
lettuce and tomato.

2 Circle the correct words to complete each sentence.

1. Hot dogs _____ on the streets in New York City.

   (a.) are sold   b. are sell   c. sells

2. They _____ by hundreds of people.

   a. are buying   b. are bought   c. bought

3. The hot dogs _____ , not fried.

   a. boils   b. is boiled   c. are boiled

4. Water _____ by vendors, too.

   a. are sold   b. is sold   c. is selling

5. The bottles of water _____ in cold water.

   a. is kept   b. are keeping   c. are kept

6. The hot dog carts _____ at the end of each day.

   a. is moved   b. are moving   c. are moved

3 Read the sentences. Write A (active) or P (passive).

1. Five different desserts are served at my favorite restaurant. ___P___

2. The vegetables are steamed, but the fish is fried. _____

3. They make the soup at the restaurant, and they serve it with a salad. _____

4. The fruit is served cold on ice cream. _____

5. The chef grills chicken and beef at your table. _____

6. The hot dogs for the company parties are bought from a vendor. _____

7. The waiter makes the salad at your table. _____

8. The cooks fry the empanadas in the morning, and they microwave them before serving. _____

9. He bakes the cake for 40 minutes. _____

4 Change the active sentences in Exercise 3 to the present passive.

1. _The soup is made at the restaurant, and it is served with a salad._

2. _____

3. _____

4. _____

5. _____

5 Complete the text with the present passive of the verbs in parentheses.

MARTY'S FINE FOOD
Come to our new restaurant on Maple Street.

- You'll love our exotic menu! The seafood is local.
  It __is brought__ (bring) to our
  restaurant three times a week.

- Our bread _____ (bake) fresh
  every morning.

- Our vegetables _____ (grow)
  on local, organic farms.

- Breakfast _____ (serve) from
  8:00 a.m. to 11:30 a.m.

- Lunch and dinner _____ (serve) all day.

- Prices _____ (list) on our website.
  See www.martysfinefood/cup.com.

Please visit us soon and let us make you a great meal!

6 Answer the questions with your own ideas. Write complete sentences with the present passive.

Example: __Hamburgers and dumplings are often fried.__

1. What are two foods that are often fried?

_____

2. What are three foods that are served at your favorite restaurant?

_____

3. What is one food that is often melted on hamburgers?

_____

4. What are two foods that are boiled?

_____

5. What is one food that is baked?

_____

6. What is one food that is steamed?

_____

B Sounds good to me.

1 Write the conversation in the correct order.

Then if I were you, I'd get the lamb chops.
That's a good idea.
I know. What are you going to have?
OK. I think I'll do that. Why don't you get the lamb chops, too?
✓This new restaurant is great. There are so many things on the menu.
Why don't you try the cheese ravioli?

Kari: _This new restaurant is great. There are so many things on the menu._

John: _____

Kari: Everything looks good. I have no idea what to get.

John: _____

Kari: No, I had pasta for lunch.

John: _____

Kari: _____

John: _____

2 Complete the conversation with the phrases from the box and food from the menu.

Sounds good to me.   My recommendation would be to . . .

MARTY'S FINE FOOD

Main Dishes

Lamb Chops	$21.00
Cheese Ravioli	$13.00
Baked Fish	$16.00
Grilled Steak	$16.00

Friend: Everything looks good. I don't know what to get.

You: _____

Friend: _____

Mix and bake

1 Circle the correct words to complete the conversations.

Mei: Do you want a pretzel? They're really
hard chips
chewy / **sweet**.
5

Lori: No, thanks. I think they're **bland** / **sticky**.
6
They don't have any taste.

Mei: How about a chocolate cookie? They're
salty / **sweet.**
7

Lori: That sounds great, thanks.

Luz: Let's get popcorn. OK?

Gi Woo: No, it's too **salty** / **sour**. How about
1
some lemon candy?

Luz: That's too **creamy** / **sour** for me!
2
Cotton candy?

Gi Woo: Too **crunchy** / **sticky**. How about the
3
Fruit Chews?

Luz: Great. They're **juicy** / **salty** and
4
wonderful!

Ming: Do you like the chili?

Raul: Well, it's really **creamy** / **crunchy**, but it's
8
too **bland** / **spicy** for me. I mean, it tastes
9
good, but it has too much red pepper in it!
How are the tacos?

Ming: They're great. They're **chewy** / **crunchy** and
10
they're not spicy at all.

2 Write the cooking directions in the correct order on the recipe card. Do the rice first. Then do the beans.

Rice
After it boils, cover the pan and ③ turn down the heat.
Cook it for 15 more minutes or ④ until the water is gone.
✓ Put the water and rice in a pan. ①
Once it is cooked, put it in a bowl until the beans are finished. ⑤
Then cook the rice until it boils. ②

Beans
As soon as they're done, pour them ④ over the rice.
Then turn down the heat, and boil ③ the beans for about 1½ hours.
Once it boils, add the beans and a ② little salt.
Put some water in a pan, and heat ① it until it boils.

RUTH'S RICE AND BEANS RECIPE

INGREDIENTS FOR RICE:	INGREDIENTS FOR BEANS:
350 ml water	1 liter water
225 grams rice	500 grams red beans
	salt

Before you cook, clean the beans and put them in cold water for 8 to 12 hours. Then pour off the water and put the beans in the refrigerator.

To start cooking, make the rice.

1. ___Put the water and rice in a pan.___
2. Then cook the rice until it boils.
3. After it boils cover the pan and turn down the heat.
4. Cook it for 15 more minutes or until the water is gone.
5. Once it is cooked, put it in a bowl until the beans are finished

While the rice is cooking, start the beans.

6. Put some water in a pan, and heat it until it boils.
7. Once it boils, add the beans and a little salt
8. The turn down the heat, and boil the beans for about 1½ hours.
9. As soon as the're done, pour them over the rice.

Serve hot.

3 Circle the correct words to complete the email.

Subject: Your new restaurant

Hi Elsa,

It's great that you're opening a restaurant. My restaurant has been very successful this year, and I'd be happy to give you advice. Here are a few tips:

- (Before) / After you make any decisions, see how much money you have for the restaurant.
  1
- Before / (After) you know how much you'll spend, find the place for your restaurant.
  2
- (As soon as) / Until you find the place, make the big decisions, like what color to paint the walls.
  3
- You can decide on the smaller things (once) / before the big decisions are made.
  4
- I'm sure you have an idea about what kind of food you want to serve. Don't make the menus **as soon as** / (until) you have tried all of the recipes! I put chicken satay
  5
  on my menu **once** / (before) I made it, and it wasn't very good. I had to change all
  6
  of my menus!

There is a lot more to tell you. Let's talk on the phone soon, and I can give you more advice.

Marty

4 Write a simple recipe for a food you know. Use time clauses with some of the words in the box.

after	as soon as	before	once	until

DISH: Chicken soup

INGREDIENTS: Chicken, Vegetables

DIRECTIONS:

After wash the chicken pull in a recipe.
As soon as pull in a recipe add water.
Boit the Chicken and before to ready add the
vegetables. Once
When the vegetable be soft turn off the stove.
Server until the chicke soup be warm.

D Chocolate!

1 Read the article. How long do you have to wait before you can eat the cake?

a. 20 minutes   b. 40 minutes   c. 60 minutes

www.yourrecipes/cup.com

Chocolate Dream Cake
by Mari Park
A delicious cake that's easy to make!

225 grams flour
225 grams sugar
75 grams cocoa powder
1 teaspoon baking soda

1 tablespoon butter, melted
80 ml oil
250 ml cold water

Before you add the liquids, mix the dry ingredients together. Once they are mixed, add the butter and oil. Pour the cold water into the mixture and stir. Bake in a round pan for 40 minutes. Let cool for 20 minutes before you serve it.

COMMENTS: + Post a comment

DiPeters26 This cake was easy to make, and it was delicious! I added a chocolate sauce over the top of the cake. Delicious!

MarcosG I made this cake, and I thought it was too bland. It needs a little salt. And DiPeters26, can you give me your sauce recipe?

DiPeters26 Sure, MarcosG. Mix 225 grams of powdered sugar, 2 teaspoons of butter, 1 teaspoon of vanilla, 200 grams of cocoa, and 125 ml of milk. Boil together until sauce starts to get thick. Then cool and pour over cake.

KloveCook I tried this recipe, but the cake was too dry. Next time, I might add more butter. I think I'll try DiPeters26's chocolate sauce, too.

MTP1987 This cake was great! My only problem was that it was too small. The next time, I doubled the recipe and baked it in two pans. My family loves this cake!

OTHER RECIPES:
No Bake Cookies
Double Chocolate
  Cake
Apple Cobbler
Mini Chocolate
  Cookies
Chocolate Surprise
Cocoa Cream Puffs
Easy Frosting

VIDEOS:
How to Make
  Healthy Desserts
How to Sift Flour
Where to Buy Good
  Chocolate

2 Read the text again. Then write T (true) or F (false).

1. For the cake, you add the butter last. ___*F*___

2. You boil the water before you add it. ___F___

3. MarcosG doesn't want the chocolate sauce recipe. ___T___

4. KloveCook hasn't tried DiPeters26's chocolate sauce yet. ___T___

5. MTP1987 made the cake more than once. ___T___

Behavior

A The right thing to do

1 Match the two parts of each phrase.

1. give __*b*__
   a. in line

2. keep __a__
   b. someone a gift

3. cut __c__
   c. someone waiting

4. talk __d__
   d. loudly in public

5. offer __g__
   e. litter *Litera, cama parir o dar a luz los animales.*

6. admit __f__
   f. a mistake *dar carr, tirar*

7. drop __e__
   g. someone your seat

8. give __h__
   h. someone a compliment

2 Complete each conversation with a kind of polite or impolite behavior.

1. **A:** Excuse me, you can't ___cut in line___ .
   I was here first.

   B: Oh, I'm sorry. I didn't see you.

2. **A:** You should ___give___ that woman
   ___seat___ . She has a lot of bags.

   B: Good idea. I don't mind standing on the subway, and
   she needs the seat.

3. **A:** Hey, you shouldn't ___drop trash___
   on the street. It's not good for the environment.

   B: Yeah, you're right. I'll pick it up.

4. **A:** You really shouldn't ___talk loudly in public___ on your cell phone.
   It's impolite. I'm trying to listen to the music.

   B: Sorry. I'll go to another place to talk.

5. **A:** John can never ___admit a mistake___ . He always says
   he's right.

   B: I know, but he's really wrong this time.

6. **A:** In the United States, do you ___invide___ a friend ___to celebred.___
   for the Fourth of July?

   B: No, but if you go to a Fourth of July party, you could take some food.

3 Complete the interview with the correct sentences from the box.

> ✓And what would you do if something bad happened?
> ✓I guess I'd like to be an astronaut!
> No, I wouldn't.
> What would you do if someone got sick?
> What would you do if you weren't a pilot?

Reporter: I'm talking to pilot Tonya Hitchcock. So, Captain Hitchcock, have you ever been in a dangerous situation?

Tonya: No, I really haven't.

Reporter: _And what would you do if something bad happened?_
1

Tonya: Well, I'd stay calm and try to find a solution.

Reporter: That's a good plan. Now, has anyone ever gotten really sick on the plane?

Tonya: No, not on one of my flights.

Reporter: No I Wouldn't
2
Would you turn the plane around?

Tonya: What Would you do if someone got sick?
3
First, I'd ask if there were a doctor on the plane!

Reporter: That's a good idea. One last question.
What Would you do if you weren't a pilot?
4

Tonya: Hmm . . . another job? I guess I'd like to be astronaut!
5

4 Put the words in the correct order to make sentences.

1. be angry / I'd / someone / If / cut in line / in front of me, / .

   If someone cut in line in front of me, I'd be angry.

2. in the library, / ask them to be quiet / people / were talking too loudly / If / I'd / .

   if in the library people were talking too loudly I'd ask them to be quiet.

3. If / I kept / "I'm sorry." / someone waiting / say, / I'd

   if I kept someone waiting I'd say I'm sorry.

4. I'd / if / be happy / gave me / a compliment, / someone / .

   if someone geve me a compliment I'd be happy.

5. were dropping litter / What / if / would you do / your friend / out of your car / ?

   What would you do if your friend wee dropping litter out of you car?

6. you say / your parents / gave you / If / what / a lot of money, / would / ?

   What Would you say if you parents gave you a lot of money?

5 Circle the correct words to complete each question.

How polite are you?

1. What **would you do** / **did you do** if your friend **would talk** / **were talking** loudly at a movie?

2. If you **would see** / **saw** someone drop litter on the ground, what **would you say** / **did you say**?

3. If you **would like** / **liked** a stranger's jacket, **would you give** / **you gave** him or her a compliment?

4. What **would you do** / **did you do** if an elderly person **would need** / **needed** a seat on a train?

5. What **would you do** / **did you do** if your friend **asked** / **would ask** you for a lot of money?

6. If you **make** / **made** a mistake, **did you admit** / **would you admit** it?

7. If you **are** / **were** impatient to get your concert ticket, **would you cut** / **did you cut** in line?

8. What **would you do** / **did you do** if someone **would want** / **wanted** directions to a place in your town?

6 Answer the questions from Exercise 5 with your own information.

Example: *I'd feel embarrassed, but I wouldn't say anything.*

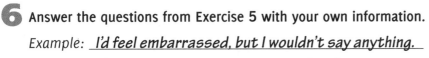

1. I Would ask to him speak less loudly
2. I Would don't drop litter on the ground.
3. I Wouldn't say anything Probabibly.
4. I Would let an elderly person sit.
5. I wouldn't give money
6. _____
7. _____
8. _____

B I didn't realize that.

1 Complete the sentences with the correct words.

1. It's the c<u>ustom</u> to leave a tip.

2. Oh, I d<u>idn't realize in korea we didn't do</u> that.

3. Oh, r<u>ight</u> ? I wasn't a_____ of that.

4. You're s<u>hould</u> to pay the waiter.

5. Really? I didn't r<u>ealize</u> that.

6. You're e<u>xpect</u> to leave 15 to 20 percent of the amount on the check.

2 Complete the conversation with the sentences from Exercise **1**. Sometimes more than one answer is possible.

Tracey: This food was great.

Yae Wan: I agree, and it wasn't very expensive. It's $24, so that's $12 for me, and $12 for you.

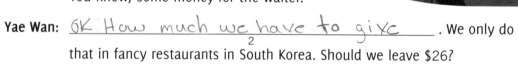

Tracey: We need to give more than $24.

<u>It's the custom to leave a tip</u> .
1
You know, some money for the waiter.

Yae Wan: <u>OK. How much we have to give</u> . We only do
2
that in fancy restaurants in South Korea. Should we leave $26?

Tracey: No. That's not enough.

<u>The service service and the food was great.</u>
3

Yae Wan: <u>You right</u> . Let's leave
4
20 percent. The waiter was great.

Tracey: OK. How much is that?

Yae Wan: Let's see . . . 20 percent of $24 is $4.80, so it's $28.80 total. Let's just give $30. Do we pay at the front of the restaurant?

Tracey: No. <u>Let's pay here</u> .
5

Yae Wan: <u>I'll ask for the ticker</u> . OK, here
6
he comes.

Tracey: Excuse me . . . We're ready to pay.

Doing things differently

1 Cross out the word that doesn't belong in each list.

turn down = to reject to deny

1. **make:** a request an excuse ~~a favor~~
2. **offer:** an apology <u>a request</u> an explanation
   Make
3. **ask for:** an explanation a favor <u>a compromise</u>
   Agreen
4. **accept:** ~~an opinion~~ an apology a compliment
5. **turn down:** a request an invitation <u>an excuse</u>
   or the volume

2 Circle the correct word(s) to complete each conversation.

1. **A:** Jack told me he liked my new haircut.

   B: Really? He doesn't **accept** / **give**
   compliments often.

2. **A:** I think there's too much pollution in this city.

   B: Really? **I disagree with** / **agree with** your
   opinion. It's much cleaner than a lot of cities
   that I've visited.

3. **A:** Thanks for helping me with my homework.

   B: No problem. I'm happy **to return** / **ask for** the favor. Remember that you   *return = come back*
   helped me last week!   *give back something*

4. **A:** I don't know if we'll ever agree. You want a lot of things I don't want.

   B: Well, let's try to **suggest** / **reach a** compromise.

5. **A:** Did you **accept** / **turn down** Mark's invitation to dinner?

   B: Yes, I did. I have to stay home with the kids that night.

6. **A:** Jenny kept me waiting for an hour yesterday.

   B: **Did you ask her for** / **offer her** an explanation?

   A: Yes, I did. She said she had to stay late at work to finish a report.

7. **A:** I'd like to **turn down** / **make** a request for a window seat.

   B: No problem, sir. You can sit in seat 14F. That's a window seat. Enjoy your flight.

3 Look at the pictures. Check (✓) TWO possible sentences for each picture.

1. ☑ "I shouldn't have lent my sister all my money."

   ☐ "I could have bought two pizzas."

   ☑ "I should have remembered to bring my money."

   Shoulld + have + P.P.

2. ☑ "It would have been best to apologize." *be*

   ☐ "I would have stayed home."

   ☑ "I shouldn't have gotten so upset."

   get

3. ☑ "I should have taken the subway."

   ☑ "I could have driven to work today." *drive*

   ☐ "I wouldn't have stayed home today."

Modal Could, Shouldn't

4 Write sentences with the words in parentheses and past modals.

1. (I / shouldn't / borrow / Julie's car)
   P.P
   __I shouldn't have borrowed Julie's car__ .

2. (What / could / I / do / differently)
   What Could I have done diferently?

3. (I / could / take / the bus) *P.P*
   I could have taken the bus .

4. (I / should / drive / more slowly)
   I should have driven more slowly. .

5. (Julie / wouldn't / drive / so fast)
   Julie wouldn't have driven so fast .

6. (She / would / see / the stop sign)
   She would have seen the stop sign. .

7. (Should / I / offer to pay Julie / to fix the car)
   Should I have offered to pay Julie to fix the car. ?

8. (What / would / you / do)
   What Would you have done? ?

5 Complete the letters with the correct form of the word pairs in the box.

Pedria   *Deberia*

could / give	could / microwave	✓should / do	shouldn't / say

Dear Henry Helper,

My wife was really upset last night. She made a nice dinner, and I said that it was cold.

I don't understand why she got so angry. It <u>was</u> cold! What _____**should**_____
                                                                                        1

I _**have done**_____ ? *–Confused in Chicago*
     1

Dear Confused in Chicago,

Your wife made you a nice dinner. You _____Could have given_____ her
                                                        2

a compliment. You _____Couldn't have said_____ the dinner was cold.
                                3

You _____Shouldn't say_____ it to make it hot enough! *–Henry Helper*
          4

could / do	should / talk	would / reach	wouldn't / get

+ have + P.P.

Dear Henry Helper,

My roommate and I often disagree. Last week, we argued about keeping the kitchen

clean. We're not talking to each other now. What _____Could_____ we
                                                                5

_____have done_____ differently? *–Angry Anita*
          5

Dear Angry Anita,

I _____Wouldn't have gotten_____ so upset. You and your roommate
          6

_____Should have talked_____ about the problem quietly. It's important
          7

for roommates to work together, so I _____Would have reached_____ a
                                                        8

compromise. Try to stay relaxed the next time you don't agree. A dirty kitchen isn't a

good reason to lose a friend! *–Henry Helper*

6 Look at the letters in Exercise 5. Write responses with your own ideas. Use past modals.

Example: _**I wouldn't have said anything.**_ or _**You could have said thank you.**_

1. Dear Confused in Chicago,

   You Wouldn't have said dinner was cold.

2. Dear Angry Anita,

   You Wouldn't have argued about keeping the kitchen clean.

D Acts of kindness

1 Read the article. In what places does the Random Acts of Kindness Foundation try to inspire kindness?

Something to THINK ABOUT

The Random Acts of Kindness Foundation is an organization that inspires people to be kind. It started in 1995, and its goal is to spread kindness. The people of the Foundation want us to be kind to others. And if someone is kind to you, they want you to "pay it forward" by doing something nice for someone else. Their website gives people ideas on how to be kind in schools and at work.

People post ideas on the Foundation website about ways to be kind. Several people have posted ways they are kind at work. A manager at a company in Texas brings cake to work for each employee's birthday. A manager at a company in California had a "Not-Going-Away" pizza party. She said that they used to celebrate only when people left the company. She decided to have a "Not-Going-Away" party for the employees who worked there and didn't leave. It was fun, and the employees felt appreciated. Another manager in Illinois bought a vacation apartment for her employees. They get points for good things

they do at work, and each weekend one of her 45 employees uses the apartment. They take family or friends for a weekend vacation.

Some companies inspire employees to do kind things for each other. One company has "Secret Pals." Each employee fills out information about his or her interests and hobbies, and the information is given to another employee who is their "Secret Pal." The Secret Pal does kind things for the other person, like giving them gifts or kind notes. The employees know the person they are doing kind things for, but they don't know who is doing kind things for them. Another company in Iowa sold bags of candy and flowers to their employees. The employees bought the candy and flowers and gave them to each other. It was a way for employees to give each other small gifts to say thank you. The company made over $700. They could have kept the money, but they "paid it forward," and gave the money to a charity.

2 Read the text again. Then check (✓) the items that are random acts of kindness mentioned in the reading.

1. ☑ posting ideas on a website

2. ☑ bringing cake for people's birthdays

3. ☑ having a Not-Going-Away party for employees

4. ☐ going on vacation

5. ☑ giving a small gift to someone at work

6. ☑ giving money to charity

Travel and tourism

A Cities

1 Complete Wendy's notes about her vacation. Use the correct words from the box.

culturally diverse ✓	highly educated ~Adj~	slow-paced ✓
densely populated ✓	high-tech ✓	well-planned ✓
fun-loving ✓	open-minded ✓	✓ world-famous

October 7: I'm traveling in South America!
Right now I'm in Quito, Ecuador. It's a
beautiful and mountainous city. Yesterday, I
went to the ___**world-famous**___ place
                          1
called Mitad del Mundo. I met people from
all over – France, Canada, Brazil, and more!
Mitad del Mundo means the middle of the
world. I had one foot in the northern half
of the world and one in the southern half!
Last week, I was in Guayaquil. It's a
___fun loving___ city. People like to
          2
dance, and there are parties in the streets
after soccer games!

October 10: Colombia is amazing!
Yesterday, I flew to Bogotá. Bogotá is a
very ___densely populated___ city. ~Adj.~
                    3
There are so many people here!

Tomorrow, I'm going to the rain forest.
It will be ___slow placed___
                      4
compared to Bogotá. I'm going to relax
there, but I'll also learn a lot about the
environment from the people who live in
                 NOUN
the rain forest. (Jungle)

enviromental → Adj

October 15: I'm in Brazil now. Portuguese,
not Spanish, is spoken here. Right now I'm in
Curtiba. It's a ___well planned___ city.
                      5
There is a great bus system, and there are
bus stops next to most of the important
buildings. There are also many parks here.
It's a ___culturally diverse___ city, and
               6
many of the parks have items from different
cultures in them. The people here are
___highly Educated___. There are many
          7
universities in the city.

October 28: Now I'm in Santiago, Chile. It's
the most ___high tech.___ city
                    8
I've visited. It's very modern, and there are
Internet cafés and people using new cell
phones everywhere. The people are
___Open minded___. They like to
          9
talk about different ideas, opinions, and
experiences. People speak Spanish, English,
and German here.

2 Write sentences with the words in parentheses and the comparative form of
the adjectives. (+ *more*, – *less*, = *as . . . as*, ≠ *not as . . . as*).

1. (Seattle / wet + / Las Vegas)

   ___*Seattle is wetter than Las Vegas.*_____

2. (New Orleans / slow-paced + / New York)

   New Orleans is slower - paced than New York.

3. (Kyoto / expensive – / Tokyo) or isn't expensive   as expensive as Tokyo

   Kyoto is less expensive than Tokyo

4. (Small cities / usually / dangerous ≠ / big cities)

   Small cities are usually not as daugerus as big cities.

5. (The subway system / good + / the buses / in this city)

   The subway system is better than the buses in this city

6. (The international restaurants / bad + / the traditional restaurants / in this town)

   The international restaurants are worse tha the traditional restaurants
   in this town.

7. (Paris / famous = / New York City / for its great museums)

   Paris is famous as New York city for its great museums.

3 Complete the text with the superlative form of the words in parentheses.

Homer, Alaska, is one of my favorite cities. It's a slow-paced city,
and it's ___*the most relaxing*_____ (relaxing) city
I've ever visited. It was The least stressful
(stressful) vacation I've ever had. I had a lot of time to myself,
and I felt very calm. Homer isn't very densely populated. There
are only about 145 people per square kilometer. The mornings
are _____busiest_____ (busy) time of the day
because many people fish in the mornings. The restaurants in Homer have
some of __the more deliciours_____ (delicious) seafood in
the world. There was only one thing I didn't like. I had problems getting to
Homer. In fact, it was _____the ____ worst_____ (bad)
travel experience I've ever had! But I still think Homer is
___the best_____ (good) city in Alaska.

4 Circle the correct word(s) to complete each conversation.

1. **A:** What's _____ city in the world?

   B: I don't know, but I think it might be Bangkok. When I was there, it was very hot.

   a. hottest   b. hotter than   c. the hottest

2. **A:** What's the biggest city in the world? Is it New York City?

   B: No, many cities are _____ New York, like Tokyo or Mexico City.

   a. bigger than   b. the biggest   c. big

3. **A:** Did you know that Mumbai is _____ Tokyo?

   B: No. That's really interesting. It must have a very large population.

   a. the most densely populated   b. more densely populated than   c. the least densely populated

4. **A:** Hesperia is one of _____ cities in California.

   B: Really? Maybe I'll move there. Los Angeles is so expensive!

   a. less expensive than   b. the least expensive   c. cheaper than

5. **A:** New York is the best city in the United States!

   B: I disagree. I think Chicago is _____ New York.

   a. better than   b. the best   c. better

6. **A:** What's _____ city in the world?

   B: I think it's Seoul. I read that somewhere before.

   a. less high-tech than   b. more high-tech than   c. the most high-tech

5 Look at the chart. Then answer the questions. Use complete sentences.

India

	New Delhi	Kolkata	Mumbai
Size	1,482 square km	1,380 square km	440 square km
Population density	28,438 per square km	27,462 per square km	23,088 per square km
January average temperature	21°C	26°C	29°C
August average temperature	33°C	32°C	29°C

1. Which city is bigger – New Delhi or Kolkata? _New Delhi is bigger than Kolkata._

2. Which city is the smallest? Mumbai is the more smallers than Kolkata and ND

3. Which city is the most densely populated? New Delhi is the most densely populated.

4. Which city is warmer in January – New Delhi or Kolkata? Kolkata is more warner than New Delhi

5. Which city is the coolest in August? Mumbai is the coolerst in August.

B I'll let someone know.

1 Read the sentences and check (✓) the correct column.

	Reporting a problem	Responding to a problem
1. There's a problem with this pasta.	✓	☐
2. I'll let someone know right away.	☐	✓
3. I'm having a problem with my menu.	✓	☐
4. There seems to be a problem with our food.	✓	☐
5. I'll get someone to take care of it.	☐	✓
6. I'll have someone get on it right away.	☐	✓

2 Complete the conversations with the sentences from Exercise 1. Sometimes more than one answer is possible.

A. **Carl:** Excuse me . . .

There's a problem with this pasta.
1

Waiter: What's wrong with it?

Carl: It's cold!

Waiter: I'm sorry. I'll to take care
2
of it.
2

Carl: Thank you.

B. **Isabella:** Uh, hello . . . Can you help me?

Waiter: Of course. What's the problem?

Isabella: I Can't... Understand The menu. this lenguage.
1

Look! It's in French. I can't read it.

Waiter: I take care about it I'm speak french.
2

C. **Truong:** Excuse me . . .  I have a little problem with the menu.
1

Waiter: What is it?

Truong: Well, I asked for it an hour ago, and it's not here!

Waiter: I'm sorry. I'll have someone get on it right away
2

Travel experiences

Crossword Puzzle

1 Complete the puzzle with the correct words that complete the sentences.

Across

3. This restaurant is overrated _____ . I can't believe it got five stars. I'd give it two!

5. When I went to Seoul, I was upgraded _____ to first class!

7. Our hotel was overbooked _____ , but the manager found us a room in another hotel.

8. The museums in Spain are usually packed on the weekends. They're less crowded during the week.

9. Paul's flight to Vancouver was delayed for two hours. He worked on his laptop while he waited.

Down

1. My ticket to Australia was $3,120! I know it's expensive to fly there, but I think my ticket was over priced

2. I was guaranteed _____ a seat on the train, but when I got there, my seat was taken.

4. We got a Discounted _____ price on our airline tickets, but the hotels were expensive.

6. My visa Expired _____ last year, and I haven't gotten a new one yet.

waranty → for cars
Guaranteed → for other things.

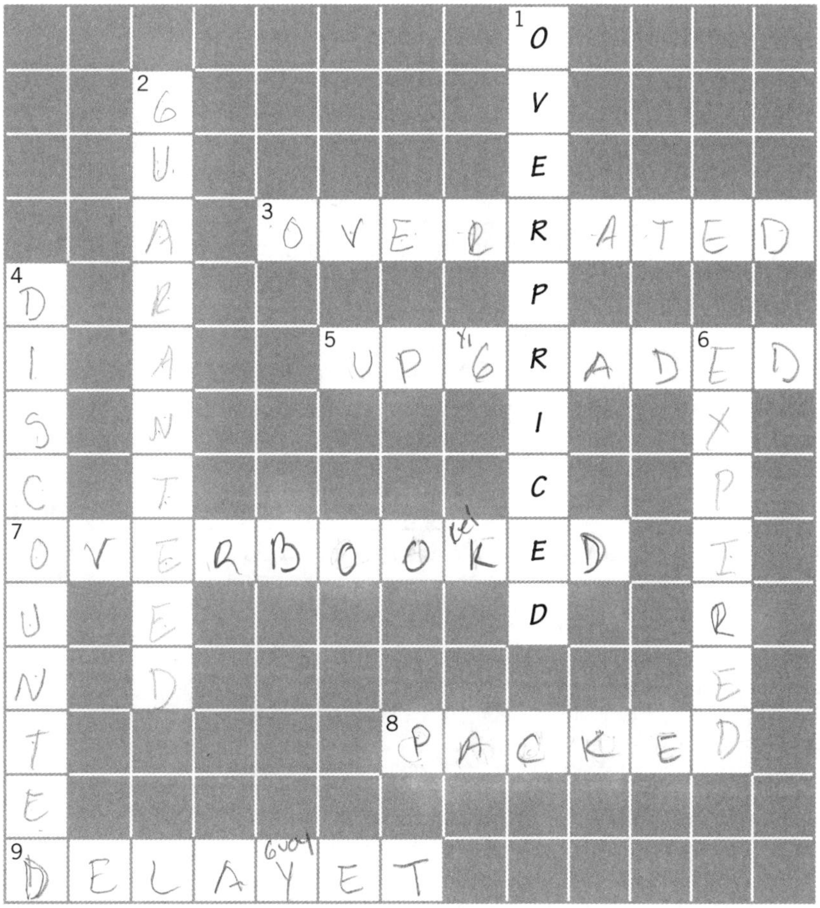

Crossword grid filled in:
1 Down: OVERPRICED
2 Down: GUARANTEED
3 Across: OVERRATED
4 Down: DISCOUNTED
5 Across: UPGRADED
6 Down: EXPIRED
7 Across: OVERBOOKED
8 Across: PACKED
9 Across: DELAYET

2 Jill is planning her trip. Put her words in the correct order to make sentences.

1. Thomas / to / me / that was priced right / told / find a ticket / .

   Thomas told me to find a ticket that was priced right.

2. advised / upgrade / at the airport / Pam / me / to / my ticket / .

   Pam Advised me to ungrade my ticket at the airoport   ~cambiar

3. a discounted ticket / Seth / reminded / to buy / me / .

   Seth reminded me to buy a discounted ticket.
                                             Adj   (NOUN)

4. let my visa / expire / not / me / to / reminded / Isabel / .

   Isabel reminded me not to let my visa expide.

5. travel alone / not / advised / My grandmother / me / to / .

   My grandmother advised me not to travel alone.

6. at night / She / to / me / take / not / the subway / warned / .

   She warned me not to take the subway at night.
                                Infinitive

3 Look at the website. Then write sentences about the underlined advice. Use the simple past of the verb in parentheses.

on → day/on Saturday
in → time of day
at → time 3:00

Hi friends! I'm going to Sydney, Australia, in June. I don't know much about Sydney. What should I pack? What should I do there? Thanks! –Heather

JaneB92: It isn't very warm in Sydney in June. <u>Take a sweater!</u>

MelvinJones: <u>See the Sydney Opera House!</u> It's amazing.

Ahmet1986: <u>Don't forget your passport!</u> Last time I traveled, I forgot mine. I missed my flight!

LingLee: Do you like wildlife? <u>Go whale watching.</u> It's incredible!

LoriTravel: <u>Don't forget an umbrella.</u> It might rain a lot while you are there.

FreddyD: Do you like nature? Well, <u>don't go to the Royal Botanic Gardens.</u> I think you should go hiking in the Blue Mountains. You can see flowers and plants in the mountains.

---

comandos and advised use not to

1. (Jane / advise)   _Jane advised her to take a sweater._

2. (Melvin / advise)   Melvin advised her to see the Sydney Opera House.

3. (Ahmet / warn)   Ahmet warned her to not forget her passport.

4. (Ling / tell)   Ling told her to go whale watching.

5. (Lori / remind)   Lori remied her not to forget an umbrella

6. (Freddy / tell)   Freddy told her not to go to the Royal Botanic Gardens.

4 Mateo and Pilar are talking on the phone and will meet at the airport. Write what they said. Use reporting verbs.

1. **Mateo:** "Pilar, use the big bags for the clothes."

   (advise) *Mateo advised Pilar to use the big bags for the clothes.*

2. **Pilar:** "Mateo, bring enough cash."

   (remind) Pilar remined Mateo to bring enough cash.

3. **Mateo:** "Pilar, remember the passports."

   (tell) Mateo told pilar to remomber the passports.

4. **Pilar:** "Mateo, don't forget to pick up our tickets."

   (remind) Pilar remiend Mateo to remied, not to forget to pick up their tickets.

5. **Mateo:** "Pilar, don't forget to lock the doors!"

   (tell) Mateo told pilar not to forget to lock the doors.

6. **Pilar:** "Mateo, don't be late to the airport!"

   (warn) Pilar warned Mateo not to be late to the airport.

5 What commands or advice have people given you in the past? Use reporting verbs with your own ideas or some of the expressions from the box.

Example: *My friend reminded me to take an umbrella on my trip to Seattle.* or
 My mother warned me not to stay out late.

be careful driving ✓	get a visa	not stay out late
call someone ✓	not forget something	remember a key to something
do your homework ✓	not go out alone	take something on vacation

1. My friend Ann advised me be careful driving in the city.
2. My Mother warned me don't call someone, how I don't know.
3. Jose called me Yesterday and remembed about do my homework
4. My friend told me be carreful with choose where do you eat.
5. My teacher advised me not to be late after work.
6. _____

D | *My town, the best town*

1 Read the travel information. Then answer the questions.

1. Which city is colder in the winter? _Moscow Russia is cooler that. Moscow Idaho_

2. Which city is warmer in the summer? _Moscow Idaho is warmer that. Moscow Russia in the summer_

Moscow, Russia
Moscow is a world-famous city with many sights to see. You'll want to spend at least a week here.

Geography and Population: Moscow is 130 meters above sea level. The population is 10.5 million with about 9,800 people per square kilometer.

Climate: The average temperature is –5°C in the winter and 16°C in the summer.

Getting around: The worst way to get around Moscow is by car. Take the subway (called the Metro) or a bus or tram instead. The Metro is usually faster.

Things to see and do: Moscow has many museums, and you can visit historic sites like the Bolshoi Theater, the most famous theater in Russia. There are also many parks. Don't forget to take a boat trip on the Moscow River!

For more information, call 1-800-555-4310 or visit www.visitmoscow/cup.com.

Moscow, Idaho, the United States
Moscow is a safe and friendly town in Idaho. All seasons are beautiful, and it's an easy getaway for a weekend trip.

Geography and Population: Moscow is 786 meters above sea level in a mountainous area. It is a small town with a population of about 23,000 and about 1,440 people per square kilometer.

Climate: The average temperature in the winter is 2°C, and in summer it is 18°C.

Getting around: The best way to get around in Moscow is to drive. You can also call the Dial-A-Ride bus company to pick you up and take you where you want to go.

Things to see and do: In the summer, Moscow is a great place to hike and ride bikes. In the winter, you can ski or ride snowmobiles. Every February, Moscow hosts a jazz festival.

For more information, call 1-866-555-6000 or visit www.travelmoscowus/cup.com.

2 Read the travel information again. Then read the sentences and write where each person went. Write *Russia* or *the United States.*

1. Susan went to the city that is higher above sea level.   _the United States_

2. Carlos went to the city that has fewer people.   _____

3. Ji Sung and Lilly took the subway around the city.   _Moscow, Russia_

4. Bianca went to a concert in a famous theater.   _____

5. Dan and Ken went to a music festival in February.   _the U.S._

6. Marcia and Mel took a boat trip on a river.   _Moscow, Russia_

The way we are

A *Who are you?*

[handwritten notes:] Adjetivo → Primero | habits → NOUN

[handwritten notes:] annoying = Molestar habits | deasive - Adj.

[handwritten note:] Adjetive describe people

1 Put the letters in the correct order to make words for character traits.

1. y o l a l — *loyal*
2. c e g r e e n t i — *energetic*
3. a i l d t e i i s c — *idealistic*
4. a l l g i o c — *Logical*
5. d u u s o i s t — *studious*
6. v c i e p t m i o t e — *competitive*
7. e a t m i a i i g n v — *imagnative = creative*
8. n n d d e e i p n e t — *independent*
9. r s u e b l l e i o — *rebellious*

2 Daisuke is going to meet Yumiko's family. Complete the conversation with words for character traits.

Daisuke: So, Yumiko, what is your family like?

Yumiko: Well, my parents are great. They're very _____ *loyal* _____ *[handwritten: Confiar]*. They always

support me! My older sister is an artist. She's very _____ *imaginative* _____ and has a lot of interesting ideas. She can also be very _____ *idealistic* _____. She thinks her art is going to save the world!

Daisuke: That's funny! What's your younger sister like?

Yumiko: She's great, too, but we're very _____ *competitive / independent* _____. I'm only a year older than she is. We both want to be the best player on our soccer team.

Daisuke: My brother and I are like that, too, especially with math. We're both _____ *Logical* _____ when we make decisions, too. But he's more _____ *studious* _____ than I am. I don't spend very much time studying.

Yumiko: I know! Maybe that's why you're always so _____ *energetic* _____! I never have energy at school because I stay up so late studying.

Daisuke: Anyway, tell me about your brother. What's he like?

Yumiko: He's nice, but he's very _____ *independent / competitive* _____. He's 21, and he doesn't do a lot with the family now. When he was younger, he was pretty _____ *rebellious* _____ and didn't want to follow the rules.

3 Complete the sentences with *who* or *which*.

1. Danielle is the kind of person _____ *who* _____ likes to be with her family.

2. Her parents are people ____ who ____ are very energetic.

3. They took a vacation ____ which ____ was very adventurous.

4. Danielle has a brother ____ who ____ is pretty rebellious.

5. She has a sister ____ who ____ is sensitive and quiet.

6. Her sister has a job ____ which ____ is difficult.

7. She works in an office ____ which ____ is often busy.

8. Danielle has a lot of friends ____ who ____ enjoy coming to her house.

4 Rewrite the sentences about Lea and Omar. Change *that* to *who* or *which*.

1. Lea and Omar have a house that is near the ocean.

   Lea and Omar have a house which is near the ocean.

2. Lea is someone that loves the ocean.

   Lea is someone who loves the ocean.

3. But Omar is the kind of person that doesn't like the water.

   But Omar is the kind of person who doesn't like the water.

4. They have a boat that he never uses.

   They have a boat which he never uses

5. Omar is a person that likes to play golf.

   Omar is a person who likes to play golf

6. Lea and Omar are people that don't always do things together.

   Lea and Omar are people who don't always do thing together

5 Read the text and look at the underlined pronouns. Cross out the pronouns that are optional.

My friend Paul is a person who other students want to work with. He has personality traits that people like. For example, he's the kind of student that usually knows the answers to the teacher's questions, and he's someone who always finishes his work. He's also a person who doesn't mind helping his classmates with their work.

Outside of class, Paul is a person who is a good friend. People say he's a friend that they can talk to. Paul is also the kind of person who is interested in a lot of things. He's a great musician. The instrument that he plays best is the guitar, but he plays the piano, too. He's the kind of musician that I want to be!

6 Check (✓) TWO phrases that can complete each sentence.

which and that for things.
Who. for people

1. Burak has imaginative ideas . . .

   ☑ that are hard to understand.

   ☑ which are useful for his job.

   ☐ who is also logical.

2. My parents are energetic people . . .

   ☑ that like adventure.

   ☐ are idealistic.

   ☑ who do many interesting things.

3. Penelope is a person . . .

   ☑ teachers like.

   ☐ is my best friend.

   ☑ who sings really well.

4. TSmart is a new cell phone . . .

   ☑ that I have to have.

   Which ☑ has a small camera.

   ☐ people are buying. → *cosa*

5. Chicago is a city . . .

   ☑ people travel to for fun.

   ☑ that gets a lot of snow.

   ☐ who is very windy.

6. I have a lot of friends . . .

   ☑ who are loyal.

   ☑ want to be musicians.

   ☑ that like to be independent.

That → que People
Who → Quien People

which → El cual Cosas

7 Complete the sentences with your own ideas. Use *who*, *which*, or *that*.

Example: I like cities __*that are exciting*__ . or I like cities __*which are small and quiet*__ .

1. I like cities __Which are cleaning and Quiety__ .

2. I dislike people __Who are impolite and don't respect others.__

3. I want a job __Which can I have off Weekens__ .

4. A loyal person is someone __Who is very Polite and Wisdow.__ .

B Sorry, but can I ask something?

Complete the conversation with the correct words.

Paulo: Listen to this. This article says your favorite color says a lot about your personality.

Amelia: Really? What does it say?

Paulo: Well, first tell me your favorite color.

Amelia: It's yellow.

Paulo: OK, it says you are idealistic. It also says . . .

Amelia: S*orry* ___ , but c*an* ___ I ask s*omething* ___ ?
        (1)   (1)   (1)

Paulo: Y*es* ___ , of c*ourse* ___ .
       (2)   (2)

Amelia: What does it mean by idealistic?

Paulo: You know, you're determined to make good things happen.

Amelia: Oh, OK. What else does it say?

Paulo: It says you are good at making plans, but you're often not energetic enough to do them. And it says . . .

Amelia: B*efore* ___ you g*oing* ___ on, could I a*ask* ___ something?
        (3)   (3)   (3)

Paulo: OK. S*ure* ___ .
        (4)

Amelia: What magazine is this from? It sounds kind of crazy.

Paulo: It's a psychology magazine. Let me tell you more. It says . . .

Amelia: I'm sorry, b*ut* ___ could I ask o*some/one t*ing* ___ ?
         (5)   (5)   (5)

Paulo: You mean, one more thing? Sure. G*go* ___ a*head* ___ .
                          (6)   (6)

Amelia: What's the name of the magazine?

Paulo: *Modern Psychology*. OK, now let me finish. It says you are logical and you like to know the facts. Now, doesn't that sound like you?

Amelia: Well, yes, but . . .

Wishing for change

1 Label each picture with a sentence made from the correct phrase from the box.

balance work and play ✓	find time to relax	✓live within a budget
be more organized ✓	✓lead a healthier lifestyle	✓manage time better

1. *He needs to manage time better.*

2. Live within a budget

3. lead a healthier lifestyle

4. be more organized

5. balance work and Play

6. find time to relax.

2 Answer the questions with your own information.

Example: _I try to do something fun for an hour every day after work._

1. How do you balance work and play?

   I try made time in the day after work.

2. Do you manage your time well? How could you manage your time better?

   I could more organized

3. Do you usually live within your budget? How could you save more money?

   I do with my budget. Don't spelling in necesary things.

4. Do you find time to relax during the week? What's your favorite way to relax?

   _____

5. Are you more organized at work or at home? What could you do to be more organized?

   _____

6. Do you lead a healthy lifestyle? What could you do to be healthier?

   _____

3 Match each situation with the correct wish.

at = time —— seasons, Months
in = specific time of day
on = day
_   holidays_
_   special days._

wish + Verb in Past tense

1. I can't find anything in my office! __f__

2. I can't go to the concert with you. __a__

3. I'm really thirsty. __d__

4. I never feel like exercising. __b__

5. I don't understand how this puzzle works. __h__

6. I really like music. __g__

7. I only got 34% on my history test. __e__

8. I got so angry when we lost the soccer game. __c__

a. I wish I didn't have plans on Friday.

b. I wish I were more energetic.

c. I wish I weren't so competitive.

d. I wish I had a glass of water.

e. I wish I could take it again.

f. I wish I could be more organized.

g. I wish I could play an instrument.

h. I wish I were more logical.

4 Circle the correct word to complete each wish.

Top Ten Wishes

What do you wish for? We took a survey and here are
the top results. Have you ever said any of these things?

1. "I wish I **travel** / (could travel) around
   the world."

2. "I wish (I **had**) / **have** a new car."

3. "I wish (I **were**) / **am** rich."

4. "I wish I **not have** / (**didn't have** to) work."

5. "I wish I (**weren't**) / **were** so stressed."

6. "I wish I **can see** / (**could see**) my future."

7. "I wish I **live** / (**lived**) within a budget."

8. "I wish I **could lost** / **could lose** weight."

9. "I wish I (**were**) / **are** healthier."

10. "I wish I (**didn't spend**) / **don't spend**
    so much money."

5 Read the sentences. Write wishes with the opposite information.

1. I'm not imaginative. *I wish I were imaginative.*

2. My sister is extremely talkative. *I wish my sister weren't* so talkative .

3. My travel budget is small. I wish my travel budget wasn't small or was bigger

4. I'm not studious. ~was~ I wish I were studious. or more studious.

5. My soccer team isn't competitive. I wish My soccer team was more competitive

6. I'm always busy on weekends. I wish I weren't always busy on weekends.

6 Read the sentences. Write complete sentences with your own information.

Example: *I wish I could read fast.*

1. Write two things you wish you could do.

   I wish I could speak English better.
   I wish I could have vacation right now.

2. Write two things you wish you had.

   I wish I had time for go to my country
   I wish I had to visit in Arizona el gran canon

3. Write two personality traits you wish you had or didn't have.

   I wish I was more happier.

D Alternative therapies

1 Read the text. What is the name of the job for a person who uses music to help people?

_____

Music Heals

Music therapy is using music to help people with a variety of problems. For example, it can help people with communication and speech problems speak better. It can help people with memory problems remember things from their past. Music therapy can also help people manage stress and be more relaxed. It can even make people with bad pain feel better.

In music therapy, a music therapist works with one person alone or with small groups. The therapist meets with the person and does tests to find out what the problem is and what the person can do with music. Then the therapist decides what kind of music therapy to use. Some people sing, and others might compose music, but a person doesn't need to know about music to be helped by music therapy. There are options such as listening to music and dancing to music. Research shows that these activities are good for the body and for the mind.

Homes that take care of elderly people often have music therapy programs. The programs help the elderly be more energetic and also help with memory problems. Some hospitals have music therapy for patients who are in a lot of pain. Music can affect a part of the brain that reduces pain.

Trevor Gibbons is one example of a person who was helped by music therapy. In 2000, he was putting in windows on the fourth floor of a building when he fell. He was in the hospital for over a year. He was in a lot of pain, and he couldn't talk. He went from the hospital to a rehabilitation center that has a music therapy program, and a music therapist worked with him for several years. He could sing more easily than he could talk. Trevor says that music also helped him manage loneliness, sadness, and pain after he was hurt. Music and the music therapist inspired him, and he has written and sung many songs. He has even recorded CDs and performed at Lincoln Center in New York.

2 Read the text again. Then write T (true), F (false), or NI (no information).

1. Music therapy can help people with many different problems. ___T___

2. You do not have to be good at music to benefit from music therapy. ___T___

3. Music therapy is only for very old people. ___F___

4. Music therapy didn't help Trevor with his pain. ___F___

5. It took Trevor five years to get better. ___F___

New ways of thinking

A Inventions

1 Put the letters in the correct order to make adjectives. Then write the negative forms with *in-* or *un-*.

1. t n c e n o e v i n   *convenient*   *inconvenient*
2. e n i c t o n n a l v o   conventional   unconventional
3. f s i i a n c n i t g   significant   insignificant
4. g i n v i m t a i a e   imaginative   unimaginative
5. i c r e v a e t   creative   increative
6. u l c u c e f s s s   successful   unsuccessful
7. v e c f e i f e t   effective   ineffective
8. v e e f u t l n   eventful   uneventful

2 3 6 4 5

2 Complete the text with the word in parentheses or its negative form.

Ansafone

Today, people think answering machines are _____*inconvenient*_____
(convenient) because they are used to voice mail. But when Willy Müller
made the first automatic answering machine in 1935, it was a
_____*significant*_____ (significant) invention. In 1960, the Ansafone,
invented by Dr. Kazuo Hashimoto, was the first
_____successful_____ (successful) answering machine sold in the
U.S. It was followed by the PhoneMate in the 1970s. However, many of
these early answering machines were _____inefective_____ (effective) because they
were so big and heavy! Then a man named Gordon Matthews changed everything.
Matthews was an _____imaginative_____ (imaginative) man who looked at things in new
and _____unconventional_____ (conventional) ways. In 1979, he started VMX, the company
that made the first voice mail system. Voice mail is _____effective_____ (effective)
because you can listen to your messages using your phone. The system is more
_____convenient_____ (convenient) than an answering machine.

3 Put the words in the correct order to make sentences.

Handwritten note top right:
So - very + Adjective
Such -
(a/an) + adjective
that - to show a result

1. great / a / is / designer / My sister / such / .

   My sister is such a great designer.

2. creative / She / so / is / .   Adj.

   She is so creative.

3. Her / are / interesting / ideas / so / .   Adj.

   Her ideas are so interesting.

4. She / she decided to open / that / imaginative / so / is / her own store / .

   She is so imaginative that she decided to open her own store.

5. online store / good / a / such / idea / was / Her / .

   Her online store was a such a good idea.

6. It / successful / her other job / that / she quit / was / so / .

   it was so successful, that she quit her other job.

7. ten people working for her / is / a big company / that / she has / such / Now it / .

   She has ten people working for her such a big that is a big company. Now it. such

8. She / I / hardly ever see her / that / busy / so / is / .

   She is so busy that I hardly ever see here.

4 Complete the conversation with *so* or *such*.

Dennis: Hey, Laila. Did you see that list of cool ideas for cell phones on the Internet the other day? It was _____**such**_____ (an) amazing list.
1

Laila: No, I didn't see it.

Dennis: Well, some of the ideas were _____**So**_____ creative, and there was _____**Such**_____ (a) cool picture of one of them, too.
2   3

Laila: Tell me about it.

Dennis: Well, it was _____**Such**_____ (a) great idea. It was a cell phone that is only five square centimeters.
4

Laila: That's _____**So**_____ small!
5

Dennis: Yes, it is. But it opens and gets bigger! It was _____**such**_____ an imaginative idea that the inventor won an award for it.
6

Laila: Wow. I love new inventions. The list sounds _____**So**_____ interesting . . . What's the website?
7

5 Rewrite the sentences with *so* or *such* in the correct position.

1. Wow! That salesman is enthusiastic about the Easy Broom.

   Wow! That salesman is so enthusiastic about
   the Easy Broom.

2. But it looks like an ineffective product!

   But it looks like such an ineffective product

3. The inventor's idea is unimaginative.

   The inventor's idea is so unimaginative.

4. His design is conventional.

   His design is so conventional

5. He'll have a difficult time getting people to buy it.

   He'll have such a difficult time getting people to buy it.

6 What do you think of the invention in Exercise 5? Write your own opinion with some of the words in the box. Use *so* or *such*.

convenient / inconvenient	design
creative / uncreative	idea
significant / insignificant	invention

Example: _It's so creative, but it's such an insignificant invention._

_____

7 Make one sentence. Use *so . . . that* or *such . . . that*.

1. That new phone is popular. There aren't any left in the store.

   That new phone is so popular that there aren't any left in the store.

2. Daniel is creative. He won an award for his idea.

   Daniel is so creative, that he won an award for his ideas

3. Eva is a successful businessperson. She got two promotions this year.

   Eva is such a successful businessperson that she got two promotions this year.

4. That new car is cheap. I might be able to buy it.

   that new car is so cheap that I might be able to buy it.

5. The Internet is a great invention. People all over the world are using it.

   the Internet is such a great invention, that people all over the world are using it.

Got any suggestions?

Read the pairs of questions and responses. Complete each conversation with the correct pair.

Do you have any ideas? One idea could be to invite her.	Got any ideas? One solution might be to keep it in the refrigerator.	✓Got any suggestions? Something we could try is to put them on top of each other.

A. Hee Jin: You have such a big book collection!

Debbie: I know. There isn't room for all of the books on my bookshelf.

Got any suggestions?
1

Hee Jin: Something we could try is to
2
put them on top of each other.
2

Debbie: What do you mean?

Hee Jin: You know, instead of standing them up, put them on each other, like this.

Debbie: Oh, I see. Good idea.

B. Lydia: Hey, my cell phone isn't working.

Josh: Oh, no. What are you going to do?

Lydia: Hmm . . . I don't know. Do you have any ideas?
1

Josh: One solution might be to keep it in the refrigerator. fridge freezer
2

Lydia: That's a weird idea. Why?

Josh: Well, it really works. But it only keeps the phone working for a while. You'll probably have to get a new one soon.

C. Mario: Hey, do you want to go to a concert on Friday?

Hank: Yes! But I can't. I have plans with Jill.

Mario: But it's our favorite band . . . The Pines.

Hank: Oh, no! I have to go. But what about Jill?

Got any ideas?
1

Mario: One idea could be to invite her.
2

Hank: That's a good idea. I think she'll like the band, too. Thanks!

Accidental inventions

(tall) such + a /an + adj
(very) so + Adv.

1 Circle the correct words to complete the texts.

Something New to Eat!

Noun
The (invention) / invented of the ice cream cone was an accident!
1   *—Verb*

It was invention / (invented) in 1904 at the World's Fair in
p   2

St. Louis, Missouri. Arnold Fornachou's ice cream stand was such
Noun   *Verb*

a (success) / succeeded at the fair that he ran out of dishes. Next
3

to Arnold, Ernest Hamwi was selling waffles – a flat type of cake.

When Arnold ran out of dishes, Ernest rolled one of his waffles

and creation / (created) a dish. Ernest put the ice cream in the
4

waffle. This (innovation) / innovated became the ice cream cone!
5

After the fair, Ernest Hamwi development / (developed) a new company that sold ice
6

cream in waffle cones. His company success / (succeeded). The (design) / designed has
7   8

changed over the years, but waffle cones are still popular.

A New Color

cambia de color

In 1856, William Perkin was a young scientist. He introduction / (introduced) a new
9

dye to the world – by accident! Dyes are used to change the color of cloth. Perkin

was trying to make a new medicine, but by accident he made a beautiful purple

dye. Perkin's dye was the first that was not made from a plant or an animal. It was

an (improvement) / improved over other dyes because it was less expensive and
10

easier to make. The dye (proved) / proof to be successful. Perkin's (creation) / created
11   12

was also a new color. He called it *mauve*.

2 Answer the questions with your own information.

Example: __I designed a tree house for my yard. My parents helped me make it.__

1. Have you ever designed anything? What was it? __I never have been designed anything.__

2. What's your biggest success in life? _____

3. What do you think is the best invention in the past ten years? _____

4. Have you ever been asked for proof of who you are? When? _____

3 Circle the correct phrase to complete each sentence.

1. The crossword puzzle _____ by Arthur Wynne in 1913.

   a. is invented   (b.) was invented   c. have been invented

2. At first, Arthur's puzzle _____ a word-cross.

   a. is called   (b.) was called   c. have been called

3. Crossword puzzles _____ in newspapers for about 100 years.

   a. is printed   b. was printed   (c.) have been printed

(4.) The first crossword puzzle book _____ in 1924.

   a. is made   (b.) was made   c. have been made

5. Today, some crossword puzzles _____ online.

   (a.) are done   b. were done   c. have been done

6. *The New York Times* newspaper _____ for its crossword puzzles. Many people
   buy the newspaper because they want to do the crossword puzzle.

   (a.) is known   b. was known   c. were known

Handwritten margin notes:
Passive Past of the Participle
The lightbulb (was invented)
by thomas Edison.
was invented in 1913
Past Participle
At first was called.
Active
[Thomas Edison]
invented the ligthbulb

Handwritten labels: Active (by sentence 1b), Passive (by sentence 2b), Passive (by 2), Present Perfect (by sentence 3/4)

4 Complete the text with the correct form of the verb in parentheses. Use the passive form
of the simple present, simple past, or present perfect.

www.history/inventions/cup.com

Fun facts about the zipper

- The zipper _was invented_ (invent) in 1913 by Gideon Sundback.
  ₁
- It _was called_ (call) the "Hookless Fastener" for over ten years.
  ₂
  Then, in 1925, it _was named_ (name) the zipper. A person using a
  ₃
  zipper on a boot said "zip" because that was the sound that it made. It
  has been called (call) the zipper ever since that time.
  ₄
- Zippers _are used_ (use) today on all types of clothing. In the past,
  ₅
  they _were used_ (use) on clothing for people in World War I.
  ₆
- Zippers _have been made_ (made) of metal since 1913. Today, many of
  ₇
  them _are made_ (made) of plastic.
  ₈
- Pants with zippers _have been worn_ (wear) by men for many years, and
  ₉
  they still wear them today. But women's clothing did not have zippers until about 1930.
  Then zippers _were put_ (put) on women's clothing, too.
  ₁₀

5 Write sentences with the words in parentheses and the passive form of the simple present, simple past, or present perfect.

[handwritten notes top right: (is) used P.P / (was) used P.P. / (have been) used P.P]

windshield

windshield wiper

1. (Today, / car windshields / make / of glass)

   Today, car windshields are made of glass.

2. (Windshield wipers / invent / in 1905 by Mary Anderson)

   Windshield wipers were invented in 1905 by Mary Anderson.

3. (The design of windshield wipers / improve / since 1905)

   The design of windshield wipers has been improved since 1905

4. (Windshield wipers / put / on the front of cars / for many years)

   Windshield wipers have been put on the front of cars for many years.

5. (Today, / windshield wipers / find / on the front and the back of some cars)

   Today, windshield wipers are found on the front and the back of some cars.
   Present P.P

6 Rewrite the sentences in the passive form.

1. Alexander Graham Bell invented the telephone.
   Active

   The telephone was invented by Alexander Graham Bell.

2. People have used telephones since 1876.

   telephones since 1876 have been used by People

3. Someone made the first cell phone call in 1973.

   The first cell phone call was made in 1973, by Someone

4. 1.4 billion people used cell phones in 2003.

   Cell phone in 2003, were used by 1.4 billion people.

5. Over 4.6 billion people use cell phones today.

   Cell phones today are used Over 4.6 billion people

6. People develop new kinds of cell phones every year.

   New Kinds of cell phones are developed every year.
   Every year, new kind of cell phone are developed

Making life easier

1 Read the text. Then number the items in the order they were invented.

___3___ refrigerator   _____ vacuum cleaner   ___1___ sewing machine   _____ microwave

Remember when?

Many inventions make life easier. We forget what life was like before these things were invented. Here are some inventions that made life easier at home.

The Refrigerator   The refrigerator was invented in 1876 by Carl von Linde. Before that, many people had icehouses. They bought ice and kept it in a building outside of the house. People put their food in the icehouse to keep it cold and fresh. But the icehouse didn't keep things fresh for long. The refrigerator makes keeping food fresh much easier.

The Vacuum Cleaner   Before the vacuum cleaner was invented, people used brooms to clean their floors. The first vacuum cleaner was invented in 1860 by Daniel Hess, but it was very heavy. One person had to move the base of the machine, and another person moved the part that picked up dirt and dust. Many people improved Hess's design, but vacuum cleaners were still expensive and heavy. In 1908, James Spangler made an effective and less expensive vacuum cleaner. After that, people started buying them for their homes.

The Sewing Machine   Imagine not being able to buy clothing in a store! Before the invention of the sewing machine, everyone made their clothing at home by hand. Many people tried to invent a sewing machine in the 1800s, and Elias Howe invented the first useful sewing machine in 1846. Others followed. The invention of the sewing machine allowed companies to make large amounts of clothing that could be sold in stores.

The Microwave   The microwave was invented by accident. Percy Spencer was working with radar waves at his job. The radar waves cooked a candy bar that was in his pocket! This gave him an idea, and he created the microwave oven in 1945. The first microwave was called the Radar Range. It was used mostly in restaurants.

2 Read the text again. Then rewrite the sentences to correct the underlined mistakes.

1. Carl von Linde invented the microwave.   *Carl von Linde invented the refrigerator.*

2. You needed only one person to use the first vacuum cleaner.
   You needed two people to used the fist vacuum cleaner.
   You needed One person for moved the bas and another persone moved The part that picked up dirt and dust.

3. Daniel Hess made a cheaper vacuum cleaner. Jaims spangler made an effective and less expensive vacuum.
   Jan

4. Before sewing machines were invented, people made their clothes in stores.
   → Everyone made their clothing at home by hand.

5. The first microwave was called the Percy Spencer Oven. The first microwave was called the Radar Range

Lessons in life

A *Why did I do that?*

Prefixes (beginning of the word)
Suffixes (end)
-ly
-tion
-ed (pensar otra vez)

1 Write new words with the correct prefixes. Add *dis-*, *mis-*, or *re-*. *un*

Juzgar mal

1. judge   _**misjudge**_   4. think   _rethink_   *(pensar otra vez)*

2. continue   _discontinue_   5. regard   _disregard_   *(igrorar)* _ignore_   *Ingorar*

3. spell   _misspell_   6. make   _remake_   *(rehacer)*

2 Complete the conversations. Use the words in the box with the correct prefixes: *dis-*, *mis-*, or *re-*.

dis | agree   *re* consider   *re* do   *dis* ✓like   *mis* pronounce   *mis* understand

Pronunciar mal

A.   **Carla:** Let's go to a Tom's Hamburgers for lunch.

    Dae Ho: I'd rather not. I _____**dislike**_____₁
red meat.

    Carla: Really? Please _reconsider_₂ *(rethink)*.
They have good salads there, too.

    Dae Ho: Oh, OK. We can go to Tom's, then.

B.   **Mary:** This painting is beautiful!

    Jill: I _disagree_₁ *(No agreen)*. I think it's ugly!

C.   **Claire:** I'm sorry. I didn't mean to _mispronounce_₁ your name.

    Sean: That's OK. It's hard to say. You say, "Shawn," but it's spelled S-E-A-N.

D. **Mr. Ito:** Did you _misunderstand_₁ the directions, Kelly? Your homework
is completely wrong.

    Kelly: I understood the directions, but I think I did the wrong page.
Can I _redo_₂ it?

    Mr. Ito: OK. Give it to me tomorrow.

3 Complete the conversation with the past perfect of the verbs in parentheses.

Sheila: How was the movie with Amanda last night, Felipe?

Felipe: The movie was OK, but I was really embarrassed. I started to pay for the movie, but I realized I _had left_ (leave) my money at home.

Sheila: So, did Amanda pay for the movie?

Felipe: Yes, she did. I _had also forgotten_ (also / forget) to turn off my cell phone before we went into the theater. My mom called!

Sheila: Did you answer it?

Felipe: Yes. The movie _had not started yet_ (not start / yet), so I went outside. When I got back, it _had already begun_ (already / begin).

Sheila: Oh, no!

Felipe: Then I realized I _had not brought_ (not bring) my glasses, so we moved to the front of the theater. It was really uncomfortable.

Sheila: I'm sure Amanda didn't mind.

Felipe: I don't know. I emailed her. I checked an hour ago and she _had not responeded yet_ (not respond / yet).
or _responeded yet_

4 Write sentences with the words in parentheses. Tell what Kim *had done* and *had not done* by the time the guests arrived for her party. Use the past perfect with *yet* or *already*.

1. (Kim / not take out / the garbage) *Kim hadn't taken out the garbage yet.*
2. (she / wipe off / the kitchen counters) *She had already wiped off the kitchen counters*
3. (she / wash / the dishes) She had washed the dishes.
4. (she / do / the laundry) She had done the laundry
5. (she / not hang up / the clothes) She hadn't hung up the clothes yet
6. (she / go / grocery shopping) She had gone grocery shopping
7. (she / not put away / groceries) She hadn't put away groceries yet
8. (she / not make / the pizza) She hadn't made the pizza yet.

5 Write sentences with the words in the chart. Use the simple past and the past perfect in each sentence.

had + P.P.

Happened first	Happened second
1. Ms. Jones / mispronounce / my name	she / ask / me how to spell it
2. she / know / his brother for two years	Sandra / meet / Jake
3. Jackie / call / her dad ten times	she / heard his message / on her voice mail
4. we / already / ask / him a lot of questions	we / agree / to John's idea
5. he / think about it / carefully	Hai / disregard / Tim's advice
6. the company / borrow / a lot of money	it / close

1. _Ms. Jones had mispronounced my name_

   before _she asked me how to spell it_ .

2. By the time _Sandra met Jake_ *Simple Past* ,
   She had *not* Known, his brother for two years. *Past Perfect*

3. Jackie had called her dad ten times
   before She heared his message on her voice mail

4. By the time We agreed to John's idea. We
   had already ask him a lot of questions.

5. Before Hai disregarded Tim's advise.
   He had already thought about it.

6. The Company had borrowed a lot of
   money before it closed .

mispronounce – mispronounced, misspell – misspelled.

6 Write sentences with your own information. Use the past perfect and simple past.

Example: _I'd taken English classes before I began this class._ or
I hadn't taken English classes before I began this class.

1. (not) take English classes / before / begin this class
   I had taken English classes before, I began this class

2. (not) thought about other cultures / before / start studying English
   I hadn't thought about other cultures before, I started studying English.

3. (not) often misspelled English words / before / take this class
   I hadn't often misspelled English words before I took, this class.

4. (not) mispronounced a lot of English words / before / practice them in this class
   I hadn't mispronounced, a lot of English words before I practiced Them in this class.

5. (not) read my email / by the time / do my homework last night
   I hadn't read my email by the time I did my homework last night.

B *I'm sure you'll do fine.*

1 Complete the conversation with the sentences from the box.

> ⌐ Do you have a list of their names?
> ✓ Hi, Tia. How are you?
> ⌐ I know Mandarin. I can help you.
> ⌐ I'm pretty nervous about it.
>   Really? That would be great!
> ⌐ Well, I don't want to mispronounce their names.
>   I'm sure you'll do fine tomorrow.

Chao: _Hi, Tia. How are you?_

Tia: I'm OK, I guess. But people are coming to my office tomorrow from China, and
I'm pretty nervous about it   nervous
                                                             anxious

Chao: Really? Why?   I have stressed

Tia: _I don't want to mispronounce their names_

Chao: _Do you have a list of their names?_

Tia: Yes, I do. Why?

Chao: _I know Mandarin. I can help you_

Tia: _Really? That would be great._

Chao: We'll practice tonight, and _I'm sure you'll do fine tomorrow._

2 Complete the conversations with phrases for expressing worry and for reassuring someone.

A. **John:** I have to meet Sue's parents tomorrow, and I'm kind of
worried about it .
        1

Mark: I'm _sorry about it_ .
                    2

B. Mi Yon: I have an English test tomorrow, and I'm a little
anxious .
       1

Brenda: _Do will be fine_ .
             2
Evrything will be OK. .
             3

60 **Unit 8** Lesson B

C What if . . . ?

1 Complete the chart with *get* or *make* and the correct phrases from the box.

esfuerzo (handwritten above "an effort")
eliminar (handwritten above box, right)
hacer decision (handwritten, right)

| ✓ a big deal | an effort | mistakes | out of | rid of things |
| a fool of myself | into trouble | on my nerves | over it | up my mind |

obtener (handwritten under box)

get . . .	make . . .
	Hacer (handwritten) **make a big deal**
get into trouble	*Make a fool of myself*
get on my nerves	*Make mistakes*
get out of	*Make an affort*
get over it	*Make up my mind*
something. (handwritten) *get rid of thing*	

2 Complete the email with expressions with *get* and *make*. Use the simple present.

Subject: Oh, no!

Hi Sharon!

How are you? I'm OK, but I need some advice. I'm having a problem with my roommate. Jack _**gets on my nerves**_ a lot. First of all, he's very messy. He never ___*gets rid of things*___[1] he doesn't need. I try not to ___*make a big deal*___[2] about it, but I might have to say something. No one is perfect. We all ___*Make mistakes*___[3], but I would just like him to ___*gets an effort*___[4]. You know, try a *little*!

Oh, and he always tries to ___*gets out of*___[5] doing the chores. I wash the dishes, I take out the garbage, and I even hang up *his* clothes! I know I should try to ___*get over it*___[6] and disregard his behavior. He's a really nice person. He lent me $100 last week and said it was no problem. What's your advice? I have a hard time with decisions, and I can never ___*Make up my mind*___[7]. I don't want to say the wrong thing. What should I do?

Write soon!

Ian

3 Read the sentences. Then answer the *yes / no* questions. Use short answers.

1. If Dana had listened to her parents, she wouldn't have gotten into trouble.

   Did Dana listen to her parents? _No, she didn't._

   Did she get into trouble? _Yes, she did_

2. If Carlos had made up his mind, he would have a new car right now.

   Did Carlos make up his mind? _No, He didn't_

   Does he have a new car? _No, He doesn't._

3. If Paul had said he was sorry, Carolina would have gotten over it quickly.

   Did Paul say he was sorry? _No, He didn't._

   Is Carolina still upset? _Yes, She is._

4. Mona wouldn't have made a fool of herself if she hadn't sung so loudly at the party.

   Did Mona sing loudly? _Yes, She did._

   Did she make a fool of herself? _Yes she did._

5. Vicky would have understood the homework if she hadn't been late for class.

   Was Vicky late for class? _Yes She was._

   Did she understand the homework? _No, she didn't._

4 Circle the correct forms to complete the conversation.

I had + P.P
I would have + P.P.

Hiro: Hi, Lydia. Did you and Kyle get home OK last night?

Lydia: Not really. It took us over an hour.

Hiro: Really? Didn't you drive home?

Lydia: Well, if I **hadn't dropped** / wouldn't have dropped
my keys out the window by mistake, we
had driven / **would have driven** home.
    (1)   (2)

Hiro: Oh, no! Did you look for your keys?

Lydia: Yes, but we couldn't find them. We probably
had found / **would have found** them if it
            (3)
hadn't been / **wouldn't have been** so dark.
    (4)

Hiro: So, did you take the bus home?

Lydia: No. If we **had left** / would have left earlier, we
                    (5)
had taken / would have taken the bus. But
    (6)
it was too late, so we walked home!   pag. 79

5 Complete the story. Change the main clause of the last sentence to an *if* clause in the next sentence.

If I hadn't gone to the concert, I wouldn't have seen Julia.

1. <u>If I hadn't seen Julia</u>, she wouldn't have gotten on my nerves.

2. <u>If she hadn't</u> gotten on my nerves, I wouldn't have made a fool of myself.

3. <u>If I hadn't made a fool of myself</u>, Julia would have invited me to her party.

4. <u>If Julia had invited me</u>, I would have talked to Brenda.

5. <u>If I had talked to Brenda</u>, I would have asked her to dinner tonight.

6. <u>If I had asked her dinner tonight</u>, I wouldn't have had a boring night watching TV alone!

6 Look at each picture. Then write a third-conditional sentence about it with words from the box.

✓buy the computer	get rid of some things	⌐have room for the sofa	rain
forget her credit card	⌐go to the baseball game	✓pass the test	✓study

1. <u>If she had studied, she would have passed the test.</u> or <u>She would have passed the test if she had studied.</u>

2. <u>If they had gotten rid of sofa, they would have room for the sofa.</u>

3. <u>If she hadn't forgotten her credit card, she would have bought new computer</u>

4. <u>If it hadn't rained, they would have gone to the baseball game</u>

D A day to remember

1 Read the text. What three types of memory are mentioned?

_____   _____   _____

What will you remember?

Patricia Sanders remembers the day she met her husband perfectly. It was over 50 years ago. She remembers that it rained the day that they met in a bookstore. She remembers he was wearing a blue raincoat, and she was wearing a red dress. She even remembers what he said to her. But she can't remember what she had for lunch today.

The brain has different ways to store memories. It stores some information in short-term memory, which can only keep the information for about 30 seconds. For example, if you look up a phone number, you can store the number in your brain long enough to make the phone call. But a minute later, you might forget the number. The brain also stores information in what some people call "recent memory." This allows you to remember what you had for lunch or what you did yesterday. Important information is stored in long-term memory. Some information is stored in long-term memory after you repeat it a lot. For example, if you call the same phone number over and over again, your brain will remember it for a long time. If you read one book on a subject, you may forget a lot of it. But if you read several books and articles about the subject, you will remember the information for a lot longer. Significant events are also stored in long-term memory. So a year from now, you might forget what you had for lunch today, but you will remember the first time you met your husband or wife or got a promotion at work.

Research shows that it's natural for people to have recent memory loss as they get older. People often experience this memory loss after the age of 50. So, it's normal that Patricia remembers the day she met her husband. It's in her long-term memory. And it's normal that she can't remember what she did yesterday. Her brain's recent memory is not working as well as it used to. Some people have severe memory loss, but Patricia's problems are normal.

> **Tips to help with "recent memory" loss:**
>
> • Make a list of things you want to remember.
>
> • Take medicine at the same time every day.
>
> • Put your keys in the same place every day.
>
> • Don't make a big deal about forgetting things. Relax, be honest, and laugh about the problem.

2 Read the text again. Answer the questions.

1. What has Patricia forgotten? _*what she had for lunch today*_

2. How long can the brain store information in short-term memory? _only keep information for about 30 seconds_

3. What kind of memory stores information that is repeated often? _Phone number_

4. Which type of memory is it normal for older people to lose? _memory loss_

5. How could an older person remember to take his or her medicine? _Take medicine at the same time every day_

Can you explain it?

 A ***Everyday explanations***

1 **Add -*less* or -*ful* to the word in parentheses to complete each sentence.**

1. I just broke my cell phone. Now it's
   _____**useless**_____ (use)!

2. I got _meaningful_ ~~significativo~~ (meaning) information from
   Dr. Jacobs. I think I will be healthier if I follow her advice.

3. A lot of trees fell last night in that ___powerful___ ~~poderoso~~
   (power) windstorm.

4. Benny and Tom went bungee jumping. They're
   ___fearless___ ~~No temen~~ (fear)!

5. Laura is such a ____careless____ (care) driver. She always drives too fast.

6. Air pollution is ___harmful___ ~~Perjudical~~ (harm). It can make you sick.

7. I don't know how to help you. I feel so ___powerless___ (power).

8. Penny has a big dog, but it's ___harmless___ (harm). It won't hurt you.

9. Mr. Garcia's explanation was very ___useful___ (use). I finally
   understand algebra!

10. You can borrow my computer, but please be ___careful___ (care) with it.

11. Sue is very ___fearful___ (fear) of animals. She won't even go to a zoo!

12. That question was completely ___meaningless___ (meaning). No one knew
    how to answer it.

2 **Write your own ideas.**

1. Two things that are useful for school: ___**a computer**___ and ___notebook___
2. Two things that are harmful to the environment: ~~Perjudical~~ ___pollicions___ and
   ___imqructo___
3. Two things you should be careful doing: ___driven___ and ___swimming___
4. Two people who are fearless: _____ and _____
5. Two meaningful classes you have taken: ~~significative~~ ___Math.___ and ___sciencies___
6. Two inventions that are useful: ___Light power___ and ___cp___

3 Complete the webpage with past modals of the verbs in parentheses.

www.localmysteries/cup.com

KimKim: Last night I saw a strange light in the sky. Did anyone see it?

What could it _**have been**_ (be)? ~~1~~

DonRJ: The city might _have had_ (have) ~~2~~ some fireworks.

Rita86: Fireworks make noise. It was too quiet last night. You couldn't _have seen_ (see) fireworks. ~~3~~

QT007: I saw the light, too. I think something could _have fallen_ (fall) from an airplane. ~~4~~

CindyT: It couldn't _have come_ (come) from a plane. Look at the ~~5~~ picture . . . It's going *across* the sky, not *down*.

WhyMe: OK. KimKim must _have taken_ (take) this picture with her ~~6~~ camera open for a long time. I'm sure she's kidding!

* * *

PeteOP: Did anyone hear a strange noise on Main Street last night? I think it might _have been_ (be) a wild animal! ~~7~~

Jeff1982: You couldn't _have heard_ (hear) a wild animal, PeteOP. ~~8~~ There aren't any wild animals around here.

4 Complete the sentences with past modals. Use *must, couldn't,* or *could* and the correct form of the verb in parentheses.

1. I don't know why Patricio wasn't in class today. He _**could have been**_ (be) sick.

2. Tracey was at a concert last night, and she saw her favorite band. I'm sure she _must have had_ (have) fun!

3. Jackie _couldn't have drunk_ (drink) milk. She can't have dairy at all.

4. My sister hasn't called me all week. She usually calls me every day. I wonder if she _Could have lost_ (lose) her cell phone.

5. I've been waiting for Tonya at the airport for an hour. I'm sure her plane _Must have left_ (leave) late.

6. Marianna is really good at math. She _Couldn't have gotten_ (got) a bad grade on the test.

7. Oh, no! My mother _Must have tried_ (try) to call me. My cell phone has been off, and there's a missed call. She always calls me at this time.

5 Why wasn't Larry in class yesterday? Complete the sentences with past modals. Use *must, couldn't,* or *might* and the correct form of the phrases in the chart.

Bebe no podria – podria

Modal Verbs
_____

Should
Could
Must → Estronger
Might → NEstronger
May
Would

	Not sure	Sure
Steve	be sick	be at home
Clara	go out with friends	not stay at home
Diana	miss the bus	have a good reason
Ken	watch the baseball game on TV	forget about class
Tina	go to a job interview	need to miss class
Mr. Anderson	think there was no class	not check the class schedule

1. Steve thinks Larry __might have been sick__ .

   He __must have been at home__ because his car was there.

2. Clara thinks Larry Might have   gone out with friends.

   She says he Couldn't   have stayed at home because she went to

   his house after school, and he wasn't there.

3. Diana thinks Larry Might have missed the bus.

   She says he Could have had a good reason for not coming.

4. Ken thinks Larry Might have watched the baseball game on tv,

   He says Larry Must have forgotten about class,

5. Tina thinks Larry Might have gone to a Job interview. ?

   She says he Must n't have needed to miss class — ?

6. Mr. Anderson thinks Larry Might have thougth there was no class.

   He says Larry Couldn't have checked the class schedule

6 Look at each picture. Write what you think happened. Use past modals.

Bebe

Example: __She must have broken her arm.__

1. She must have been in the hospital. *She must have felt pain*

3. He must have missed the bus.

2. She must have felt pain in her arm.

4. He must have tired. of Waiten for the bus.

B I'm pretty sure that . . .

1 Complete the chart. Write the sentences from the box in the correct column.

> ✓ But it's likely that there is water on Mars. ~ *Probable*
> / But it's very probable that some kind of life was there. ~ *duda*
> ✓ I doubt that people ever lived on Mars.
> ─ I'm pretty sure that there used to be trees on Mars.
> It's highly unlikely that there were trees on Mars. ~ *improbable*
> / Well, it's doubtful that I would ever get the chance. ~ *dudoso*

Likely – Probable / doub – duda
very probable / unlikely – impobable
doubtful – dudoso

doubtful – duda
doubtless No duda.

Expressing probability	Expressing improbability
But it's likely that there is water on Mars.	*I doubt that people ever lived on Mars.*
But it's very probable that some kind.	It's highly unlikely that there were
I'm pretty sure that there use to be.	Well, It's doubtful that I would ever

2 Complete the conversation with the sentences from Exercise 1.

Josh: Look at this article, Brian. It says that at one time there might have been life on Mars. Do you believe that's possible?

Brian: Well, _I doubt that people ever_
lived on Mars ₁ . I mean,
scientists would have figured that out.

Josh: I agree that people couldn't have lived on Mars. But it's very probable that some kind of life was there ₂

Life on Mars?

Brian: What do you mean?

Josh: Well, you know, like plant life. I'm pretty sure that there ved to use trees on Mars.

Brian: No way! It's highly unlikely that there were trees ₃ on Mars. Scientists . . .

Josh: OK, OK. Maybe you're right. I'm pretty sure that there use to be ₅ water ₄ Mars. I think there are rivers or maybe even a lake.

Brian: Well, *maybe* in the past, but I don't think there's that much water now. . . .
Hey, would you go to Mars if you had the chance?

Josh: Well it's doubtful that I would ever get the ₆ chance. But if I did get the chance, I guess I would go!

C History's mysteries

1 Complete the news report with the words from the box.

abduction	discovery	explosion
✓disappearance	escape	theft

"Coming up tonight on PSB news in Miami . . . Our first story, from Houston, Texas, is

about the ___**disappearance**___ of Terrance Wellington, a well-known Houston
　　　　　　　　　　1

artist. His family says they haven't seen him since Tuesday morning. Next, Jamie

Sanders is in Mexico, and she'll tell you about the ___discovery___ of a new
　　　　　　　　　　　　　　　　　　　　　　　　　　　2

pyramid near Mexico City. That's exciting news because a new pyramid has not been

found in several years. In San Francisco, we have news about a big

___explosion___. People in the area say the noise was frightening and
　　3

extremely loud. Two restaurants burned. And don't miss this story . . . There was a

___theft___ in a museum in New York on Saturday. Robbers took a
　　4

painting worth 15 million dollars. We also have a local story that happened right here

in Florida. Carl Frey will tell you about a prison ___escape___. Two men
　　　　　　　　　　　　　　　　　　　　　　　　　　　　　　5

broke out of a prison in Jacksonville. Fortunately, police caught them a few hours later.

And our last story tonight is about an alien ___abduction___. Is it true or not?
　　　　　　　　　　　　　　　　　　　　　　　　　6

Dan Alvarado interviews two people in Phoenix, Arizona, who claim they were taken

aboard a UFO by aliens. All this and more after these messages."

pickpocket

Action
Theft =
robbery =
burglary

Person
thief
robber
burglar

2 Label each picture with the number and word from the correct news story in Exercise 1.

4 Theft

2 discovery

5 Escape

6 Abduction

1 disappearance

3 Explosion

3 Circle the correct words to complete the conversation.

Greg: Hi, Ahn. Do you have any idea (what) / if a total solar eclipse is?

Ahn: Sure. It's what happens when the moon is between the sun and earth.

Greg: Oh, OK. Do you know **how** / (if) that's why the sky gets black?

Ahn: Yes, it is. You can't see light from the sun because of where the moon is.

Greg: And can you tell me (how long) / what it lasts?

Ahn: Well, it depends. The shortest eclipses are usually about a minute.

Greg: Do you have any idea (how long) / how many the longest eclipse can be?

Ahn: It can be over seven minutes, but that hardly ever happens.

Greg: Do you know **how tall** / (if) solar eclipses happen every year?

Ahn: Yes, they do.

Greg: And can you tell me (how many) / if there are each year?

Ahn: There can be between two and five eclipses each year, but there can never be more than two total eclipses.

Greg: Interesting. Thanks, Ahn.

4 Write embedded *yes / no* questions with the words in parentheses. Use the simple past.

1. (Can you tell me / Zorro / be / a real person)
   Can you tell me if Zorro was a real person?

2. (Do you know / anyone / find / Amelia Earhart's plane)
   Do you know if anyone found Amelia Earhart's plane

3. (Do you have any idea / the Egyptians / build / the first pyramid)
   Do you have any idea if the Egyptians build the first pyramid.

4. (Can you tell me / people / find / an underwater pyramid in Japan)
   Can you tell me if people fund an underwater pyramid in Japan.

5. (Do you have any idea / anyone / escape / from Alcatraz prison)
   Do you have any idea if anyone escaped from Alcatraz prison.

6. (Do you know / the abduction / be / on the news)
   Do you know if the abduction was on the news.

5 Look at B's responses. Use *Can you tell me* or *Do you know* to write embedded *Wh-* questions about these famous places.

1. **A:** _Can you tell me how long the Tsing Ma Bridge is?_

   B: Yes, I can. The Tsing Ma Bridge is about 1.4 kilometers long.

2. **A:** _Do you know_ how tall is the Eiffel tower?

   B: Yes, I do. The Eiffel Tower is 324 meters tall.

3. **A:** Can you tell me people escaped from Alcatraz prison,

   B: Yes, I can. Two people escaped from Alcatraz prison.

4. **A:** Can you tell me if the Sphinx is 60 meters long?

   B: Yes, I can. The Sphinx is 60 meters long.

5. **A:** Do you know how tall is the Pyramid of the sun?

   B: Yes, I do. The Pyramid of the Sun is about 75 meters tall.

6. **A:** Do you know how many taxis Are they in New York city?

   B: Yes, I do. There are about 13,000 taxis in New York City.

6 Answer the questions with *Yes* or *No*. Add more information.

Example: _No. But I know there are over one million._ or
Yes, There are 2.5 million people in my country.

1. Do you know how many people there are in your country?

   No But I guess there are more that 80 Millions

2. Do you have any idea what the population of your city is?

   No,

3. Do you know if there are any mysteries about people or places in your country?

   No

4. Do you have any idea what famous writers are from your country?

   No

5. Do you know where famous people go for vacation in your country?

   No

D Explanations from long ago

1 Read the magazine interview. What is rongorongo? Circle the correct answer.

a. the name of a people   b. the name of a writing system   c. the name of an island

Lisa Olsen talks about rongorongo with Dr. Gomez . . .

EASTER ISLAND, in the Pacific Ocean, is famous for its large stone statues that were made hundreds of years ago. But not many people know about rongorongo. It is the name of the writing found on tablets, large pieces of wood, on Easter Island. I spoke with Dr. Ramiro Gomez about this mysterious writing system.

Q: Dr. Gomez, what is rongorongo?

A: Rongorongo is a writing system found on Easter Island. It doesn't have letters like English. It uses *glyphs*, which are pictures or symbols, to represent different things. In the 1860s, people discovered wooden tablets with the rongorongo glyphs on them. Today, there are only 21 of these tablets. The rest have disappeared.

Q: Can you tell me what the tablets say?

A: Many people have tried to figure out what the different glyphs mean. But so far, no one has figured out rongorongo completely. Some of the glyphs look like different animals in the area . . . birds, sea turtles, and fish. It also seems that some of the glyphs represent plants. We're pretty sure that one of the tablets has a calendar on it, but no one has figured out exactly how the calendar works.

Q: Do you know how and when the tablets were made?

A: We know that the glyphs were carved with shark's teeth. We also know that they are very old. Researchers say they might have been made in the late 1600s.

Q: If we can't read the language, are the tablets useless?

A: Definitely not. They still tell us a lot about the people who made them. For example, they had their own written language and wanted to record their history.

Q: Is there more to learn from the tablets?

A: Yes, there is. People will be studying rongorongo for many years. Hopefully, someone will solve the mystery of what is on the tablets.

2 Read the interview again. Write T (true), F (false), or NI (no information).

1. Rongorongo has 21 ~~letters.~~ →tablets _F_
2. Some of the symbols in rongorongo look like animals. __T__
3. There are sea turtles near Easter Island. __NI__
4. The symbols were made with shark's teeth. __T__
5. Rongorongo doesn't tell us anything. __F__
6. Dr. Gomez will continue researching rongorongo. __NI__

Perspectives

A A traffic accident

1 **Put the words in the correct order to make sentences.**

1. Brenda / care / her sister's cat / takes / on weekends / of / .

   Brenda takes care of her sister's cat
   on weekends.

2. with / up / comes / great ideas / Larry / .

   Larry comes up with
   great ideas.

3. doesn't put / send text messages in class / students / Ms. Nelson / up / with / who / .

   Ms. Nelson ~~students~~ doesn't put up with who send text messages in class.
   No soportan *students*

4. friends / with / up / on the Internet / catches / Paulina / . Paulina catches up on the internet with friends.

   Paulina catches up with friends on the internet.

5. going through / shouldn't get / Drivers / away with / a red light / through a red light.

   Drivers shouldn't get ~~going~~ through away with a red light.
   —away with going

6. looks / to / Arturo / his favorite musician / up / .
   Admirar
   Arturo looks up to his favorite musician.

7. along / all of his classmates / gets / Omar / with / .
   llevarse bien
   Omar gets along with all of his classmates.

8. to their trip / forward / Sandra and Mike / are looking / to Peru / .
   esperar
   Sandra and Mike are looking forward to their trip to peru.

2 **Write sentences with your own information.**

*Example: **I get along with my sister and my friend Josh.***

1. Two people you get along with: I get along with my neighbords.
   llevarse bien
2. Two characteristics you can't put up with: I don't put up people impolite.
   Soportar
3. One person you look up to: I look up people nice with everybody
   Admirar
4. Two things you're looking forward to: I looking forward a new job and finish
   esperar   to pay my debts.

3 Circle the correct verb form to complete each sentence.

1. **Kendra:** "I saw an accident on Main Street."

   Kendra said that she _____ an accident on Main Street.

   a. sees   b. has seen   (c.) had seen

2. **Jack:** "I look up to my grandfather."

   Jack told me he _____ to his grandfather.

   a. will look up   (b.) looked up   c. would look up

3. **Shan:** "I will take care of my brother's daughter."

   Shan said she _____ of her brother's daughter.

   (a.) would take care   b. won't take care   c. is taking care

4. **Sibel:** "The driver of the car has disappeared!"

   Sibel told me that the driver of the car _____ .

   (a.) had disappeared   b. were disappearing   c. disappear

5. **Matt:** "I'm getting along well with my roommates."

   Matt told me that he _____ with his roommates.

   a. has gotten along well   (b.) was getting along well   c. would get along well

6. **Ricardo:** "I have a doctor's appointment."

   Ricardo said he _____ a doctor's appointment.

   a. has had   b. had had   (c.) had

4 Match each sentence to the correct picture.

1. She said that she was working on Tuesday.
2. She said that she had worked on Tuesday.
3. She said that she worked on Tuesday.
4. She said that she would work on Tuesday.

"I work on Tuesday."

"I am working on Tuesday."

"I worked on Tuesday."

"I will work on Tuesday."

5 Complete the sentences. Use *said* or *told* and reported speech. Use *that* if you wish.

1. **Olivia:** "I have an important meeting, Doug."

   Olivia _____*told*_____ Doug *(that) she had an important meeting* ____. *Past*

   did — Past
   had + P.P

2. **John:** "I did well on my test."

   John *said that He had done on his test.*

3. **Paula:** "I'm riding my bicycle to the movie theater, Sue."

   Paula *Told* Sue *that she was riding her bicycle to the movie theater Sue.*

4. **Victor:** "I'll tell the police about the accident."

   Victor *told* me *that He would tell the police about the accident*

5. **Fred:** "I have come up with a great idea for your birthday."

   Present   *had P.T*

   Fred *said that He had come up with a great idea for my birthday.*

6. **Sally:** "A UFO is sitting in front of my house."

   Sally *Said that AUFO was sitting in front of Her house.*

6 Read the news story. Then write what each person said.

Told — Cuando hay otra Persona.

ROBBER ESCAPES WITH EXPENSIVE PAINTING

Last night there was a theft at the art museum. The museum director said, "A robber has taken a painting worth $2 million." Many people were visiting the museum at the time. Oliver Jones, 52, told a police officer, "I saw a man leave the museum with a large bag." Cindy Milton, 33, was there with her two sons but could offer no help. "I didn't see anything," she said. The theft is surprising because the museum is in a quiet, safe neighborhood. Jen Kennedy, a 25-year-old art student, told reporters, "I am surprised and a little scared." Tom Weston, 76, said, "The robber won't get away with it!" Donna Lawrence, who works at the museum, agrees with Weston. She told reporters, "The police are already looking for the robber." Then she said, "He will get caught." If you saw anything that might help catch the robber, please call the police.

were

Said — Cuando no hay otra Persona.

didn't — had P.P

was

will — Negativo Won't

1. The museum director *said that a robber had taken a painting worth $2 million* .

2. Oliver Jones *told a police officer that* ____ .

Raul Castro said that cuba would have 5 Million tourists next year.

3. Cindy Milton *Said that she hadn't seen anything* .

4. Jen Kennedy *Told reporters that she was suprised* .

5. Tom Weston *said that the robber wouldn't get* .

6. Donna Lawrence *told reporters that the police were already looking*

7. Then she *then she said he would get caught.*

↓ Past

B As I was saying, . . .

Complete the conversations with the sentences from the box.

> To get back to what I was saying, I'm really upset with Melanie.
> ✓ By the way, I saw a great movie on Friday.
> ✓ I just thought of something.
> ✓ That reminds me, I chatted with Ellie online last night.
> To finish what I was saying, I'm going on vacation next week.
> But as I was saying, the Internet is a great way to connect with old friends.

A. **Ana:** I love catching up with friends online.

Lei: _That reminds me, I chatted with Ellie_
1
online last night.
1
We talked for an hour!

Ana: Really? How is she doing?

Lei: She's great. She told me she had moved to Canada.

Ana: Wow. That's interesting.

But as I was saying, the Internet is a great way to connect with old friends
2

Lei: It really is. I wonder if my old friend Blanca ever chats online.

Ana: I bet you could find her by using one of those websites for finding old friends.

B. **Sarah:** You know, I can't put up with people who lie.

Drew: Who lied to you?

Sarah: Well, Melanie told me she couldn't go the movies with me because she was sick, but then Tom told me they went to the movie together.

Drew: _By the way I saw a great movie on friday._
1

Sarah: What did you see?

Drew: That new Brad Pitt movie.

Sarah: That sounds great. _To finish what I was saying. I'm going on vacation next week_
2

C. **Carl:** Martin is taking care of my plants while I'm on vacation.

Tito: Hey, _I Just thought of something._
1

Carl: What?

Tito: I heard that Joe's Green Place is having a sale on plants. Do you want to go?

Carl: Sure. We could go tomorrow. _To get back what I was saying. I'm really upset with Melanie._
2

C There's always an explanation.

1 Complete the puzzle and the sentences with the correct verbs.

Across

1. I don't __Plan__ on going to the restaurant with you tonight. It's too expensive.
4. We can't __decide__ on a dress. Do you like the blue one or the red one?
6. I don't __believe__ in UFOs, but my brother thinks they are real.
7. I never __Worry__ about my problems. It always seems to be OK in the end.
8. You can __Dependent__ on me. I'll help you with anything.

depender
dependiente.

Down

1. Carmela doesn't _____ in many sports, but she plays tennis with her family.
2. Don't _____ about your mother. You have to pick her up at the airport today.
3. Nick can __rely__ on his sister. She is always helpful when he needs her.

confiar

4. I didn't _____ about anything while I was sleeping last night.
5. Did you _____ about Brendon? John said that he was going to Spain!

Crossword grid:
¹P L A N
A
R
T
²F I ³R
O
R ⁴D E C I D E
⁵H ⁶ R I L
⁶B E L I E V E P Y
A T A A
⁷W O R R Y M T
⁸D E P E N D E

2 Answer the questions with your own information.

Example: __I worry about my classes.__ or __I worry about my children.__

1. What or who do you worry about?   I worry about my future
2. What sports do you participate in?   I participe in...
3. Who can you depend on?   I depend on
4. What do you plan on doing this weekend?   I plan on going to church.
5. What have you dreamed about more than once?   I dream about have grandchildre

3 Read about Brianna and Rafael's conversation. Then write T (true) or F (false).

> Brianna asked Rafael if he was OK. Rafael said he was fine. Then Rafael asked Brianna if she had gone to the Wakes concert last night. Brianna told him that she hadn't gone. Rafael said that he had gone to the concert and it had been great. Brianna said she was sorry she hadn't gone. Then she asked if the Wakes were playing again soon. Rafael told her that they were. He said they would play at the CC Café on Friday. Brianna said that she would definitely go on Friday. Then she said she was looking forward to it.

1. Brianna wanted to know how Rafael was. ___T___

2. Brianna went to the concert last night. ___F___

3. Rafael went to the concert last night. ___T___

4. Rafael thought the concert was bad. ___F___

5. The Wakes aren't playing on Friday. ___F___

6. Brianna is planning to go to the next concert. ___T___

4 Circle the correct verb form to complete the reported speech in each sentence.

1. **Jim:** "Hey, Dina, do you plan on going to Doug's party?"

   Jim asked Dina if she **is planning** / **planned** on going to Doug's party.

2. **Larissa:** "Did you hear about the big storm, Kayla?"

   Larissa asked Kayla if she **had heard** / **was hearing** about the big storm.

3. **Nancy:** "Will you take care of my cat next week, Janet?"

   Nancy asked Janet if she **would take care of** / **took care of** her cat next week.

4. **Jason:** "Are you driving to Chicago, Tiago?"

   Jason asked Tiago if he **drives** / **was driving** to Chicago.

5. **Linda:** "Hey, Tim, have you tried the dumplings yet?"

   Linda asked Tim if he **would try** / **had tried** the dumplings yet.

6. **Sakura:** "Are you nervous about the test, Dan?"

   Sakura asked Dan if he **is** / **was** nervous about the test.

7. **Mario:** "Hi, Lori. Do you want to go shopping?"

   Mario asked Lori if she **wanted** / **had wanted** to go shopping.

5 Complete the sentences with the correct pronouns.

1. **Jennifer:** "Mom, are you tired?"

   Jennifer asked her mother if _____*she*_____ was tired.

2. **Carol:** "Joe, have you seen my sister?"

   Carol asked Joe if ___*She*___ had seen ___*her*___ sister.

3. **Jack:** "Will you help me with my homework?"

   Jack asked me if I would help ___*him*___ with ___*his*___ homework.

4. **Debbie:** "Hi, Mr. and Mrs. Lee. Are you going to buy a new car?"

   Debbie asked Mr. and Mrs. Lee if ___*them*___ were going to buy a new car.

5. **Mr. Garza:** "Good morning, students. Have you done your homework?"

   Mr. Garza asked the students if ___*them*___ had done ___*their*___ homework.

I | me, my, mine
We | us, our, ours
You | your, Yours
she | her, hers,
he | him, his
it | its
They | them their, theirs

6 Read the conversation. Then rewrite the underlined questions as reported questions.

Erica: I'm really worried.

Paul: Are you worried about Ben? He wasn't in class yesterday.

Erica: Yes, I am. Have you talked to him?

Paul: No, I haven't, but I'm sure he's OK.

Erica: Will you call him?

Paul: I guess so. Why? Is your phone at home?

Erica: No, but I don't want to call him. I'm embarrassed.

Paul: Embarrassed? What's going on? Did you and Ben have a fight?

Erica: Oh, no. I had a dream about him last night. He was in an accident in the dream, and now I want to make sure he's OK.

Paul: OK. I'll call him. Do you have Ben's number?

Erica: It's 820-555-2962. Are you going to tell Ben about my dream? Please don't!

1. Paul asked Erica *if she was worried about Ben* .
2. Erica asked Paul *if He had talked to him.* .
3. Erica asked Paul *if He would call him* .
4. Paul asked Erica *if was his phone at home.* .
5. Paul asked Erica *if She and Ben had a fought* .
6. Paul asked Erica *if Sh had Bens number?* .
7. Erica asked Paul *if He was going to tell Ben about her dream.*

D Thoughts, values, and experiences

1 Read the story. Who is in the audience during the TV show?

_____

Inside the Actor's Studio

James Lipton is a TV host in the United States. He has a TV show called *Inside the Actor's Studio* that has been on TV since 1994. He interviews actors and actresses about their careers. He's also a teacher at a university. The audience is always students from his acting classes. The hour-long interviews are always interesting, but people really look forward to the end of the show. At the end, Lipton asks his guests questions based on the Proust Questionnaire. He asks each guest the same ten questions every week. Some of the questions are: *What's your favorite word?*, *What's your least favorite word?*, *What sound or noise do you love?*, and *What sound or noise do you hate?*

Many actors have given similar answers to the questions. When actress Gwyneth Paltrow was on the show, Lipton asked her what sound or noise she loved. She said that she loved the sound of her mother's voice when she said "goodnight." When Johnny Depp answered the same question,

he said that he loved the sound of his daughter's voice. Angelina Jolie said she loved the sound of her son when he couldn't stop laughing. Jolie said her least favorite sound was children in pain. Comedian and actor Dave Chappelle said he didn't like the sound of children crying.

Depp told Lipton that his favorite word was *why* and his least favorite word was *no*. Chappelle, Jolie, and actor Will Smith also said their least favorite word was *no*. Jolie said her favorite word was *now*.

Lipton has also heard some interesting and unique answers to the questionnaire over the years. Singer Jennifer Lopez said her favorite word was *love* and her least favorite word was *can't*. British actor Hugh Laurie said that his favorite word was *marsupial*, which is a word that describes animals with a pouch, like a kangaroo. Several of Laurie's answers were funny. He said his favorite noise was someone playing a guitar badly. Lipton asked him why, and Laurie said he couldn't explain it.

After the questions are finished, Lipton's students get to come up with their own questions to ask the guest. Lipton wants to entertain his audience, but he believes in giving his acting students an interesting way to learn.

2 Read the story again. Then write T (true), F (false), or NI (no information).

1. Before *Inside the Actor's Studio*, James Lipton used to be an actor. __*NI*__

2. Lipton asks all guests the same questions based on the Proust Questionnaire. __T__

3. Johnny Depp has a son, but he doesn't have a daughter. __F__

4. Many of the guests mentioned in the story said their favorite word was *yes*. __f__

5. Hugh Laurie's favorite word is *kangaroo*. __F__ marsuptial

6. Lipton's students ask the guests interesting questions. __NI__

The real world

A Getting it done

1 Complete the text with the correct phrases from the box.

Aceptado

accepted the job offer	printed the email	researched the job
applied for the job	✓ proofread and formatted his résumé	sent a thank-you note
prepare for the interview	provide references	translate a letter

corregir formateado.   *investigando*

John Torres didn't have a job after he finished college, but he worked hard to find one. First, he wrote his résumé. His friend Kyle _**proofread and formatted his résumé**_ for him. John had forgotten to _provide references_ (1) on his résumé, so Kyle added them. John looked for jobs on the Internet. He saw an ad for a translator, and he _applied for the job_ (2). Mrs. Baker from TB Trans called him to schedule an interview. Kyle helped him _prepare for the interview_ (3). He asked John questions that he thought Mrs. Baker would ask. John _researched the job._ (4), and he read a lot of information about the company. Before the interview, he _printed the email_ (5) from Mrs. Baker with the directions to her office. His interview went really well. He went home and _sent a thank-you note_ (6) to Mrs. Baker. Two days later, Mrs. Baker offered him a job. John _accepted the job offer_ (7). His first assignment was to _translate a letter_ (8) from English to Spanish. (9)

2 Answer the questions with your own information.

Example: _Yes, I have. I looked up information about the company online,_
and I practiced answering questions.

1. Have you ever had a job interview? What did you do to prepare for it?

_____

2. Have you ever made a résumé? Who proofread it?

_____

3. Have you ever accepted a job offer? What job was it?

_____

3 Read each sentence. Then check (✓) the correct answer to the question.

1. John gets Pete to print the business cards.

   Who prints the business cards? ☐ John ☑ Pete

2. Martha has her clothes washed at Mindy's Laundry.

   Does Martha wash her own clothes? ☑ Yes ☐ No

3. Yoko had her reference letter translated.

   Did someone translate Yoko's reference letter? ☐ Yes ☑ No

4. Mr. Clark gets Ned to photocopy his important papers.

   Who photocopies the papers? ☐ Mr. Clark ☑ Ned

5. Frank has Ben wash his car on the weekends.

   Who washes the car? ☑ Frank ☐ Ben

6. Jennifer plans to get her hair cut on Tuesday.

   Will Jennifer cut her own hair? ☐ Yes ☑ No

4 Complete the text with the correct phrases from the box.

get a friend to help you	have someone clean
get a neighbor to take care of	have your bank pay
get your clothes washed	✓ have your clothes dry-cleaned

Create More Time at Home ·····································

- Are you tired of doing laundry? Do you have nice suits and dresses?

  Have your clothes dry-cleaned . You can also
  ₁

  _____ at many places.
  ₂

- Don't stress about a clean house. _____ your house
  ₃

  for you. It's a little expensive, but it will give you time for other things.

- If you have children, get some help. _____
  ₄

  your children for a few hours. Then you can get things done.

- _____ with jobs around the house. Later,
  ₅

  you can help your friend. It is sometimes more fun to work together.

- Set up automatic payments and _____ your bills
  ₆

  automatically. It's easy and saves you time. You don't have to worry about late bills.

5 Circle the correct word to complete each sentence.

1. Rachel **has** / **gets** her sister translate letters for her.

2. Sammy **has** / **gets** Jeff to do the laundry.

3. Mario and Camila **have** / **get** FoTake print their photos.

4. I usually **have** / **get** my father to drive me to the airport.

5. Asami **has** / **gets** Jessie to help her with her homework.

6. We **have** / **get** Park Press print our business cards.

7. Do you **have** / **get** anyone proofread your résumé?

8. Who do you **get** / **have** to clean your house?

9. Josh **has** / **gets** Pam feed his cat when he's on vacation.

10. Mona **has** / **gets** her neighbor to pick up her mail when she's in London.

6 Look at Michio's "To Do" list. He has checked (✓) the things that he has already gotten done. Write sentences about what he has already had done and what he still needs to have done. Use the verbs in parentheses.

TO DO

1. suits – dry-clean ✓
2. shirts – iron
3. hair – cut ✓
4. apartment – clean
5. résumé – proofread ✓
6. résumé – translate into English
7. business cards – print ✓
8. car – fix

DRY CLEANERS

1. (have) _Michio had his suits dry-cleaned._

2. (get) _He needs to get his shirts ironed._

3. (get) He had his hair-cut

4. (have) He needs to have his apartment-clean.

5. (get) He gets his résumé-proofread

6. (have) He needs to have his résumé-translate into English.

7. (have) He needs to have his business cards-print.

8. (get) He needs to get car-fix.

B *Let me see . . .*

1 Three people are interviewing for a job as a salesperson. Complete the interviews with sentences from the box. Sometimes more than one answer is possible. Use each sentence only once.

Hmm, let me think.	Well, it's been great talking to you.
✓ Oh . . . let's see.	Well, it's been nice meeting you.
Um, let me see.	Well, I've really enjoyed talking to you.

A. **Interviewer:** One more question, Ms. Jones. What is your greatest strength?

Ms. Jones: Well, I really enjoy working with people.

Interviewer: OK. And what do you like best about working with people?

Ms. Jones: *Oh . . . let's see.*
<u>1</u>
I like to learn new things from them. I also like to help other people get things done.

Interviewer: Very good. <u>Well I've really enjoyed talking to you.</u>
<u>2</u>
We'll call you in a few days.

B. **Interviewer:** I have one last question, Mr. Harris. What is your greatest strength?

Mr. Harris: <u>Um, let me see</u>
<u>1</u>
I know . . . I'm very outgoing. I love to talk to people.

Interviewer: <u>Well, It's been talking to you.</u>
<u>2</u>

Mr. Harris: Thanks. Did I get the job?

Interviewer: We have a few more interviews. We'll call you in a few days.

C. **Interviewer:** OK, I have only one more question. What is your greatest strength?

Mr. Gomez: I'm very responsible. I'm always on time. I'm also energetic and hardworking. Oh, and I'm very good with computers.

Interviewer: OK. And if you had to pick one thing . . . which one would it be?

Mr. Gomez: <u>Hmm, let me think</u> I guess that I'm
<u>1</u>
responsible. I think it's important to be on time and to get your work done.

Interviewer: <u>Well It's been nice meeting you</u> Thank you
<u>2</u>
for coming in for this interview, Mr. Gomez. We'll call you in a few days.

2 Who do you think would be best for the job? Check (✓) your answer.

☐ Ms. Jones   ☐ Mr. Harris   ☐ Mr. Gomez

C Future goals

1 Complete the text with the correct phrases from the box.

~~doing volunteer work~~	~~I'm working as a journalist~~
~~having a big wedding~~	~~preparing for my exams~~
~~live in the countryside~~	~~studying abroad~~
✓ 'm already financially independent	~~write travel books~~

About me:

Birthday:
October 22

Current City:
Boston

I finished school two years ago, and I *'m already* ₁ *financially independent* ₁. I have my own apartment, and I have a great job. I **am** ₂ **Working as a Journalist** ₂ I go to a lot of different countries for my job, and I want to **Write travel** ₃ **books** ₃ about the places I've been. I love living in the city, but I hope to **live in the countryside** ₄ someday!

rural = Countryside
urban = City

Claudia Rodriguez [is going to Seoul!]

Jen Lewis: Have a great trip, Claudia! Send me a postcard. I'll be **Preparing for my exams** ₅ while you're gone! I have three big tests next week.

Claudia Rodriguez: Thanks, Jen, and good luck with your tests!

Peng Liu: Will you be back by April 3? I'm getting married! We're **having a big wedding** ₆ I hope you can come.

Claudia Rodriguez: I'm sorry, Peng. I won't be home until April 15. Near the end of my trip, I'm **doing Volunteer work** ₇. I'm teaching English at a Korean high school for two weeks, and I'm also giving free classes about how to be a good journalist.

Peng Liu: Too bad. Well, I'll show you pictures when you get home!

Mark Goldman: Hey, Claudia. I'm **studying abroad** ₈ = outside the country right now. I'm taking classes in Incheon. Maybe you can visit me when you're in Seoul!

Claudia Rodriguez: That's great, Mark! I could come to Incheon on March 29. Is that good for you?

Mark Goldman: Yes, it is! We can have lunch in Jayu Park, my favorite place here.

2 Circle the correct verb form to complete each sentence.

1. What _____ next year?

   a. will you be   b. were you doing   (c.) will you be doing   *will + be + ting*

2. Jacob _____ Chinese at a university next year.

   (a.) will be studying   b. be studying   c. was studying

3. Tonya _____ her new car by next week.

   a. having   b. will be having   (c.) will have   *will + have*

4. Larry and Samantha _____ financially independent in a year.

   a. were being   (b.) will be   c. will be being

5. _____ with Mr. Harding this week?

   (a.) Will you be working   b. You are working   c. Working

6. I'm sure that Kyle _____ his goals.

   a. will be achieving   (b.) will achieve   c. achieving

   to accomplish

3 Check (✓) the sentences that are correct. Change the sentences that are not correct to the future with *will* and write the new sentence.

1. ☐ Will you ~~be~~ remembering my birthday in two months?

   Will you remember my birthday in two months?

   continue action

2. ☐ Min Woo will be preparing for his exams this weekend.

   _____

   _____

3. ☐ Susana will be being financially independent when she gets a job.

   Susana will be financially independent

4. ☐ Will you be achieving your goals in two years?

   Will you achieve your goals in two years

5. ☑ Beatriz will be doing volunteer work on Saturday.

   Beatriz will be doing volunteer work on Saturday

6. ☑ Do you think they'll be having a good time in Spain?

   Do You think they will have a good time in Spain?

7. ☑ Tim will be working as a doctor in Los Angeles for the next three years.

   Tim will be working as a doctor in los angeles for the next three years

8. ☑ We'll be believing your story when you prove it.

   We will believe your story when you prove it

4 Complete the email with the future ~~continuous~~ *progressive* of the verbs in parentheses.

Hi Fatih!

How are you? Will you be home soon? We miss you in class. This week we had to write about what we think our lives will be like in the future. I started thinking about it a lot. Five years from now, I _won't be working_ (not / work) for a large company. Instead, I _Will be working_ [1] (work) as a travel writer. I _Will be living_ [2] (live) in a large apartment in the city. I _Will be traveling_ [3] (travel) a lot for work. I _I Will be going_ [4] (go) to Mexico and Brazil. I don't know if all this will happen, but it's OK to dream, right?

What do you think you _Will be doing_ [5] (do) in five years? _Will_ [6] you _studing_ [7] (study) abroad?

Your friend,

Nick

5 Complete the email with the future with *will* of the verbs in parentheses.

Hey Nick!

It was great to hear from you. I _'ll be_ [1] (be) home on Tuesday. I'm having a great time in Spain. Your question was interesting. Let's see . . . in five years, what will I be doing? Well, first I _Will finish_ [2] (finish) school next year, but then I _Will go_ [3] (go) to work for my father. In five years, I _Won't be_ [4] (not / be) his assistant. I _Will have_ [5] (have) to make the decisions! I hope I _'ll meet_ [6] (meet) someone really nice in the next few years, but I _won't be_ [7] (not / be) married in five years. I do think that I'll be living in the countryside. _Will_ [8] you _visit_ [8] (visit) me there?

See you soon!

Fatih

6 What will you be doing in five years? Write two sentences about each topic.

Example: _I'll be studying abroad in Canada. Maybe I'll learn French!_

1. School: _I won't be at the school._
2. Work: _I'll be working_
3. Travel: _I'll be traveling._

D My career

1 Read the article. What is causing some jobs to disappear?

DISAPPEARING JOBS

Have you ever thought about jobs disappearing? As technology improves and new things are invented, some jobs are no longer needed. For example, before the invention of the automatic elevator, there were elevator operators. The operator controlled the elevator as it went up and down, and he or she opened and closed the doors of the elevator. Once elevators became automated, this job was no longer needed. Here are some other jobs that might disappear some day.

Travel Agents: In the past, people had travel agents plan their trips and buy their tickets. Today, it is easy to buy plane tickets online. It's also easy to research different places to go, find hotels, rent cars, and much more. There will be fewer travel agents in the future because more and more people will be planning their vacations online.

Bank Tellers: Bank tellers inside a bank help you get cash, deposit your checks, and transfer money. But since the invention of automated teller machines (ATMs), online banking, and banking by phone, many people rarely go inside a bank. They don't need to get help from the bank teller because they can use new technologies to do those things at the ATM, online, or by phone.

Photo Processors: Photo processors develop and print pictures. With the invention of digital cameras, the need for this job has been reduced. Many stores now have machines that print digital pictures. Even these types of stores are disappearing because many people now print their pictures at home.

Video Store Clerks: People don't have to go to video stores to rent movies anymore. They can rent them from companies that send movies in the mail. Many videos can also be streamed online. It's possible that there won't be any video stores in the future.

We'll know in time which of these jobs will last and which ones won't. We'll also see what other jobs might disappear as technology improves. Even though some jobs are lost, technology also creates new jobs. For example, someone has to put money in ATM machines and repair them when they break.

2 Read the article again. Write T (true), F (false), or NI (no information).

1. The automatic elevator was invented 100 years ago. _NI_

2. There are no travel agents now. _F_

3. Because of ATMs, people never go into banks now. _F_

4. A lot of people print photographs at home. _T_ *(Many)*

5. It's very expensive to stream videos online. _NI_

6. New jobs are often created when old ones disappear. _T_

Finding solutions

A Environmental concerns

1 Complete the sentences and the puzzle with the correct verbs. What's the mystery word?

1. Dana wants to _recycle_ her old computer, but she doesn't know where to take it.
2. Lydia _purchase_ tasks when she goes out in her car. For example, she buys food at a store near her office.   *Tareas*
3. Don't _spill_ oil on the ground.
4. Jack's car is in great condition. He _____ it by checking the oil often.
5. You should _____ where the recycling room is in your new apartment building.

Puzzle:
1. R E C Y C L E
2. C O M B A C t
3. M
4. M A I N T A I N
5. I D E N T I F Y

2 Complete the text with the correct verbs from the box.

avoid *evitar* *conservar*	conserve	limit	store
commute	discard *descartar*	purchase	✓recycle

Simple Ways You Can Reduce Pollution

- ___Recycle___ items like newspapers, magazines, and plastic bottles from your home.
  1

- ___avoid___ products that are harmful for the environment. *Perjudicial*
  2
  Instead, ___purchase___ "green" products for your home.
  3

- ___discard___ old batteries and printer ink properly. Be sure you
  4
  ___store___ them in a safe place until you find the right place to throw
  5
  them away.

- How do you ___commute___ to work? Can you walk, take a bus, or ride a
  6
  bicycle to work? If you have to drive, try to go to work with other people in your car.

- ___conserve___ water. When you wash your hair or brush your teeth, turn
  7
  the water off until you are ready to use it again. In this way, you can
  ___limit___ how much water you use.
  8

3 Complete the sentences with the present continuous passive of the verb in parentheses.

STAYING GREEN

Many hotels do things that are not good for the environment. For example, water

<u>is being wasted</u> (waste) every day in many hotels, and many items

<u>doesn't being recycle</u> ¹ (not / recycle). The good news is that there is a

growing number of "green" hotels around the world. The Alto Hotel in Melbourne, Australia, is

one that is making a difference. For example, the lights at the hotel are powered by wind energy,

and the guests' newspapers are recycled every day. Other environmentally friendly things

<u>is doing</u> ³ (do) every day at the Alto Hotel, too. If you go

there, you'll see that "green" cleaning products <u>are using</u> (use)

to clean the rooms. Rain water <u>is being collected and stored</u> ⁴ (collect and store) at

the hotel and then used later for cleaning and for watering plants. Hotel guests

<u>are teaching</u> ⁵ (teach) how to help the environment, too.

The hotel gives people free parking if they drive electric or hybrid cars. And guests

<u>are being reminded</u> ⁶ (remind) that they can walk to places close

to the hotel. Not only is the hotel environmentally friendly, it's a beautiful place to stay, too.

4 Write sentences with the verbs in parentheses. Use the simple present with the infinitive passive.

1. (Something / have / do / about the parking problem)

<u>Something has to be done about the parking problem.</u>

2. (More "green" buildings / need / create)

<u>More green buildings need to be create</u>

3. (Chemicals / have / store / in safe containers)

<u>Chemicals have to be store in safe containers</u>

4. (Batteries / have / discard / properly)

<u>Batteries have to be discard properly</u>

5. (More water / need / conserve)

<u>More water need to be conserve</u>

6. (Newspapers / need / recycle)

<u>Newspapers need to be recycle</u>

5 Circle the correct words to complete the conversation.

Rosa: Something has (to be done) / is being done
_1_
about the pollution in this city.

Jake: I agree that the problem needs

(to be taken care of) / is being taken care of,
_2_
but it's too big for us to do anything about it.

Rosa: We can help a lot! A lot of pollution

to be made / (is being made) by our cars.
_3_

Jake: But we have to get to work!

Rosa: There are other ways to go. You know, in some cities cars

not to be allowed / (aren't being allowed) on the road with only one person.
_4_

Jake: Hmm, that's interesting. I guess if changes have (to be made) / are being made,
_5_
people will make them!

Rosa: Maybe we can talk to people at work and start a carpool . . . you know,
ride together.

Jake: That's a good idea. That new highway to be built / (is being built) right now.
_6_
It will be easy for me to pick up you and Tonya on my way to work.

Rosa: That'd be great. But don't remind me about the new highway! Think of all the
pollution that (to be created) / is being created by all those cars!
_7_

6 Complete the sentences with your own ideas about your country. If you need help, you
can use some of the words in the box.

clean	fix	paper	pollution	technology
conserve	health clinics	parks	recycle	trash
education	newspapers	plastic	recycling programs	waste

Example: _Something has to be done about maintaining our bridges._ or

Something has to be done about the pollution in our air.

1. Something has to be done about _____ .

2. Not enough money is being spent on _____ .

3. A lot of money is being spent on _____ .

4. _____ is / are being recycled.

5. _____ isn't / aren't being recycled.

6. The highways need to be _____ .

B That's a good point.

1 Complete the conversation with the sentences from the box.

> I see it a little differently.
> It's better to pay more for something that doesn't harm the environment.
> Thanks. I like the idea of "green" products.
> That's great, but these products are really expensive.
> ✓This store is great. They only sell "green" products.
> Wow. You make a very good point.
> Yes, but you have the money to pay more.

Ken: _This store is great. They only sell "green" products._

Bill: That's great, but these products are really expensive.

Ken: I think that's OK. I see a little differently

Bill: Yes, but you have the money to pay more.

I think everyone should be able to buy products that help the environment.

Ken: Well, I don't mind paying more!

Bill: It's better to pay more for something that doesn't harm the environ

What about people who don't have the money? They should be able to buy "green" products, too.

Ken: Wow. You make a very good point

Bill: Thanks. I like the idea of green products.

I just think they should be cheaper.

2 What do you think about these opinions? Use a phrase from the box to give your own response.

> Actually, I have a different opinion.   I see what you mean.
> I don't see it that way.   That's a good point.

1. **Ken:** People should have to drive with two or more people in their cars.

   You: _____

2. **Bill:** People shouldn't have to recycle if they don't want to.

   You: _____

My community

1 Label each picture with the correct community improvement phrase.
Use one word from each box.

✓beautification	employment	neighborhood	recreation
community	health	public	recycling

center	center	garden	✓project
center	clinic	library	watch

1. _beautification project_   2. employment center   3. neighborhood watch

4. recreation center   5. Public library   6. health clinic

7. recycling center   8. community garden

2 Put the words in the correct order to make sentences.

1. don't recycle / a recycling center here, / Although / there's / many people / .

   Although there's a recycling center here, many people don't recycle.

2. after school / Jen goes / Jen's mom / so / works late, / to a recreation center / .

   So after school Jen goes. Jen's mom works late to a recreation centre

3. a city rule / because of / We / about maintaining cars / have cleaner air / .

   A city rule about maintaining cars because we have cleaner air.

4. a beautification project / so that / this area / We / will look better / should start / .

   We should start a beutification project so that this area will look better.

5. Our yard / at the garden center / we / if / will look nice / get plants / .

   if we got plants at the garden center, Our yard will look nice.

3 Circle the correct words to complete the email.

Dear Councilman Sunders:

I am a concerned citizen in your area. So / **(Although)** [*a pesar de que*] the city council office is working
1
to fight crime in our neighborhood, we still need more help. This is a significant
problem, and many people in the neighborhood no longer go out at night
if / **(because of)** [*porque*] the crime. A few of my neighbors and I want to try to help solve the
2
problem. We feel things will get better if / **(so)** we start a neighborhood watch. But we
3
don't think that's enough. We think the police need to be in our neighborhood more
because of / **(so)** criminals know they will get caught. We're dedicated to changing
4
things, **(so)** / although we will be at the next community meeting on May 8 at
5
7:00 p.m. in the Oakmont Community Center. We hope you or someone from your
office will be there because of / **(so that)** [*asi que eso*] you can help. **(Although)** / If this email may
6   7
seem negative, we appreciate your work on the city council. I'm asking for your help
so that / **(because of)** what you have done in the past for our great city.
8

Please contact me if you have questions or if you'd like more information about our
plan for a neighborhood watch.

Thank you,

Brenda Quinton
–Concerned citizen

4 Combine the phrases to make sentences. Add *although, because of, if, so,* or *so that*. Add a comma when necessary.

1. you should go to the health clinic / you don't feel well

   You should go to the health clinic if you don't feel well.

2. Dennis doesn't like sports / he plays basketball with his brother once in a while

   Although Dennis doesn't like sports, he plays basketball with his brother once in a while.

3. Carla loves sports / she plays soccer and tennis at the recreation center

   Carla loves sports so she plays soccer and tennis at the recreation center.

4. my mother enjoys being outside / she works a lot in the community garden

   My mother enjoys being outside because of she works a lot in the community garden.

5. Mr. and Mrs. Quinton don't go out at night / the crime in the neighborhood

   Mr and Mrs Quinton don't go out at night because of the crime in the neighborhood.

6. I'll go to the employment center tomorrow / I don't get this job today

   I'll go to the employment tomorrow although I don't get this job today.

7. we should ask for volunteers / the beautification project won't be too expensive

   We should ask for volunteer so that the beutificantion project won't be too expensive.

8. we have a great public library here / some people rarely read a book

   Although we have a great public library here, some people rarely read a book.

5 Read the text. Then answer the questions.

Neighbors! Although I'm happy that we have a new recycling center in the neighborhood, I think it needs to be improved. The containers aren't big enough, so there are always items on the floor. The area would be much cleaner if the containers were bigger. There is also no place to recycle newspapers, so I think that needs to be added. Someone told me the recycling center is small because of a lack of money. We need to write to Councilman Steven Sunders and tell him how important this center is so that something can be done about it. Neighbors – please help yourselves, and write a letter today so we can get this problem fixed! Email Shawn Davis for more information at SDavis@cup.com.

1. Is Shawn happy that there is a new recycling center?   _Yes, he is._

2. Are the containers at the center big enough?   _No, they not._

3. Is the recycling center clean?   _No, it not_

4. What needs to be added to the center?   _A bigger containers_

5. Why is the recycling center small?   _because of a lack of money_

6. Why does Shawn want people to write to Steven Sunders?   _for get this problem fixed._

D Getting involved

1 Read the text. What are three benefits of mobile health clinics?

They <u>help people who are sick</u>(1), <u>give patients information</u>(2), and <u>test people for medical problems</u>(3)

Health Clinics on the ~~Move~~

Health care is a concern around the world. There are often too many people at hospitals, and in some areas people have to commute a long way to get to them. One solution to this problem is mobile health clinics. Mobile health clinics are like a small doctor's office in a van. The van drives to different locations so that people can get to it easily. Mobile clinics don't provide everything that a doctor's office or a hospital can, but there are a lot of services they do have. Doctors and nurses in mobile health clinics help people who are sick, test people for medical problems, and give patients information.

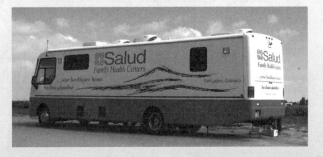

One benefit of mobile health clinics is that they can save money. When people are being checked at a mobile health clinic, they can avoid expensive trips to the emergency room. For example, in the United States, a trip to a mobile health clinic in Boston, Massachusetts, costs about $120. A visit to an emergency room in the same area is usually about $970.

Mobile health clinics can also help people avoid serious health problems. The St. Joseph Mobile Health Clinic in Santa Rosa, California, helps over 1,400 families every year. These are people who might not go to a doctor regularly if there weren't

any mobile health clinics. They would only go to a hospital if they had serious problems. The mobile health clinic can catch problems before they get serious.

Mobile health clinics also bring care to people who don't live near medical services. For example, in Kenya, the clinics, hospitals, and doctors' offices are in large cities. So the mobile health clinics take the doctors and nurses to communities that are not near the large cities.

One program in Peru has mobile health clinics that include dental care. The program brings dentists to small communities with no dentists and educates people on how to take care of their teeth. Then they can keep their teeth healthy after the clinic leaves the area.

2 Read the text again. Then answer the questions.

1. What are three things doctors do in mobile health clinics? _*help people who are sick, test people for medical problems, and give patients information*_

2. How much does it cost to go to a mobile health clinic in Boston? <u>About $120</u>

3. How many families go to the St. Joseph Mobile Clinic every year? <u>1400 families</u>

4. Why don't some people in Kenya go to doctors' offices or hospitals? <u>are only in large cities</u>

5. What is one kind of medical service provided by mobile clinics in Peru? <u>dental care</u>

Credits

Illustration credits

Kveta Jelinek: 5, 6, 29, 44, 52, 58, 69, 84; Andrew Joyner: 27, 36, 62, 70, 76; Greg Paprocki: 12, 28, 42, 79, 92; Garry Parsons: 21, 30, 45, 59, 67, 83; Rob Schuster: 8, 17, 68; Richard Williams: 9, 25, 39, 51, 63, 73, 91

Photography credits

2 ©Media Bakery; 3 ©Shutterstock; 4 ©Paul Cooklin/Getty Images; 7 ©Thomas Barwick/Getty Images; 10 ©Bill Brooks/Alamy; 13 ©Image Source/Getty Images; 14 ©Media Bakery; 18 ©Photo Library; 19 ©Jupiter Images; 24 ©Bon Appetit/Alamy; 26 ©Media Bakery; 30 ©Euro Style Graphics/Alamy; 34 ©Kathryn O'Dell; 40 *(left to right)* ©Lilyana Vynogradova/Alamy; ©Per Breiehagen/Getty Images; 41 ©Michael Hitoshi/Getty Images; 43 ©Chris Ryan/Alamy; 46 ©Media Bakery; 48 ©Newscom; 49 ©Gail Baker/SureWest; 50 ©Emir Rifat Isik; 53 ©Elena Elisseeva/Alamy; 55 *(top to bottom)* ©Caro/Alamy; ©The Bridgeman Art Library/Getty Images; 56 *(top to bottom)* ©Media Bakery; ©Shutterstock; ©Shutterstock; ©D. Hurst/Alamy; 57 ©Media Bakery; 60 ©Alamy; 65 ©Istock Photos; 66 ©James Porto/Getty Images; 70 ©Jamie Cooper/SSPL/Getty Images; 71 ©Ryan Cheng/Getty Images; 72 ©Shutterstock; 74 *(all)* ©Media Bakery; 80 ©Bravo/Everett Collection; 85 *(top to bottom)* ©Media Bakery; ©Radius Images/Alamy; ©Media Bakery; ©Shutterstock; ©Media Bakery; ©Shutterstock; ©Brownstock/Alamy; ©Media Bakery; ©Brownstock/Alamy; 86 ©Garry Gay/Alamy; 88 ©Photo Library; 93 *(top row, left to right)* ©Jim West/Alamy; ©Yellow Dog Productions/Getty Images; ©Lana Sundman/Alamy; *(middle row, left to right)* ©Adrian Sherratt/Alamy; ©David Cordner/Getty Images; ©Media Bakery; *(bottom row, left to right)* ©Superstock; ©Tony Anderson/Getty Images; 96 ©John Moore/Getty Images

Level 4
Kosta.
404-901-0506
Kdalageorgas @gmail. com

The aztecas left the territory
They was looking for a Sing.
(This is a Mistery

Network: LAA-LAB
Password LAA-L@bs123?

Network: LAA-LAB
Password LAA-L@bs123?